# Berlitz®

# *German*
## BUSINESS
## PHRASE BOOK

### WITH BUSINESS DICTIONARIES
### BY P.H. COLLIN

---

**Easy to use features**

Handy the

Quick reference pronu

Country factf

Question and multiple

# How best to use this Phrase Book

This business phrase book has been designed to provide the handiest
reference source to suit your business needs — whether you're on a trip
to a German-speaking country, entertaining a German-speaking visitor,
or corresponding by telephone, fax or letter with a German-speaking
business partner.

- Consult the **Contents** pages (3-4) to locate the section you need.
  Separate, descriptive contents lists are included at the beginning of
  each chapter, to help you find your way around.

- Your fastest look-up is via the **English-German dictionary** (pp. 125-160),
  which contains over 2,500 essential business terms. For help in
  translating German documents, use the **German-English dictionary**
  (pp.161-191).

- For more technical terminology, consult **Industries and professions**
  (pp. 97-124). This section contains specific terms for use in 12 major
  business fields.

- Practical guidelines and the essential phrases for telephoning and
  introducing yourself and your company are provided in the section on
  **Making contact** (pp. 5-32).

- For more complex business situations, consult **Communication skills**
  (pp. 33-64). Sequenced phrases provide a progressive framework for
  developing meetings and negotiations successfully.

- For day-to-day business transactions, **Company departments**
  (pp. 65-96) provides the essential terms and model phrases for dealing
  effectively with your German-speaking counterpart.

Note: noun plurals are indicated in parentheses, e.g. **Import(e)**
*plural* **Importe**; **Treffen(-)** *plural* **Treffen**; **Plan(-ë)** *plural* **Pläne**.
Feminine forms of masculine nouns are indicated in square brackets,
e.g. **Verwalter(-) [-in]** *feminine noun* **Verwalterin**. For the feminine plural
add **-nen**: *Verwalterinnen*.

2nd printing 1996                                                           Printed in Spain

# CONTENTS

### Acknowledgements

This material was developed in association with Nick Brieger and
Jeremy Comfort of York Associates, and JOHN GREEN TEFL TAPES;
business dictionaries were compiled by Peter Collin Publishing Ltd; our
thanks also to Able Translations Ltd – a division of Berlitz International
Inc. and Oxford Brookes Language Services for their help in the
preparation of this book.

# Making Contact

## BUSINESS COMMUNICATION

### On the Telephone

| | |
|---|---|
| answering machine | **der Anrufbeantworter(-)** |
| code | **die Vorwahl** |
| conference call | **die Sammelgesprächsschaltung** |
| direct line | **die Direktverbindung(en)** |
| engaged/busy | **besetzt** |
| extension | **der Apparat(e), der Anschluß** |
| get through | **durchkommen** |
| international call | **das Ferngespräch(e)** |
| local call | **das Ortsgespräch(e)** |
| switchboard | **die Vermittlung(en)** |
| telephone (n)/(v) | **das Telefon(e)/telefonieren** |
| telephone directory | **das Telefonbuch(¨-er)** |

### Identifying yourself

| | |
|---|---|
| ● Hallo, ... Co./Inc. here. | ● **Firma ..., guten Tag.** |
| ▶ Good morning/afternoon. | ▶ **Guten Tag.** |
| ▶ My name is ... | ▶ **Mein Name ist ...** |
| ▶ This is ... here. | ▶ **Hier ist ...** |

### Asking to speak to someone

| | |
|---|---|
| Could I speak to ... please? | **Könnte ich bitte mit ... sprechen?** |
| Could you put me through to ... please? | **Könnten Sie mich bitte zu ... durchstellen?** |
| Can I have extension 351 please? | **Könnten Sie mich bitte mit Apparat 351 verbinden?** |

INTRODUCTIONS, see page 23

| Could I speak to someone who deals with ...? | Könnte ich bitte mit jemandem sprechen, der für ... zuständig ist? |
|---|---|
| ▶ Who's calling? | ▶ Mit wem spreche ich, bitte? |
| ▶ Could you tell me what it's about? | ▶ Worum handelt es sich, bitte? |
| ▶ Can I help you? | ▶ Kann ich Ihnen behilflich sein? |
| ▶ Who would you like to speak to? | ▶ Mit wem möchten Sie sprechen? |
| ▶ Speaking. | ▶ Am Apparat. |

## Giving the reason for the call

| It's in connection with ... | Es geht um/handelt sich um ... |
|---|---|
| I'm calling about ... | Ich rufe wegen ... an. |
| I'm phoning to tell you ... | Ich rufe an, um Ihnen zu sagen ... |
| The reason I'm calling is ... | Der Grund meines Anrufs ist ... |

## Making excuses

| I'm afraid _____ is ... | Es tut mir leid, aber _____ ... |
|---|---|
| not available at the moment. | ist momentan leider nicht zu sprechen. |
| in a meeting. | ist in einer Sitzung. |
| with a customer at the moment. | ist mit einem Kunden. |
| on holiday/vacation. | ist im Urlaub. |
| not in the office. | ist nicht im Büro. |
| on the other line at present. | spricht gerade am anderen Apparat. |
| no longer with the company. | ist nicht mehr in dieser Firma. |
| I'm afraid his line's engaged/busy. | Ich fürchte, sein Anschluß ist (gerade) besetzt. |
| Do you want to hold? | Möchten Sie warten? |
| Can I pass you to his/her ... | Darf ich Sie mit seinem[-er] ... verbinden? |
| assistant/colleague/replacement | Assistenten[-in]/Kollegen[-in]/Nachfolger[in] |

## Taking a message

| Would you like to leave a message? | Möchten Sie eine Nachricht hinterlassen? |
|---|---|
| May I take a message? | Soll ich etwas ausrichten? |
| Can I take your name and number? | Können Sie mir Ihren Namen und Ihre Telefonnummer geben? |

INTRODUCING YOUR COMPANY, see pages 28 & 45

| | |
|---|---|
| Can I get him to call you back? | **Soll er Sie zurückrufen?** |
| ● Please leave a message after the tone. | ● **Bitte hinterlassen Sie einen Nachricht nach dem Bibton.** |

### Leaving a message

| | |
|---|---|
| Could you give him a message? | **Könnten Sie ihm etwas ausrichten?** |
| Could you ask her to call me back? The number is ... | **Könnten Sie sie bitten, mich zurückzurufen? Die Telefonnummer ist ...** |
| Could you tell her I'll call back later? | **Könnten Sie ihr ausrichten, daß ich später noch einmal anrufen werde?** |

### Showing you understand

| | |
|---|---|
| I see/understand. | **Ich verstehe.** |
| Right/Fine/Okay. | **Gut/Alles klar/Okay.** |

### Communication problems

| | |
|---|---|
| Could you repeat that? | **Könnten Sie das bitte wiederholen?** |
| I'm sorry, I didn't catch your name. | **Entschuldigen Sie, aber ich habe Ihren Namen nicht verstanden.** |
| Could you speak a little slower/ louder? | **Könnten Sie bitte etwas langsamer/lauter sprechen?** |
| It's a very bad line. I'll call you back. | **Die Verbindung ist sehr schlecht. Ich rufe Sie zurück.** |
| Could you spell that please? | **Könnten Sie das bitte buchstabieren?** |
| Let me just repeat that: ... | **Lassen Sie mich das noch einmal wiederholen: ...** |

### Ending the call

| | |
|---|---|
| Thanks very much for your help. | **Vielen Dank für Ihre Hilfe.** |
| I'm grateful for your assistance. | **Ich danke Ihnen für Ihre Hilfe.** |
| I look forward ... | **Ich würde mich freuen ...** |
| to seeing you soon. | **Sie bald zu sehen.** |
| hearing from you. | **von Ihnen zu hören.** |
| See/Speak to you soon. | **Bis bald./Bis dann.** |
| Good-bye/Bye. | **Auf Wiederhören/Tschüß.** |
| Thanks for calling. | **Vielen Dank für den Anruf.** |

TELEPHONE NUMBERS, see page 18

## Correspondence

Business correspondence should be kept brief and to the point. The text should be blocked, not indented. A typical letter would be addressed:

---

### BRAUN & WINTER GmbH
Postfach 16608 ● D-80307 München

Herrn
Hans-Dieter Huber
Computech GmbH
Hauptstraße 12
D-6000 Frankfurt/Main 1

| **Ihre Zeichen** | **Ihre Nachricht/Ihr Schreiben vom** | **Datum** |
|---|---|---|
| BA/1h | 12.05.9- | München, (den) 18.05.199_ |

**Betreff**
Ihre Bestellung vom 12.05.199-

---

For a fax, the essential details are:

---

### Peter Schumann KG                     *Telefax*

**An:** Worldwines
**z. Hd. (zu Händen):** Paul Braun
**Fax:** +44 171 647 2815
**Von:** Peter Schumann
**Fax:** 49 89 3 42 67
**Seiten:** 1
**Datum:** 23. März 199_

---

### The Greeting

| | |
|---|---|
| Dear Sirs *(impersonal)* | **Sehr geehrte Herren,** |
| Dear Sir *(if name not known)* | **Sehr geehrter Herr,** |
| Dear Madam *(if name not known)* | **Sehr geehrte Frau,** |
| Dear Mr Müller *(if name known)* | **Sehr geehrter Herr Müller,** |

### The start

| | |
|---|---|
| Thank you for your letter of _____ (date), ... | Vielen Dank für Ihr Schreiben vom _____, ... |
| I have received your letter of _____ (date), ... | Ich habe Ihr Schreiben vom ____ erhalten, ... |
| asking if/about ... | in dem Sie fragen, ob/über ... |
| enclosing ... | in dem als Anlage ... beilag. |
| in which you asked ... | in dem Sie fragen, ... |
| I have recieved your letter concerning ... | Ich habe Ihr Schreiben bezüglich ... erhalten. |

### Explaining the purpose

| | |
|---|---|
| We are writing to inquire about/whether ... | Wir möchten uns mit diesem Schreiben über ... erkundigen./ erkundigen, ob ... |
| I am writing in connection with ... | Mein Schreiben bezieht sich auf ... |
| In response to ... | In Beantwortung ... |
| With reference to ... | Bezugnehmend auf ... |
| Further to ... | Im Anschluß an ... |
| With regard to ... | Hinsichtlich ... |

### Requesting

| | |
|---|---|
| We would be very grateful if you could ... | Wir wären Ihnen sehr dankbar, wenn Sie ... könnten. |
| I would be much obliged if you could ... | Ich wäre Ihnen sehr verbunden, wenn Sie ... könnten. |
| We would appreciate it if you could ... | Wir würden es sehr schätzen, wenn Sie ... könnten. |
| Please could you ... (*informal*) | Könnten Sie bitte ... |

### Giving information or replying to a request for information

#### Positive

| | |
|---|---|
| Please find enclosed ... | Anbei erhalten Sie ... |
| We are happy to enclose ... | Wir freuen uns, Ihnen als Anlage ... übersenden zu können. |
| We wish to inform you that ... | Wir möchten Ihnen mitteilen, daß ... |
| We are pleased to inform you that ... | Wir freuen uns, Ihnen mitteilen zu können, daß ... |

### Negative

| | |
|---|---|
| We regret to inform you that ... | **Zu unserem Bedauern müssen wir Ihnen mitteilen, daß ...** |
| We are sorry to tell you that ... | **Es tut uns leid, Ihnen mitteilen zu müssen, daß ...** |

### Thanking

| | |
|---|---|
| I am much obliged to you for sending me ... | **Ich bin Ihnen sehr verbunden, daß Sie mir ... übersendet haben.** |
| I am grateful to you for ... | **Ich bin Ihnen sehr dankbar, daß Sie ...** |
| We are much obliged to you for ... | **Wir sind Ihnen zu äußerstem Dank verpflichtet für ...** |
| Thank you for ... (*informal*) | **Vielen Dank für ...** |

### Apologizing

| | |
|---|---|
| We were extremely sorry to hear about the problem. | **Es tut uns außerordentlich leid, von diesem Problem zu müssen hören.** |
| We regret that this problem has happened. | **Wir bedauern, daß ein derartiges Problem aufgetreten ist.** |
| We apologise for ... | **Wir müssen uns entschuldigen, daß ...** |

### Linking ideas

The following linking words show the relationship between your sentences and can make your letter easier to read.

*cause*
therefore/so/consequently      **deshalb/so/folglich**

*comparison*
similarly/in the same way      **ähnlich, ebenso/auf die gleiche Weise**

*contrast*
however/nevertheless      **jedoch/trotzdem, nichtsdestoweniger**

*addition*
in addition, also      **außerdem, auch,**
too      **auch**

| *equivalence* | |
| --- | --- |
| in other words/that means | **mit anderen Worten/das heißt** |
| *inclusion* | |
| for example/e.g. | **zum Beispiel/z. B.** |
| such as /as follows | **wie zum Beispiel/wie folgt** |
| *highlight* | |
| in particular/especially/mainly | **besonders/speziell/** |
| | **hauptsächlich, in erster Linie** |
| *generalization* | |
| usually/normally/as a rule | **gewöhnlich/normalerweise/in** |
| | **der Regel** |
| *stating the obvious* | |
| obviously/naturally/of course | **offensichtlich/natürlich/** |
| | **selbstverständlich** |
| *summary* | |
| in summary, to sum up | **zusammenfassen(d)/** |
| overall/in brief, in short | **insgesamt/kurz** |
| *conclusion* | |
| in conclusion/finally/lastly | **zum Abschluß/abschließend,** |
| | **zum Schluß/schließlich** |

## The closing

| | |
| --- | --- |
| Please don't hesitate to contact if you need any further information. | **Sie können sich jederzeit mit uns in Verbindung setzen, wenn Sie weitere Informationen benötigen.** |
| We look forward to meeting you/ hearing from you. | **Wir würden uns freuen, ein Treffen mit Ihnen vereinbaren zu können/von Ihnen zu hören.** |
| We look forward to receiving the proposal/your order/your reply. | **Wir würden uns freuen, ein Angebot/den Auftrag/eine Antwort von Ihnen zu erhalten.** |

## The farewell

| | |
| --- | --- |
| Yours sincerely | **Mit freundlichen Grüßen/ Hochachtungsvoll** |
| With best wishes/regards | **Mit freundlichen Grüßen** |

## The enclosures

| | |
| --- | --- |
| Encl. | **Anlage(n)** |

## ARRANGING APPOINTMENTS

Appointments are generally made through the secretary. Visitors are expected to be punctual.

| | |
|---|---|
| appointment | der Termin(e) |
| date | das Datum (pl Daten) |
| diary | der Terminkalender |
| meeting | das Treffen(-) |
| schedule | der Terminplan(¨e) |

### Opening

| | |
|---|---|
| You may remember, ... | Sie erinnern sich vielleicht daran, daß ... |
| we met at ... | wir uns bei ... getroffen haben. |
| ... suggested I contact you. | ... gab mir den Rat, mich mit Ihnen in Verbindung zu setzen. |
| Mr/s .... said he/she would like to talk about ... | Herr/Frau ... sagte, daß er/sie gerne über ... sprechen würde. |
| I'd like to tell you about ... | Ich würde Ihnen gerne über ... berichten. |
| I'd like to arrange a meeting. | Ich würde gerne einen Termin vereinbaren. |
| Let's fix a date. | Lassen Sie uns ein Datum ausmachen. |
| Could we meet? | Können wir uns treffen? |

- ● Could you tell me what it's about?
- ● Könnten Sie mir sagen, worum es sich handelt?
- ● Why do want to see Herr Schäfer?
- ● Weshalb möchten Sie mit Herrn Schäfer sprechen?
- ▶ I'd like to discuss something./ to discuss how ...
- ▶ Ich würde gerne etwas besprechen./besprechen wie ...
- ▶ We need to talk about ...
- ▶ Wir müssen über ... sprechen.

### Arranging a time

| | |
|---|---|
| Could you manage next week? | Paßt es Ihnen nächste Woche? |
| What about Friday afternoon? | Wie sieht es mit Freitag nachmittag aus? |
| Would Monday suit you? | Würde Ihnen Montag passen? |
| Shall we say 2 o'clock? | Sagen wir um 14 Uhr? |
| ▶ I'm afraid I can't manage Friday. | ▶ Es tut mir leid, aber Freitag paßt es mir nicht. |

DATES, see page 15/TIME, see page 16

| | |
|---|---|
| ▶ Next week is out. | ▶ Nächste Woche geht leider nicht. |
| ▶ Can you make the following week? | ▶ Paßt es Ihnen die folgende Woche? |
| ▶ Tuesday would suit me better. | ▶ Dienstag würde mir besser passen. |
| ▶ 4 o'clock would be fine. | ▶ 16 Uhr würde mir gut passen. |

## Duration

| | |
|---|---|
| It'll have to be short. I've got another meeting at 5. | Es muß schnell gehen. Ich habe um 17 Uhr einen anderen Termin. |
| It won't take more than an hour. | Es wird nicht länger als eine Stunde dauern. |

## Place

| | |
|---|---|
| Where do you suggest? | Welchen Ort schlagen Sie vor? |
| I'll come to your office. | Ich komme in Ihr Büro. |
| Shall we meet in my office? | Wollen wir uns in meinem Büro treffen? |

## Directions

| | |
|---|---|
| Can you give me some directions? | Können Sie mir den Weg beschreiben? |
| Will you be coming by car? | Kommen Sie mit dem Auto? |
| I would take a taxi from the airport. | Ich würde am Flughafen ein Taxi nehmen. |
| I'll fax you a map. | Ich werde Ihnen eine Wegbeschreibung faxen. |
| Just ask for me at the reception desk. | Fragen Sie einfach am Empfang nach mir. |
| My office is on the fifth floor (US sixth floor). | Mein Büro ist im fünften Stock. |

## Ending

| | |
|---|---|
| Let me just confirm that. Friday 24th, 3:30 at your office. | Lassen Sie mich das bestätigen. Freitag, den 24., um 15:30 Uhr in Ihrem Büro. |
| I look forward to seeing you then. | Ich freue mich darauf, Sie dann zu sehen. |
| See you next Friday. | Bis nächsten Freitag. |

TRAVELLING AROUND, see page 19

### En route

| | |
|---|---|
| Where can I get a taxi? | **Wo finde ich ein Taxi?** |
| Could you take me to …? | **Nach/In die … bitte.** |
| Could you tell me how to get to …? | **Könnten Sie mir sagen, wie ich nach/zur … komme?** |
| ▶ Straight ahead. | ▶ **Geradeaus.** |
| ▶ Turn left/right. | ▶ **Links/Rechts abbiegen.** |
| ▶ You'll see it on your right/left. | ▶ **Sie sehen es dann rechts/links.** |

### Arriving

| | |
|---|---|
| My name's … | **Mein Name ist …** |
| I've got an appointment with … | **Ich habe einen Termin bei …** |
| ▶ Please take a seat. | ▶ **Nehmen Sie bitte Platz.** |
| ▶ Mr … will see you now. | ▶ **Herr … steht jetzt zu Ihrer Verfügung.** |
| ▶ She'll be with you shortly. | ▶ **Sie ist gleich für Sie da.** |

### Cancelling an appointment

| | |
|---|---|
| Unfortunately, I'll have to cancel our meeting on … | **Ich muß unseren Termin am … leider absagen.** |
| I'll be unable to make the meeting. | **Ich werde den Termin leider nicht einhalten können.** |
| ● Can we fix a new time? How about …? | ● **Können wir eine neue Zeit ausmachen? Wie wäre es mit … ?** |
| ▶ I'll check. | ▶ **Lassen Sie mich nachschauen.** |
| ▶ I'm afraid that's not possible. | ▶ **Ich fürchte, das ist nicht möglich.** |

### Months

| | |
|---|---|
| January | **Januar** |
| February | **Februar** |
| March | **März** |
| April | **April** |
| May | **Mai** |
| June | **Juni** |
| July | **Juli** |
| August | **August** |
| September | **September** |
| October | **Oktober** |
| November | **November** |
| December | **Dezember** |

## Date

| | |
|---|---|
| ● What's the date today? | ● Den wievielten haben wir heute? |
| ▸ It's March 1st. | ▸ Es ist der 1. (erste) Marz. |
| in May | im Mai |
| on September 7 | am 7. (siebten) September |
| from June to August | von Juni bis August |
| at the beginning of October | Anfang Oktober |
| in the middle of July | Mitte Juli |
| at the end of November | Ende November |

### Years

| | |
|---|---|
| 1996 | neunzehnhundertsechsundneunzig |
| 1998 | neunzehnhundertachtundneunzig |
| in 2001 | (im) zweitausendeins |

### Days

| | |
|---|---|
| Monday | Montag |
| Tuesday | Dienstag |
| Wednesday | Mittwoch |
| Thursday | Donnerstag |
| Friday | Freitag |
| Saturday | Samstag, Sonnabend |
| Sunday | Sonntag |

| | |
|---|---|
| today | heute |
| tomorrow | morgen |
| yesterday | gestern |
| the day before yesterday | vorgestern |
| the day after tomorrow | übermorgen |
| this Wednesday | diesen Mittwoch |
| next Friday | nächsten Freitag |
| a week on from Tuesday | Dienstag in einer Woche |
| by Thursday | bis Donnerstag |
| on Saturday | am Samstag/Sonnabend |
| every Monday/on Mondays | jeden Montag, montags |
| in 5 days' time | in fünf Tagen |
| last/next month | im letzten/nächsten Monat |
| for 5 days | für fünf Tage |

NUMBERS, see page 17

### Times of day

| | |
|---|---|
| early morning | **der frühe Morgen** |
| morning | **der Morgen, der Vormittag(e)** |
| midday | **Mittag** |
| lunchtime | **die Mittagszeit(en)** |
| before lunch | **vor dem Mittag** |
| after lunch | **nach dem Mittag** |
| afternoon | **der Nachmittag(e)** |
| late afternoon | **der Spätnachmittag(e)** |
| evening | **der Abend(e)** |

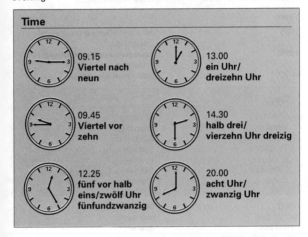

**Time**

09.15 **Viertel nach neun**

13.00 **ein Uhr/ dreizehn Uhr**

09.45 **Viertel vor zehn**

14.30 **halb drei/ vierzehn Uhr dreizig**

12.25 **fünf vor halb eins/zwölf Uhr fünfundzwanzig**

20.00 **acht Uhr/ zwanzig Uhr**

- What time does it start/end?
  - at 9 a.m./p.m.
- How long will it last?
  - 10 minutes
  - ¾ of an hour
  - until 7:30 p.m.

from ... up to ...
about ...
... exactly
... at the latest

- **Wann beginnt/endet es?**
  - **um 9 Uhr vormittags/abends**
- **Wie lange wird es dauern?**
  - **10 Minuten**
  - **eine Dreiviertelstunde**
  - **bis 19:30 Uhr**

**von ... bis ...**
**um etwa ...**
**... genau**
**... spätestens**

## Numbers

| | | | |
|---|---|---|---|
| 0 | null | 50 | fünfzig |
| 1 | eins | 60 | sechzig |
| 2 | zwei (**zwo** *on telephone*) | 70 | siebzig |
| 3 | drei | 80 | achtzig |
| 4 | vier | 90 | neunzig |
| 5 | fünf | 100 | (ein) hundert |
| 6 | sechs | 110 | hundertzehn |
| 7 | sieben | 120 | hundertzwanzig |
| 8 | acht | 130 | hundertdreißig |
| 9 | neun | 140 | hundertvierzig |
| 10 | zehn | 150 | hundertfünfzig |
| 11 | elf | 200 | zweihundert |
| 12 | zwölf | 300 | dreihundert |
| 13 | dreizehn | 400 | vierhundert |
| 14 | vierzehn | 500 | fünfhundert |
| 15 | fünfzehn | 1000 | (ein)tausend |
| 16 | sechzehn | 1100 | tausendein- hundert |
| 17 | siebzehn | | |
| 18 | achtzehn | 1200 | tausendzwei- hundert |
| 19 | neunzehn | | |
| 20 | zwanzig | 5000 | fünftausend |
| 21 | einundzwanzig | 10,000 | zehntausend |
| 22 | zweiundzwanzig | 50,000 | fünfzigtausend |
| 30 | dreißig | 100,000 | hunderttausend |
| 40 | vierzig | 1,000,000 | eine Million |

### Ordinal numbers

| | |
|---|---|
| first (1st) | **erste (1.)** |
| second (2nd) | **zweite (2.)** |
| third (3rd) | **dritte (3.)** |
| fourth | **vierte** |
| fifth | **fünfte** |
| sixth | **sechste** |
| seventh | **siebte** |
| eighth | **achte** |
| ninth | **neunte** |
| tenth | **zehnte** |
| hundredth | **hundertste** |
| millionth | **millionste** |

### Fractions etc.

| | |
|---|---|
| a half | **eine Hälfte** |
| half a ... | **ein halber ...** |
| a quarter | **ein Viertel** |
| one third | **ein Drittel** |
| four fifths | **vier Fünftel** |
| one per cent | **ein Prozent** |
| three point four per cent (3.4%) | **drei Komma vier Prozent (3,4%)** |
| once/twice/three times | **ein-/zwei-/dreimal** |

### Telephone numbers

Numbers are divided into pairs from the right, or, becoming more common, are given as individual numbers.

| | |
|---|---|
| 0 52 63 - 48 57 22 | **null zwoundfünfzig dreiundsechzig achtundvierzig siebenundfünfzig zwoundzwanzig** |
| or | **null fünf zwo sechs drei, vier acht fünf sieben zwo zwo** |

### Money

| | |
|---|---|
| DM10.523,50 | **zehntausendfünfhundertdreiundzwanzig Mark und fünfzig Pfennig(e) (10.523,50 DM)** |
| $10 per unit | **10$/zehn Dollar pro Stück** |
| profits have doubled/trebled/ halved | **die Gewinne haben sich verdoppelt/verdreifacht/halbiert** |

### Reference numbers

| | |
|---|---|
| 3580/00/DG | **drei fünf acht null Strich null null Strich DG** |

### Measurements

| | |
|---|---|
| 1.2 metres/meters | **eins Komma zwei Meter (1,2m)** |
| 500 litres/liters | **fünfhundert Liter** |
| about 20 stores | **etwa zwanzig Geschäfte/Lager** |
| in the region of ⅞ths | **etwa sieben Achtel** |
| between 50 and 60 percent | **zwischen fünfzig und sechzig Prozent** |
| 30-40,000 | **dreißig- bis vierzigtausend** |
| sales have dropped/risen by 30,000 units | **der Umsatz ist um 30.000 Stück gefallen/gestiegen** |

# TRAVELLING AROUND

## Travel by plane

| | |
|---|---|
| Is there a (connecting) flight to ...? | **Gibt es einen (Anschluß-)Flug nach ...?** |
| When does it leave/take off? | **Wann geht er ab?** |
| When does it arrive/land? | **Wann kommt er an?** |
| What time do I have to check in? | **Wann muß ich einchecken?** |

### Booking and changing flights

| | |
|---|---|
| ticket | **das Ticket(s)** |
| single/one-way | **einfach** |
| economy class | **für Economy Class** |
| business class | **für Business Class** |
| I'd like to book a return/round-trip flight to ... | **Ich möchte einen Hin- und Rückflug nach ... buchen.** |
| I'd like to cancel/change my reservation on flight number ... | **Ich möchte meine Reservierung für die Flugnummer ... stornieren/umbuchen.** |

## Travel by train

| | |
|---|---|
| buffet/restaurant car | **der Büffet-/Speisewagen(-)** |
| couchette/sleeping car | **der Liege-/Schlafwagen(-)** |
| first-class compartment | **das Erste Klasse-Abteil(e)** |
| platform | **der Bahnsteig(e)** |
| ticket office | **der Fahrkartenschalter(-)** |
| ticket reservation | **die Reservierung(en)** |
| timetable | **der Fahrplan(¨e)** |

### Enquiring about rail travel

| | |
|---|---|
| When is the next train to ...? | **Wann fährt der nächste Zug nach ...?** |
| What's the fare to ...? | **Wieviel kostet eine Fahrkarte nach ...?** |
| Do I have to change? | **Muß ich umsteigen?** |
| When does it arrive at ...? | **Wann kommt der Zug in ... an?** |
| Which platform does the train leave from/arrive at? | **Auf welchem Gleis fährt der Zug ab/kommt der Zug an?** |

### Buying a ticket

| | |
|---|---|
| I'd like a single/one-way ticket to … | Ich hätte gern eine einfache Fahrkarte nach … |
| a return/round trip ticket | eine Rückfahrkarte |
| a first-class ticket | eine Fahrkarte erster Klasse |
| I'd like to reserve a seat. | Ich möchte gern einen Platz reservieren. |

### On the train

| | |
|---|---|
| Is this the right train to …? | Ist das der Zug nach …? |
| Is this seat taken? | Ist dieser Platz besetzt? |
| I think that's my seat. | Ich glaube, das ist mein Platz. |

## Travel by taxi

| | |
|---|---|
| Could you get me a taxi? | Könnten Sie mir ein Taxi rufen? |
| Where is the taxi rank/stand? | Wo ist der Taxistand? |
| Take me to the Trade Fair. | Zur Messe bitte! |
| To this address, please. | Zu dieser Adresse bitte! |
| Please stop here. | Halten Sie bitte hier. |
| Could you wait for me? | Könnten Sie auf mich warten? |
| I'll be back in 10 minutes. | Ich bin in 10 Minuten zurück. |
| How much do I owe you? | Wieviel bin ich Ihnen schuldig? |
| Keep the change. | Der Rest ist für Sie. |

## Travel by car

### Car hire/rental

| | |
|---|---|
| I'd like to hire/rent a car. | Ich möchte gern ein Auto/einen Wagen mieten. |
| a small car | einen Kleinwagen |
| a medium-sized car | einen Mittelklassewagen |
| an automatic | ein Auto/einen Wagen mit Automatik |
| with air-conditioning | mit Klimaanlage |
| Is mileage included? | Sind die Kilometer inbegriffen? |
| I'd like to leave the car in … | Ich möchte das Auto/den Wagen in … abgeben. |
| How much is the deposit? | Wie hoch ist die Anzahlung? |
| I'd like full insurance. | Ich hätte gern einen Wagen, der voll versichert ist. |

### At the petrol/gas station

| | |
|---|---|
| Could you fill it up, please? | **Volltanken bitte!** |
| petrol/gasoline | **Benzin** |
| regular/premium/unleaded | **Normal/Super/Bleifrei** |

### Garage–Breaking down

| | |
|---|---|
| My car's broken down. | **Ich habe eine Autopanne.** |
| May I use your phone? | **Darf ich Ihr Telefon benutzen?** |
| My car won't start. | **Mein Auto springt nicht an.** |
| The battery is dead. | **Meine Batterie ist leer.** |
| I've run out of petrol. | **Ich habe kein Benzin mehr.** |
| I've got a flat tyre/tire. | **Ich habe eine Reifenpanne.** |
| There's something wrong with the ... | **Ich habe ein Problem mit ...** |
| Please check the ... | **Prüfen Sie bitte ...** |
| battery | **die Batterie** |
| brakes | **den Bremsen** |
| spare tyre/tire | **den Ersatzreifen** |
| tyre/tire pressure | **den Reifendruck** |

### Accidents

| | |
|---|---|
| Where's the nearest telephone/ garage? | **Wo ist das nächste Telefon/die nächste Werkstatt?** |
| Could you call an ambulance? | **Könnten Sie einen Krankenwagen rufen?** |
| Here's my driving licence/ driver's license. | **Hier ist mein Führerschein.** |
| What's your name and address? | **Könnten Sie mir Ihren Namen und Ihre Anschrift geben?** |
| What's your insurance company? | **Wo sind Sie versichert?** |

### Directions

| | |
|---|---|
| Go straight ahead. | **Fahren Sie geradeaus.** |
| It's on the left/right. | **Es ist auf der linken/rechten Seite.** |
| opposite/behind/next to/after ... | **gegenüber/hinter/neben/ nach ...** |
| Turn left at the ... | **Biegen Sie ... links ab.** |
| next corner | **an der nächsten Ecke** |
| traffic lights | **bei der Ampel** |
| Take the B3. | **Nehmen Sie die B3.** |
| You have to go back to ... | **Sie müssen nach/zum/zur ... zurückfahren.** |

## Accommodation

### Booking a room

| | |
|---|---|
| I'd like a single room for two nights. | Ich hätte gern ein Einzelzimmer für zwei Nächte. |
| From ... to ... | Von ... bis ... |
| single room | das Einzelzimmer(-) |
| double room | das Doppelzimmer(-) |
| twin-bedded room | das Zweibettzimmer(-) |
| family room | das Mehrbettzimmer(-) |
| with bath/shower | mit Bad/Dusche |
| I'd like a room with a shower. | Ich hätte gern ein Zimmer mit Dusche. |
| It must be quiet. | Es muß ruhig sein. |
| I'll be arriving late. | Ich werde spät ankommen. |
| How much does it cost? | Wieviel kostet das Zimmer? |
| Do you accept credit cards? | Akzeptieren Sie Kreditkarten? |

### Registering at a hotel

| | |
|---|---|
| ● My name's ... | ● Mein Name ist ... |
| ● I've got a reservation for two nights. | ● Ich habe für zwei Nächte reserviert. |
| ▶ Could you fill in this form? | ▶ Könnten Sie dieses Formular ausfüllen? |
| ▶ How will you be paying? | ▶ Wie möchten Sie bezahlen? |
| ▶ May I see your credit card? | ▶ Dürfte ich Ihre Kreditkarte sehen? |

### Complaining

| | |
|---|---|
| Could I have a quieter room? | Könnte ich ein ruhigeres Zimmer bekommen? |
| My room's too small/noisy. | Mein Zimmer ist zu klein/laut. |

### Checking out

| | |
|---|---|
| May I have the bill please? | Machen Sie bitte die Rechnung fertig? |
| I'm leaving early tomorrow so could you have the bill ready? | Ich reise morgen früh ab, könnten Sie bis dahin die Rechnung fertigmachen? |
| There's a mistake in this bill. | Die Rechnung stimmt nicht. |
| Can you order a taxi please? | Könnten Sie bitte ein Taxi rufen? |

DATES, see page 15

## INTRODUCTIONS

During introductions, everybody present is introduced by their full name and title. Shake hands as you are introduced.
Some firms are beginning to relax formality and use first names, but this should not be assumed.

## Greetings

| | |
|---|---|
| Hello. | **Hallo.** |
| Good morning/afternoon. | **Guten Morgen/GutenTag.** |
| Good evening. | **Guten Abend.** |
| How do you do? | **Sehr erfreut.** |
| Pleased to meet you. | **Freut mich, Sie kennenzulernen.** |

### Introducing yourself

| | |
|---|---|
| My name's ... | **Mein Name ist ...** |
| I'm ... | **Ich bin/Ich heiße ...** |
| Please call me ... | **Nennen Sie mich ...** |
| Everybody calls me ... | **Alle nennen mich ...** |

### Responding

| | |
|---|---|
| How do you do? I'm ... | **Guten Tag/Guten Morgen/Guten Abend. Ich bin ...** |
| Pleased to meet you too. My name's ... | **Sehr erfreut. Ich bin ...** |
| Nice to meet you too. | **Freut mich, Sie kennenzulernen.** |
| I'm sorry. I didn't catch your name. | **Entschuldigung, ich habe Ihren Namen nicht verstanden.** |

### Introducing others

| | |
|---|---|
| Peter, this is ... | **Peter, das ist ...** |
| May I introduce you to ... | **Darf ich Ihnen/Dir ... vorstellen?** |
| Have you two met? This is ... | **Kennen Sie sich bereits? Das ist ...** |

### Everyday greetings

| | |
|---|---|
| ● How are you? | **● Wie geht's?** |
| ▶ Fine, and you? | **▶ Gut, und Dir/Ihnen?** |
| ▶ Not so bad. | **▶ Nicht schlecht.** |
| ▶ Could be worse. | **▶ Könnte schlimmer sein.** |

## Presenting your job

- What do you do?
- What line are you in?

▶ I'm ...
a secretary
an accountant

▶ I work in ...
an insurance company
a school

▶ I work for ...
IBM/the local newspaper
a pharmaceutical company

▶ I'm on the ... side.
technical/commercial

▶ I'm in ...
marketing
sales/finance

▶ I'm self-employed/
unemployed/retired.

- Was machen Sie beruflich?
- Was sind Sie von Beruf?

▶ Ich bin ...
Sekretär[in]
Buchhalter[in]

▶ Ich arbeite ...
bei einer Versicherung
an einer Schule

▶ Ich arbeite für ...
IBM/die Lokalzeitung
ein Pharmaunternehmen

▶ Ich bin im ... Bereich tätig.
technischen/wirtschaftlichen

▶ Ich bin im ... tätig.
Marketing
Absatz/Finanzwesen

▶ Ich bin selbständig/
arbeitslos/Rentner[in].

## Origins

- Where do you come from?

- Where are you from?
- Where do you live?

▶ I come from ...   *I'm ...*

- Aus welchem Land kommen Sie?

- Woher kommen Sie?
- Wo wohnen Sie?

▶ Ich komme   *Ich bin ...*
aus ...

| | | | |
|---|---|---|---|
| Austalia | *Australian* | **Australien** | *Australier[in]* |
| Austria | *Austrian* | **Österreich** | *Österreicher[in]* |
| Britain | *British* | **Groß-britannien** | *Brite/Britin* |
| Canada | *Canadian* | **Kanada** | *Kanadier[in]* |
| England | *English* | **England** | *Engländer[in]* |
| Germany | *German* | **Deutschland** | *Deutscher/ Deutsche* |
| Ireland | *Irish* | **Irland** | *Ire/Irin* |
| Scotland | *Scottish* | **Schottland** | *Schotte/ Schottin* |
| Switzerland | *Swiss* | **der Schweiz** | *Schweizer[in]* |
| United States | *American* | **den USA** | *Amerikaner[in]* |
| Wales | *Welsh* | **Wales** | *Waliser[in]* |

COMPANY POSITIONS, see page 29

## Socializing

After-hours socializing is usually conducted in restaurants, wine bars or the like. As with business, punctuality is expected.

### Arriving

- How was your trip/journey?
  - Not bad.
  - No problems.
  - Rather long.
- When did you arrive/get in?
- Did you ...
  take the train/fly?
  come by car/drive?
  - I came by car/I drove.

  - I took the last flight.

- Wie war die Reise?
  - Nicht schlecht.
  - Ganz problemlos.
  - Ziemlich lang.
- Wann sind Sie angekommen?
- Sind Sie ... gekommen?
  mit dem Zug/mit dem Flugzeug
  mit dem Auto
  - Ich bin mit dem Auto gekommen.
  - Ich habe den letzten Flug genommen.

### Leaving

- I'm leaving tomorrow.
  - When does your plane leave?
  - When do you have to check in?
  Could you book a taxi for me?

  I need a taxi to take me to the airport.
  How long do you think it will take?

- Ich fahre/fliege morgen ab.
  - Wann fährt Ihr Flugzeug ab?
  - Wann müssen Sie einchecken?
  Könnten Sie für mich ein Taxi bestellen?
  Ich brauche ein Taxi zum Flughafen.
  Wie lange wird es Ihrer Meinung nach dauern?

### Accommodation

- How's your hotel?
  - Yes, it's fine.
  - It's OK.
  - It's a bit noisy.

- Wie ist Ihr Hotel?
  - Hervorragend.
  - Es ist ganz gut.
  - Es ist ein bißchen laut.

### Weather

- What was the weather like when you left?
  - Much the same as here.
  - Very sunny.
  - Dreadful.

- Wie war das Wetter, als Sie zuhause weggefahren sind?
  - Genauso wie hier.
  - Sonnig.
  - Schrecklich.

TRAVELLING AROUND, see page 19/ACCOMMODATION, see page 22

▶ Lovely and warm.
▶ Cold for the time of year.
What a lovely day!
What awful weather!
What's the weather forecast?

▶ Schön und warm.
▶ Ziemlich kalt für die Jahreszeit.
Was für ein wunderschöner Tag!
Was für ein schreckliches Wetter!
Wie soll das Wetter werden?

## Family

● Are you married?
▶ Yes, my wife is …
▶ My husband is …
▶ No, I'm single.
▶ I'm divorced.

● Sind Sie verheiratet?
▶ Ja, meine Frau ist …
▶ Mein Mann ist …
▶ Nein, ich bin ledig.
▶ Nein, ich bin geschieden.

● Have you got any children?
▶ Yes, two boys and a girl.

one daughter/three sons

● Haben Sie Kinder?
▶ Ja, zwei Jungs und ein
Mädchen.
eine Tochter/drei Söhne

● How old are they?
▶ They're ten and twelve.
▶ The oldest/youngest is …
▶ Oh, they've left home.

● Wie alt sind sie?
▶ Sie sind zehn und zwölf.
▶ Der/Die älteste/jüngste ist …
▶ Oh, sie sind bereits aus dem
Haus.

## Interests

● What do you do at/on the
weekends?
● Are you interested in sports?
● Do you play any sports?
▶ I play football/golf/tennis.
▶ I don't play but I watch …

▶ I go …
fishing/swimming/walking

● Was machen Sie an den
Wochenenden?
● Interessieren Sie sich für Sport?
● Treiben Sie Sport?
▶ Ich spiele Fußball/Golf/Tennis.
▶ Ich spiele nicht aktiv, aber ich
schaue …
▶ Ich gehe …
angeln/schwimmen/wandern

## Invitations

● Would you like to come to/for
dinner?
▶ I'd love to.
▶ I'd love to but …
▶ I'm afraid I can't.
▶ I've got another engagement.

● Darf ich Sie zum Essen
einladen?
▶ Mit Vergnügen./Gerne.
▶ Gerne, aber …
▶ Ich fürchte, das geht nicht.
▶ Ich habe schon einen anderen
Termin.

● Could you manage next Tuesday?
▶ Tuesday would be fine.

● How about a drink after work?

▶ Good idea.

● Let me buy you a drink.
▶ That's very kind of you.

● Paßt es Ihnen nächsten Dienstag?
▶ Dienstag wäre gut.

● Wollen wir nach der Arbeit noch etwas trinken gehen?
▶ Gute Idee.

● Ich lade Sie auf ein Glas ein.
▶ Sehr freundlich von Ihnen, vielen Dank.

## Dining out

### Arriving & ordering

| | |
|---|---|
| We've booked a table for four. | Wir haben einen Tisch für vier Personen bestellt. |
| Are you having a starter/dessert? | Nehmen Sie eine Vorspeise/eine Nachspeise? |
| I'd recommend the fish. | Ich kann Ihnen den Fisch empfehlen. |
| What are you going to have? | Haben Sie gewählt? |
| I think I'll have the beef. | Ich glaube, ich nehme Rindfleisch. |
| Could you tell me what ... is? | Könnten Sie mir sagen, was ... ist? |

### Commenting

| | |
|---|---|
| The fish is delicious. | Der Fisch ist ausgezeichnet. |
| Are you enjoying the beef? | Ist das Rindfleisch gut? |
| Thank you for a lovely meal. | Vielen Dank für das ausgezeichnete Essen. |

### Paying

| | |
|---|---|
| Could I have the bill? | Könnte ich bitte die Rechnung haben? |
| Do you accept ... card? | Kann ich mit der ... -karte bezahlen? |
| Is the service included? | Ist die Bedienung inbegriffen? |

### Saying good-bye

| | |
|---|---|
| I'm afraid we must go now. | Wir müssen jetzt leider gehen. |
| I hope we'll meet again soon. | Ich hoffe, wir sehen uns bald wieder. |
| Good-bye/Bye. | Auf Wiedersehen/Tschüß. |

## Introducing the company

Increasingly, German companies are moving towards flatter, less hierarchical management structures.

### Sectors

| | |
|---|---|
| Heavy Industry | **die Schwerindustrie** |
| (Light) Manufacturing | **die verarbeitende Industrie** |
| Services | **der Dienstleistungssektor** |

### Types of company

| | |
|---|---|
| company | **das Unternehmen(-)** |
| firm | **die Firma(-en)** |
| sole trader | **das Einzelunternehmen(-)** |
| partnership | **die Personengesellschaft(en)** |
| limited partnership | **die Kommanditgesellschaft (KG)** |
| partnership partly limited by shares | **die Kommanditgesellschaft auf Aktien (KGaA)** |
| trading company | **die Handelsgesellschaft (HG)** |
| open/unlimited trading company | **die offene Handelsgesellschaft (OHG)** |
| limited company | **die Gesellschaft(en) mit beschränkter Haftung (GmbH)** |
| public limited/incorporated company | **die Aktiengesellschaft(en) (AG)** |
| state company | **das Staatsunternehmen(-)** |
| private company | **das Privatunternehmen(-)** |

### Parts of company

| | |
|---|---|
| Head Office/Headquarters | **der Hauptsitz, die Zentrale(n)** |
| Parent company | **die Muttergesellschaft** |
| Holding company | **die Holdinggesellschaft(en)** |
| Subsidiary | **die Tochtergesellschaft(en)** |
| Business Unit | **der Geschäftsbereich(e), die Sparte(n)** |
| Branch | **die Filiale(n), die Zweignieder-lassung(en)** |
| Sales Office | **das Verkaufsbüro(s)** |
| Division | **der Geschäftsbereich(e), die Sparte(n)** |
| Department/Section | **die Abteilung(en)** |

PERSONNEL DEPARTMENT, see page 86

### Position in a company

| | |
|---|---|
| Chairman | **der Vorsitzende(n)** |
| Managing Director/CEO | **der Generaldirektor(en) [-in]** |
| Vice President | **der Vizepräsident(en) [-in]** |
| Director | **der Direktor(en), der leitenden Angestellte(n)** |
| Board of Managers | **der Vorstand** |
| Manager | **der Manager(-) [-in]** |
| Supervisor | **der Vorgesetzte(n)** |
| Assistant | **der Assistent(en) [-in]** |
| Shop floor worker | **der Arbeiter(-) [-in]** |
| Office staff | **das Büropersonal** |

### People in a company

| | |
|---|---|
| headcount | **die Personalstärke** |
| staff | **die Belegschaft** |
| personnel | **das Personal** |
| management | **die Unternehmensleitung** |
| workers | **die Arbeiter** *pl* |

### People around the company

| | |
|---|---|
| supplier | **der Lieferant(en)** |
| customer/client | **der Kunde(n)** |
| agent | **der Handelsvertreter(-) [-in]** |
| distributor | **der Großhändler(-) [-in], der Generalvertreter(-) [-in]** |
| dealer | **der Händler(-) [-in]** |

### Location

| | |
|---|---|
| We're based in ... | **Unser Sitz befindet sich in ...** |
| Our head office is located in ... | **Unser Hauptsitz befindet sich in ...** |
| We have branches throughout the world. | **Wir haben Filialen in der ganzen Welt.** |

### Activity

| | |
|---|---|
| We're in the telecommunications field. | **Wir sind auf dem Telekommunikationssektor tätig.** |
| We're a leading company in ... | **Wir sind ein führendes Unternehmen im Bereich ...** |

| | |
|---|---|
| There are three major business units. | **Es gibt drei große Geschäftsbereiche.** |

## Size

| | |
|---|---|
| There are four partners in the firm. | **Die Firma hat vier Teilhaber.** |
| We employ 20,000 people. | **Wir beschäftigen 20.000 Mitarbeiter.** |
| We have 20,000 employees. | **Wir haben 20.000 Beschäftigte.** |
| We have an annual turnover/ annual sales of $250 million. | **Unser Jahresumsatz beträgt 250 Millionen Dollar.** |
| Annual profits are in the region of $25 million. | **Die jährlichen Gewinne bewegen sich im Bereich von 25 Millionen Dollar.** |

## Career development

| | |
|---|---|
| I started as a foreman on the shop floor. | **Ich begann als einfacher Vorarbeiter.** |
| I got promoted to plant manager. | **Ich wurde zum Betriebsleiter befördert.** |
| I was recently appointed Production Director. | **Vor kurzem wurde ich zum Produktionsleiter ernannt.** |
| I'm due to retire next year. | **Nächstes Jahr gehe ich in Rente.** |
| I've stayed with the same company. | **Ich bin immer im selben Unternehmen geblieben.** |
| I've worked for … since 1988/ for 20 years. | **Ich arbeite seit 1988/ seit 20 Jahren für …** |
| I joined the company 20 years ago. | **Ich bin vor 20 Jahren in das Unternehmen eingetreten.** |
| I've changed jobs often. | **Ich habe häufig die Stelle gewechselt.** |

## Company history

| | |
|---|---|
| The company was founded in 1884. | **Das Unternehmen wurde 1884 gegründet.** |
| We set up the company in 1982. | **Wir haben das Unternehmen 1982 ins Leben gerufen.** |
| We went public 2 years ago. | **Wir sind vor 2 Jahren an die Börse gegangen.** |
| The company was taken over by Blaskins. | **Das Unternehmen wurde von Blaskins übernommen.** |
| Later we merged with … | **Später fusionierten wir mit …** |

NUMBERS, see page 17/DATES, see page 15

## Introducing the product

| | |
|---|---|
| product line | **die Produktlinie(n)** |
| product attribute | **die Produkteigenschaft(en)** |
| product feature | **das Produktmerkmal(e)** |
| product benefit | **der Nutzen des Produkts** |
| product advantage | **der Vorteil(e) des Produkts** |
| Our main product is ... | **Unser Hauptprodukt ist ...** |
| We have two major product lines: ... | **Wir haben zwei Hauptproduktlinien: ...** |
| It is designed to ... | **Es wurde entwickelt, um ...** |

## Life & service

| | |
|---|---|
| after sales/customer service | **der Kundendienst** |
| maintenance | **die Wartung** |
| repair (n) | **die Reparatur(en)** |
| replacement | **die Auswechslung(en), der Ersatz** |
| It will last at least ten years. | **Es wird mindestens zehn Jahre halten.** |
| It should be regularly serviced. | **Es sollte regelmäßig gewartet werden.** |
| We have a 24-hour help desk. | **Unser Kundendienst ist 24 Stunden am Tag erreichbar.** |

## Delivery

| | |
|---|---|
| You can expect delivery within 2 weeks. | **Die Lieferung erfolgt innerhalb von 2 Wochen.** |
| The earliest delivery will be next month. | **Die Lieferung erfolgt frühestens nächsten Monat.** |
| The delivery may be delayed by 24 hours. | **Die Lieferung kann sich um 24 Stunden verzögern.** |

## Price

| | |
|---|---|
| low/cheap | **niedrig/billig** |
| medium/reasonable | **mittel/reell** |
| high/expensive | **hoch/teuer** |
| The product is reasonably-priced. | **Das Produkt hat einen reellen Preis.** |
| We can offer you a 15% discount. | **Wir bieten Ihnen einen Rabatt von 15%.** |

CUSTOMER SERVICE, see page 66/PRODUCTS, see page 82

## Touring the premises

| | |
|---|---|
| office building | **das Bürogebäude(-)** |
| plant/factory | **das Werk(e)/die Fabrik(en)** |

### Offices

| | |
|---|---|
| board room | **der Sitzungssaal(-säle)** |
| canteen/company restaurant | **die Kantine(n)** |
| corridor | **der Gang(¨e)** |
| floor | **die Etage(n)** |
| lift/elevator | **der Aufzug(¨e)** |
| meeting room | **das Konferenzzimmer(-)** |
| open-plan design | **das Großraumbüro(s)** |

### Office furniture & equipment

| | |
|---|---|
| desk | **der Schreibtisch(e)** |
| fax machine | **das Faxgerät(e)** |
| filing cabinet | **der Aktenschrank(¨e)** |
| PC | **der PC(s)** |
| photocopier | **der Kopierer(-)** |
| printer | **der Drucker(-)** |
| work station | **der Arbeitsplatzrechner(-), der Arbeitsbereich mit Computer** |

### Plant layout

| | |
|---|---|
| component | **die Komponente(n)** |
| despatch/dispatch area | **der Versandbereich(e)** |
| factory floor | **der Fertigungsbereich(e)** |
| machine room | **der Maschinenraum(¨e)** |
| paint shop | **die Lackiererei(en)** |
| raw materials | **der Rohstoff(e)** |

### Showing visitors around

| | |
|---|---|
| I'm pleased to welcome you to … | **Ich freue mich, Sie bei … begrüßen zu dürfen.** |
| Welcome to … | **Willkommen bei …** |
| Please come this way. | **Kommen Sie bitte hier entlang.** |
| Follow me. | **Folgen Sie mir.** |
| Be careful! | **Seien Sie vorsichtig!** |
| Over there, you can see … | **Dort drüben sehen Sie …** |
| Are there any questions? | **Haben Sie noch Fragen?** |

# Communication Skills

## BUSINESS PRESENTATIONS

### Check-list

To help you organize your presentation, it is useful to plan it around the following stages:

| | | |
|---|---|---|
| 1. The introduction | ❑ | **1. die Einleitung** |
| 2. The overview | ❑ | **2. der Überblick** |
| 3. The main part | ❑ | **3. der Hauptteil** |
| 4. The summary | ❑ | **4. die Zusammenfassung** |
| 5. The ending | ❑ | **5. Schlußbemerkungen** |
| 6. Questions and answers | ❑ | **6. Fragen und Antworten** |

### 1. The introduction

| | |
|---|---|
| Good morning/afternoon, ladies and gentlemen. | **Guten Morgen/Guten Tag, meine sehr verehrten Damen und Herren.** |
| Dear colleagues | **Liebe Kolleginnen und Kollegen** |
| Dear participants | **Liebe Seminarteilnehmer** |
| My name is ... | **Mein Name ist ...** |
| I work for Rossomon as Marketing Director. | **Ich bin Marketing-Direktor bei Rossomon.** |
| I am the Personnel Director at Rossomon. | **Ich bin Personalchef bei Rossomon.** |

INTRODUCTIONS, see page 23/COMPANY POSITIONS, see page 29

In this talk, I'd like to ...
describe the main activities of our company.

present our product range.

explain the production processes at our plant.

In meinem Vortrag möchte ich ...
auf die wichtigsten Tätigkeitsbereiche unseres Unternehmens eingehen.
unsere Produktpalette vorstellen.
die Fertigungsverfahren in unserem Werk erläutern.

### 2. The overview

I've divided my talk into 4 main parts.

My presentation is split into 4 major sections.

In the description, I aim to cover the 4 key processes.

Ich habe meinen Vortrag in 4 Hauptabschnitte unterteilt.

Mein Vortrag gliedert sich in 4 Hauptabschnitte.

In meinen Ausführungen möchte ich auf die 4 wichtigsten Verfahren eingehen.

Firstly, we'll look at ...

Secondly, I'm going to talk about ...

After that, I'll tell you about ...

Schauen wir uns zunächst ... an.

Danach werde ich über ... sprechen.

Anschließend werde ich auf ... eingehen.

| The order of points | |
|---|---|
| First(ly) | **Erstens** |
| Second(ly) | **Zweitens** |
| Third(ly) | **Drittens** |
| Fourth(ly) | **Viertens** |
| After that | **Danach** |
| Next | **Als nächstes** |
| Finally | **Schließlich** |

### 3. The main part

Now let's look at the first point.

Now I'd like to start the first part.

Kommen wir nun zum ersten Punkt.

Lassen Sie mich nun mit dem ersten Abschnitt beginnen.

NUMBERS, see page 17

### Ending a point

| | |
|---|---|
| That's all about … | **Das wäre alles zu …** |
| That's all I want to say about the first point. | **Soweit zum ersten Punkt.** |
| That brings me to the end of the first part. | **Damit möchte ich den ersten Teil abschließen.** |

### Moving on to the next point

| | |
|---|---|
| Next let's look at … | **Kommen wir nun zu …** |
| Now I'd like to move on to the next point. | **Das bringt mich zu meinem nächsten Punkt.** |
| So now I'd like to talk about … | **Lassen Sie mich nun etwas zu/ zum/zur … sagen.** |

### Visual aids

| | |
|---|---|
| As you can see on the transparency, … | **Wie Sie auf der Folie/dem Dia sehen können, …** |
| You can see the relevant information … | **Alle wichtigen Informationen finden Sie …** |
|   on the screen |   **auf der Leinwand** |
|   on the monitor |   **auf dem Bildschirm** |
|   on the transparency |   **auf der Folie/dem Dia** |
|   in the illustration |   **der Abbildung** |
|   in the drawing |   **der Zeichnung** |
|   from the model |   **dem Modell** |
|   from the plan |   **dem Plan** |

*The relevant figures are shown …*
**Die wichtigsten Zahlen werden … dargestellt.**

on the pie/bar chart
**auf dem Kreisdiagramm/ Balkendiagramm**

by a solid/broken/dotted line
**als durchgezogene/ gestrichelte/gepunktete Linie**

COLOURS/COLORS, see page 36

| The shaded boxes ... | Die schattierten Felder ... |
|---|---|
| The blue triangles ... | Die blauen Dreiecke ... |
| show the major activities. | zeigen die wichtigsten Tätigkeitsbereiche an. |

### Colours/Colors

| black | schwarz | light ... | hell ... |
|---|---|---|---|
| blue | blau | orange | orange |
| brown | braun | pink | rosa |
| dark ... | dunkel ... | red | rot |
| green | grün | white | weiß |
| grey/gray | grau | yellow | gelb |

### 4. The summary

| Well, that brings me to the end of my final point. | Damit komme ich zum Ende meines letzten Punkts. |
|---|---|
| That concludes the main part of my talk. | Damit möchte ich den Hauptteil meines Vortrags abschließen. |
| So now, I'd just like to summarize the main points. | Ich möchte nun kurz die Hauptpunkte meines Vortrags zusammenfassen. |

### 5. The ending

| That's all I have to say for now. | Ich möchte meine Ausführungen damit beenden. |
|---|---|
| I hope that ...<br>the presentation has given you all the relevant information for your needs. | Ich hoffe, daß ...<br>Sie durch die Präsentation alle Informationen bekommen haben, die Sie benötigen. |

### 6. Questions and answers

| If you have any questions, I'll be happy to answer them. | Für weitere Fragen stehe ich Ihnen gerne zur Verfügung. |
|---|---|
| Your question, please. | Ihre Frage, bitte. |
| Any more questions? | Gibt es noch weitere Fragen? |
| If there are no more questions, I'd like to thank you for your attention. | Falls Sie keine weiteren Fragen mehr haben, möchte ich mich für Ihre Aufmerksamkeit bedanken. |

# MEETINGS, CONFERENCES AND TRADE FAIRS

## Preparing for the meeting

| | |
|---|---|
| the chairperson | der/die Vorsitzende(r) |
| the participant | der Teilnehmer(-) [-in] |
| the agenda | die Tagesordnung(en) |
| the secretary | der Sekretär(e) [-in] |
| the minutes | das Protokoll(e) |
| point | der Tagesordnungspunkt(e) |
| item | der Tagesordnungspunkt(e) |
| AOB (any other business) | Sonstiges |

## The time and place

| | |
|---|---|
| I'd like to call a meeting to discuss ... | Ich möchte eine Sitzung einberufen, um ... zu besprechen. |
| I'd like to fix a time and place for the meeting. | Lassen Sie uns den Ort und das Datum der Sitzung festlegen. |
| Does Monday at ... o'clock suit you? | Wie wäre es mit Montag, ... Uhr? |
| We are planning to meet in my office/the meeting room. | Wir wollen uns in meinem Büro/ im Konferenzraum treffen. |

## Preparing the agenda

| | |
|---|---|
| I've prepared an outline agenda. | Ich habe eine vorläufige Tagesordnung entworfen. |
| Could you look through it, please? | Könnten Sie sie kurz durchsehen? |
| Could you add any points you'd like to discuss? | Sie können gerne weitere Punkte hinzufügen, die Sie besprechen möchten. |
| Could I ask you to lead item 2 on staff training? | Könnten Sie die Leitung bei Punkt 2, der Mitarbeiterschulung, übernehmen? |
| I've finalized the agenda. | Ich habe die Tagesordnung fertiggestellt. |
| You'll receive all the papers tomorrow. | Morgen erhalten Sie alle Unterlagen. |

ARRANGING APPOINTMENTS, see page 12/TIME, see page 16

COMMUNICATION SKILLS

Meetings, conferences and trade fairs

## The Chairperson's role

### Opening the meeting

| | |
|---|---|
| Good morning/afternoon, ladies and gentlemen. | Guten Morgen/Guten Tag, meine sehrs verehrten Damen und Herren. |
| If we are all here … let's start./shall we start? | Wenn alle anwesend sind, … könnten wir anfangen./dann lassen Sie uns anfangen. |
| First of all I'd like to introduce … | Zunächst möchte ich … vorstellen. |
| Would you like to say a few words about yourselves? | Möchten Sie sich vielleicht selbst vorstellen? |
| Have you all got a copy of the agenda? | Haben Sie alle eine Kopie der Tagesordnung erhalten? |
| The objective/purpose/aim/ target of this meeting is to … | Zielsetzung/Absicht/Zweck/Ziel dieser Sitzung ist … |
| Now let's look at the agenda in detail. | Lassen Sie uns die Tagesordnung im einzelnen durchgehen. |
| As you can see there are four main points/items. | Wie Sie sehen, haben wir im wesentlichen vier Tagesord- nungspunkte. |
| I think we will need about 30 minutes for point/item 1, 20 minutes for point/item 2, … | Ich denke, wir werden etwa 30 Minuten für Punkt eins, 20 Minuten für Punkt 2 … benötigen. |
| We will break for coffee/ lunch at … | Für … Uhr ist eine Kaffeepause/ Mittagspause vorgesehen. |
| We aim to finish at … o'clock. | Das Ende der Sitzung ist für … Uhr vorgesehen. |
| Is that OK for everybody? | Sind Sie alle damit einverstanden? |

### Moving to points on the agenda

| | |
|---|---|
| Let's look at the first point. | Kommen wir zu Punkt eins. |
| I'd like to start with item one. | Ich möchte mit Punkt eins anfangen. |
| OK, Marianne, over to you. | Ich übergebe an Sie, Marianne./ Jetzt sind Sie daran, Marianne. |

NUMBERS, see page 17

| | |
|---|---|
| I believe you're going to lead this one. | Ich glaube für diesen Punkt sind Sie zuständig. |
| Can I ask you to present the background information? | Könnten Sie uns bitte die notwendigen Hintergrundinformationen geben? |
| Right. Let's move on to the next point. | Gut, kommen wir nun zum nächsten Punkt. |
| Karl, would you like to introduce the next point? | Karl, könnten Sie ein paar einleitende Worte zum nächsten Punkt sagen? |
| OK, on to item 2. | Gut, kommen wir zu Punkt 2. |

## Keeping the meeting on track

### Inviting contributions

| | |
|---|---|
| What's your opinion on this, Liz? | Wie sehen Sie die Sache, Liz? |
| Helmut, we haven't heard from you yet. | Helmut, Sie haben noch nichts dazu gesagt. |
| Would you like to add anything, Veronika? | Möchten Sie noch etwas hinzufügen, Veronika? |

### Stopping people talking

| | |
|---|---|
| We can't all speak at once. Roland first, then Liz, then Helmut. | Nicht alle auf einmal. Zuerst Roland, dann Liz, dann Helmut. |
| One at a time, please! | Einer nach dem anderen, bitte! |
| Well, thank you, Veronika. I think that's clear now. Could we have some other opinions? | Danke, Veronika. Ich denke, das ist jetzt klar. Was meinen die anderen dazu? |

## Dealing with problems of comprehension

| | |
|---|---|
| I'm sorry. I didn't hear what you said. Would you mind repeating it, please? | Entschuldigung, ich habe nicht gehört, was Sie gesagt haben. Könnten Sie das vielleicht wiederholen? |
| I'm sorry. I don't quite follow you. | Ich kann Ihnen leider nicht ganz folgen. |
| Could you go over that again, please. | Könnten Sie das vielleicht noch einmal erklären? |
| What exactly do you mean by …? | Was genau meinen Sie mit …? |

### Preventing irrelevance

| | |
|---|---|
| I'm afraid that's outside the scope of this meeting. | **Ich glaube, das ist nicht mehr Thema dieser Sitzung.** |
| We're beginning to lose sight of the main point. | **Wir verlieren das eigentliche Thema aus den Augen.** |
| Keep to the point, please. | **Bleiben Sie bitte beim Thema.** |
| We're running short of time. | **Uns läuft die Zeit davon.** |
| Please be brief. | **Fassen Sie sich bitte kurz.** |

### Paraphrasing

| | |
|---|---|
| So what you're saying is … | **Sie wollen also sagen, daß …** |
| In other words … | **Mit anderen Worten …** |
| So you mean … | **Sie meinen also, daß …** |

### Controlling decision-making

| | |
|---|---|
| I'd like to (formally) propose that … | **Ich möchte (förmlich) beantragen, daß …** |
| Can we take a vote on that proposal? | **Könnten wir über diesen Antrag abstimmen?** |
| All those in favour/favor. Right. All those against. Right, thank you. | **Wer ist dafür? Gut. Wer ist dagegen? Gut, danke.** |
| So that motion has been accepted/rejected by 4 votes to 3. | **Damit wurde dieser Antrag mit 4 zu 3 Stimmen angenommen/ abgelehnt.** |

### Summarizing & minuting/recording

| | |
|---|---|
| To sum up then, … | **Zusammenfassend gesagt, …** |
| So far we have agreed that … | **Bisher sind wir also übereingekommen …** |
| Could you minute/record that, please? | **Könnten Sie das bitte ins Protokoll aufnehmen?** |
| Have you minuted/recorded that? | **Haben Sie das ins Protokoll aufgenommen?** |

### Concluding a point on the agenda

| | |
|---|---|
| Well, I think that covers everything on that point. | **Ich denke, damit ist alles zu diesem Punkt gesagt.** |

| | |
|---|---|
| So, on point one we have agreed that … | In Bezug auf Punkt eins haben wir uns also geeinigt, daß … |
| we have accepted the figures. | wir die Zahlen angenommen haben. |
| That leaves two follow-up tasks. | Daraus ergeben sich zwei Folgeaufgaben. |
| Paul, could you prepare some information for the next meeting? | Paul, könnten Sie bis zur nächsten Sitzung weitere Informationen beschaffen? |
| Helmut, when could we have the results of your survey? | Helmut, wann könnten Sie uns die Ergebnisse Ihrer Untersuchung vorlegen? |

### Closing the meeting

| | |
|---|---|
| Right. That just about covers everything. | Gut. Damit hätten wir wohl alles abgehandelt. |
| So, the next meeting will be on … (date) at … (time) | Die nächste Sitzung ist am … um … |
| I'll circulate the minutes of this meeting in the next few days. | Das Protokoll dieser Sitzung geht Ihnen in den nächsten Tagen zu. |
| Thanks for your participation. | Ich danke Ihnen für Ihre Anwesenheit. |
| Right, I declare the meeting closed. | Hiermit schließe ich die Sitzung. |

## The Participants' role

### Getting the chair's attention

| | |
|---|---|
| (Mister/Madam) chairman | Herr Vorsitzender/Frau Vorsitzende |
| Excuse me for interrupting. | Entschuldigen Sie, daß ich Sie unterbreche. |
| I'd like to comment on that. | Dazu möchte ich etwas anmerken. |

### Giving opinions

*strongly*

| | |
|---|---|
| I'm convinced/sure/positive that … | Ich bin überzeugt/sicher/absolut sicher, daß … |
| I strongly believe that … | Ich glaube fest daran, daß … |

*neutrally*

| I think/consider/feel that … | Ich denke/nehme an/habe das Gefühl, daß … |
| As I see it, … | Meiner Meinung nach … |
| From my point of view … | Meiner Ansicht nach … |

*weakly*

| I'm inclined to think that … | Ich neige zu der Auffassung, daß … |
| I tend to think that … | Ich meine, daß … |

## Making recommendations

| Shall we hear the figures now? | Vielleicht sollten wir jetzt zu den Zahlen kommen? |
| Let's discuss the results first. | Lassen Sie uns zuerst über die Resultate sprechen. |
| I suggest we postpone the decision till the next meeting. | Ich würde vorschlagen, die Entscheidung bis zur nächsten Sitzung zu vertagen. |

## Agreeing or disagreeing with others

### Full agreement

| I totally agree with you. | Ich bin ganz Ihrer Meinung. |
| I'm in total agreement with you on that point. | In diesem Punkt bin ich ganz Ihrer Meinung. |
| I'm all in favour/favor of that proposal. | Ich stimme diesem Antrag uneingeschränkt zu. |

### Partial agreement

| Up to a point, I agree with you, but … | Ich stimme Ihnen bis zu einem gewissen Punkt zu, aber … |
| Of course, on the other hand … | Sicher, andererseits … |
| You could/may be right, but … | Sie haben vielleicht recht/Sie mögen recht haben, aber … |

### Disagreement

| I don't agree with you on that point. | In diesem Punkt bin ich anderer Meinung. |
| I can't accept that proposal. | Ich kann diesem Antrag nicht zustimmen. |
| I disagree totally. | Ich bin völlig anderer Meinung. |

## Conferences

| | |
|---|---|
| congress | **der Kongreß(-sse)** |
| symposium | **das Symposium(-en)** |
| seminar | **das Seminar(e)** |
| convention | **die Konferenz(en)** |
| to attend | **besuchen** |
| to participate | **teilnehmen** |
| chairperson | **der/die Vorsitzende** |
| participant | **der Teilnehmer(-) [-in]** |
| delegate | **der/die Delegierte(n)** |
| speaker | **der Redner(-) [-in]** |
| keynote speaker | **der Hauptredner(-) [-in]** |
| presenter | **der Moderator(en) [-in]** |

### Introducing the speaker

It gives me great pleasure to introduce Dr Alfred Bermann.

**Es ist mir eine große Freude, Ihnen Herrn Dr. Alfred Bermann vorstellen zu dürfen.**

I am very pleased to present Professor Martina Meier.

**Ich freue mich, Ihnen Frau Professor Martina Meier vorstellen zu dürfen.**

He is going to present the findings of his latest research.

**Er wird über seine neuesten Forschungsergebnisse referieren.**

She will deliver a paper entitled 'Management 2000'.

**Ihr Vortrag trägt den Titel „Management 2000".**

### Research and findings

| | |
|---|---|
| finding | **das Ergebnis(se)** |
| result | **das Resultat(e)** |
| conclusion | **die Schlußfolgerung(en)** |
| outcome | **das Ergebnis(se)** |

### Addressing the audience

Ladies and gentlemen

**Sehr verehrte Damen und Herren**

Dear colleagues

**Liebe Kolleginnen und Kollegen**

It gives me great pleasure to address you today on ...

**Ich freue mich sehr, heute vor Ihnen zum Thema ... sprechen zu dürfen.**

I should also like to thank ... for sponsoring me.

**Desweiteren möchte ich mich bei ... für die freundliche Unterstützung bedanken.**

INTRODUCTIONS, see page 23

### Thanking the speaker & inviting questions

| | |
|---|---|
| I should like to thank Dr Alfred Bermann for his most interesting talk. | Ich danke Herrn Dr. Alfred Bermann für seinen außerordentlich interessanten Vortrag. |
| Dr Bermann's talk touched many important issues. | Dr. Bermann hat in seinem Vortrag viele wichtige Punkte angesprochen. |
| So now, there will be an opportunity for questions. | Sie haben jetzt die Möglichkeit, Fragen zu stellen. |
| Are there any questions or comments? | Gibt es Fragen oder Anmerkungen? |
| Yes, your question, please. | Ja, Ihre Frage, bitte. |

### Concluding the talk

| | |
|---|---|
| I'm afraid that I will have to interrupt this interesting discussion. | Leider muß ich diese interessante Diskussion hier abbrechen. |
| I'd like, once again, to thank Professor Meier. | Ich möchte mich noch einmal bei Frau Professor Meier bedanken. |
| It is now time to move on to the next speaker. | Wir kommen jetzt zum nächsten Vortrag. |
| We have scheduled a lunch/ coffee break until ... o'clock. | Für ... Uhr ist eine Mittagspause/ Kaffeepause vorgesehen. |
| The next talk will start at ... o'clock. | Der nächste Vortrag beginnt um ... Uhr. |

### Concluding the conference

| | |
|---|---|
| It has been a very interesting conference. | Dies war eine sehr interessante Konferenz. |
| We have heard a range of stimulating presentations. | Wir haben eine Reihe äußerst interessanter Vorträge gehört. |
| It has been ... inspiring intriguing provocative stimulating | Es war ... interessant abwechslungsreich eine Herausforderung anregend |
| Finally, we look forward to seeing you all again next year in Miami. | Ich würde mich freuen, Sie nächstes Jahr alle wieder in Miami begrüßen zu dürfen. |

## Exhibitions and Trade Fairs

### The Exhibitor's role

Introducing yourself and your company

| | |
|---|---|
| Good morning/afternoon. My name's ... | Guten Morgen/Guten Tag. Ich heiße ... |
| Here's my card. | Hier ist meine Karte. |
| Do you know our company? | Kennen Sie unser Unternehmen? |
| I'm sure you know our organization. | Ich bin sicher, daß Sie unser Unternehmen kennen. |
| We make/provide ... | Wir stellen ... her./bieten ... an. |
| We are the largest company in our field. | Wir sind das größte Unternehmen in unserem Bereich. |

Finding out about your visitor

| | |
|---|---|
| What do you do? | Was machen Sie beruflich? |
| Who do you work for? | Für wen arbeiten Sie? |
| What do they do? | Was macht Ihr Unternehmen? |
| Would you like some information about our products/services? | Wären Sie an Informationen über unsere Produkte/unsere Dienstleistungen interessiert? |
| Any specific product/service? | Sind Sie an einem bestimmten Produkt/einer bestimmten Leistung interessiert? |
| What exactly would you like to know? | Was genau möchten Sie wissen? |

Giving information to the visitor

| | |
|---|---|
| We have a number of products which can ... | Wir haben eine Reihe von Produkten, die ... können. |
| This product/service ... | Dieses Produkt/diese Leistung ... |
| is just right for your needs. | ist für ihre Zwecke bestens geeignet. |
| exactly covers your needs. | entspricht genau Ihren Bedürfnissen. |
| could be the answer to your problem. | könnte die Lösung für Ihre Probleme sein. |

GREETINGS, see page 23/INTRODUCING THE COMPANY, see page 28

| | |
|---|---|
| For your needs, I would recommend ... | **Für Ihre Zwecke würde ich ... empfehlen.** |
| I'm afraid we don't make anything like that. | **So etwas stellen wir leider nicht her.** |
| I'm sorry but we can't provide that service. | **Das können wir leider nicht anbieten.** |
| Please take a copy of our brochure/leaflet/prospectus. | **Nehmen Sie doch eine Broschüre/ein Informationsblatt/ einen Prospekt mit.** |
| It contains all the product information. | **Sie finden darin alle Inform- ationen zu unseren Produkten.** |

### Planning follow-up action

| | |
|---|---|
| Would you like ... | **Wären Sie an ...** |
| someone to visit your company? | **einem Besuch durch einen un- serer Mitarbeiter interessiert?** |
| us to prepare a quotation? | **einem Voranschlag interessiert?** |
| a demonstration of the equipment? | **einer Vorführung der Geräte interessiert?** |
| Would you like to discuss this over lunch/dinner/a coffee? | **Vielleicht sprechen wir beim Mittagessen/beim Abendessen/ bei einem Kaffee weiter über die Angelegenheit?** |
| Would you like to return to the stand/booth later? | **Könnten Sie vielleicht später noch einmal am Stand vorbeischauen?** |
| I/We'd be delighted to ... | **Ich würde mich freuen/Wir würden uns freuen ...** |
| visit your company. | **Ihrem Unternehmen einen Besuch abstatten zu dürfen.** |
| prepare a quotation. | **Ihnen ein Angebot unterbreiten zu dürfen.** |
| discuss this later. | **dies zu einem späteren Zeitpunkt zu besprechen.** |

### Saying good-bye

| | |
|---|---|
| We'll be in touch with you next week/month. | **Sie hören nächste Woche/ nächsten Monat von uns.** |
| Good-bye. | **Auf Wiedersehen/Tchüß.** |

INTRODUCING THE PRODUCT, see page 31

### The Visitor's role

#### Explaining your areas of interest

| | |
|---|---|
| I am interested in ... | Ich interessiere mich für ... |
| I would like to know more about ... | Ich hätte gern genauere Informationen über ... |

#### Questioning the exhibitor

| | |
|---|---|
| Could you explain exactly ... | Könnten Sie mir sagen, ... |
| what this product does? | wozu dieses Produkt dient? |
| how this machine works? | wie diese Maschine funktioniert? |
| where this service is provided? | wo diese Dienstleistung angeboten wird? |
| if this service is available here? | ob diese Dienstleistung hier angeboten wird? |

#### Planning follow-up action

| | |
|---|---|
| I/We would like ... | Ich wäre/Wir wären an ... interessiert. |
| someone to visit our company. | einem Besuch eines Ihrer Mitarbeiter |
| to have a quotation. | einem Angebot |
| to discuss this further. | einem weiteren Gespräch |
| to see a demonstration. | einer Vorführung |
| I look forward to hearing from you. | Ich würde mich freuen, von Ihnen zu hören. |

### Communication difficulties

| | |
|---|---|
| Could you speak ..., please? | Könnten Sie bitte ... sprechen? |
| a bit slower/louder | etwas langsamer/etwas lauter |
| I'm sorry, could you repeat that, please. | Entschuldigung, könnten Sie das bitte wiederholen? |
| What exactly do you mean by ...? | Was genau meinen Sie mit ...? |
| Could you explain that, please? | Könnten Sie das bitte erklären? |

#### Showing understanding

| | |
|---|---|
| I see/understand. | Ich verstehe. |
| Yes, I've got that now. | Ja, das habe ich jetzt verstanden. |
| Yes, that's clear now. | Ja, das ist jetzt klar. |

# NEGOTIATIONS

Negotiations are usually conducted in a formal manner and a written record of proceedings is normally made. Any oral agreement reached should be confirmed in writing.

---

### Check-list

To help you prepare your negotiation, it is useful to plan it around the following stages:

| | | |
|---|---|---|
| 1. Creating the right environment | ❏ | 1. Auswahl des passenden Umfeldes |
| 2. Defining the issues | ❏ | 2. Definition der Gesprächspunkte |
| 3. Establishing opening positions | ❏ | 3. Bestimmung der Ausgangspositionen |
| 4. Handling the offer and counter-offer | ❏ | 4. Angebot und Gegenangebot |
| 5. Testing the other side's case | ❏ | 5. Untersuchung der Position des Verhandlungspartners |
| 6. Strengthening your case | ❏ | 6. Stärkung der eigenen Position |
| 7. Handling stalemate | ❏ | 7. Verhalten bei festgefahrenen Verhandlungen |
| 8. Clinching the deal | ❏ | 8. Erfolgreicher Geschäftsabschluß |
| 9. Getting it in writing | ❏ | 9. Schriftliche Niederlegung |

---

### The processes

| | |
|---|---|
| to negotiate | verhandeln |
| to bargain | handeln |
| to discuss | besprechen, diskutieren |
| to persuade | überzeugen |
| to compromise | einen Kompromiß schließen |
| to make a deal | ein Geschäft abschließen |
| to strike a bargain | handelseinig werden |
| to reach agreement | sich einigen |
| to draft a contract | einen Vertrag aufsetzen |
| to sign the contract | den Vertrag unterzeichnen |

| | |
|---|---|
| to implement the agreement | **den Vertrag erfüllen** |
| to break the contract | **den Vertrag brechen** |

### The subject of negotiation

| | |
|---|---|
| price | **der Preis(e)** |
| delivery and terms | **die Lieferung(en) und die Lieferbedingungen** |
| payment and credit | **die Zahlung(en) und das Zahlungsziel** |
| discount | **der Preisnachlaß(¨-sse)** |
| licences/licenses | **die Lizenz(en)** |
| warranties and guarantees | **die Gewährleistung(en) und die Garantie(n)** |
| penalties | **die Vertragsstrafe(n)** |
| legal jurisdiction | **die Gerichtsbarkeit** |

## 1. Creating the right environment

For key phrases for introducing yourself and making small talk, see Section 1 Making Contact: Introductions and Socializing.

## 2. Defining the issues

### Stating the agenda

| | |
|---|---|
| OK. Shall we start? | **Gut. Sollen wir anfangen?** |
| Our position is as follows: | **Unsere Position sieht folgendermaßen aus ...** |
| We would like to buy ... | **Wir möchten ... kaufen.** |
| We are interested in selling ... | **Wir sind am Verkauf von ... interessiert.** |
| We need to reach agreement about ... | **Wir müssen uns über ... einigen.** |
| The aim/purpose/target/ objective of this negotiation is to solve the problem over ... | **Absicht/Zweck/Ziel/Zielsetzung dieser Verhandlungen ist, das Problem hinsichtlich ... zu lösen.** |

### Clarifying the agenda

| | |
|---|---|
| So, if we understand you correctly, you want to sell ... | **Wenn wir Sie also richtig verstehen, möchten Sie ... verkaufen.** |

INTRODUCTIONS, see page 23/SOCIALIZING, see page 25

| | |
|---|---|
| We fully understand your views/position ... | **Wir haben volles Verständnis für Ihren Standpunkt/Ihre Position ...** |
| but what would you actually like us to do? | **aber was sollen wir Ihrer Ansicht nach tun?** |
| but what precisely are you offering? | **aber was genau bieten Sie uns an?** |

## 3. Establishing opening positions

### Price

| | |
|---|---|
| In your proposal your asking price is ... | **Die ursprüngliche Preisforderung in Ihrem Angebot beläuft sich auf ...** |
| You have set the price at ... | **Sie haben den Preis auf ... festgelegt.** |
| We are willing to pay ... | **Wir wären bereit ... zu zahlen.** |
| Our initial offer is ... | **Unser Erstangebot beläuft sich auf ...** |

### Delivery and terms

| | |
|---|---|
| In addition, we/you can deliver the goods on 25th July. | **Außerdem könnten wir/Sie die Waren am 25. Juli liefern.** |
| we can supply the products by 25th July. | **könnten wir die Waren bis zum 25. Juli liefern.** |
| Our position is that we need the goods by 20th July. | **Wir brauchen die Waren bis zum 20. Juli.** |
| Can you arrange delivery to our site by truck? | **Könnten Sie den Lkw-Transport bis zu unserem Standort organisieren?** |
| However, you expect us to provide transport and insurance. | **Wir sollen also den Transport und die Versicherung übernehmen.** |
| However, you do not agree to pay for ... | **Sie sind also nicht bereit, ... zu bezahlen.** |

### Payment and credit

| | |
|---|---|
| We expect payment by bank transfer... | **Die Zahlung sollte innerhalb ... per Banküberweisung erfolgen.** |
| within 60 days. | **von 60 Tagen** |
| 90 days after invoice. | **nach Rechnungsausstellung** |
| 90 days after order. | **nach Auftragsdatum** |

PAYMENT, see page 77/DISTRIBUTION, see page 71

| | |
|---|---|
| Our normal payment terms are by letter of credit. | **Üblicherweise erfolgen die Zahlungen per Akkreditiv.** |
| Do you accept our payment terms? | **Sind Sie mit unseren Zahlungsbedingungen einverstanden?** |
| We do not normally pay ... | **Normalerweise zahlen wir nicht ...** |
| in cash. | **bar.** |
| by bank transfer. | **per Banküberweisung.** |

## Discount

| | |
|---|---|
| However, we can offer an initial discount of 5%. | **Wir können Ihnen einen Preisnachlaß von 5 Prozent anbieten.** |
| But we are prepared to reduce the total price by 5%. | **Wir sind allerdings bereit, den Gesamtpreis um 5 Prozent zu senken.** |
| What discount can you offer? | **Welchen Preisnachlaß könnten Sie uns anbieten?** |

## Licences/Licenses

| | |
|---|---|
| What licence/license can you offer? | **Welche Lizenzen können Sie anbieten?** |
| We are prepared to offer a licence/license to sell the product. | **Wir könnten Ihnen eine Verkaufslizenz für das Produkt anbieten.** |
| We cannot grant a licence/license to manufacture the product. | **Wir können keine Fertigungslizenz für das Produkt erteilen.** |
| The licence/license will initially be limited to 5 years. | **Die Laufzeit der Lizenz ist zunächst auf 5 Jahre beschränkt.** |

## Warranties and guarantees

| | |
|---|---|
| What warranties and guarantees do you offer? | **Welche Gewährleistungen und Garantien bieten Sie an?** |
| We warrant the goods for a period of 5 years. | **Unsere Gewährleistungszeit für diese Produkte beträgt 5 Jahre.** |
| We cover all parts and labour/labor for 1 year. | **Für ein Jahr übernehmen wir sämtliche Ersatzteil- und Arbeitskosten.** |

PRICING, see page 84/DATES, see page 15

| In that case, we … | In diesem Fall werden wir … |
| will replace the goods. | die Waren ersetzen. |
| repair the equipment free of charge. | die Geräte kostenlos reparieren. |
| We cannot guarantee the goods against … | Wir können keine Garantie geben für … |
| breakdown | einen Betriebsausfall |
| normal wear and tear | normalen Verschleiß |

### Penalties

| What happens if anything goes wrong? | Was geschieht, wenn Probleme auftreten? |
| What compensation will you pay if …? | Welche Entschädigungen zahlen Sie im Falle von …? |
| We will claim compensation if … | Wir werden eine Entschädigung fordern, falls … |
| you don't deliver on time. | Sie nicht termingerecht liefern. |
| the goods are delayed. | sich die Lieferung der Waren verzögert. |
| the equipment breaks down. | die Anlage ausfällt. |

### Legal jurisdiction

| What happens if there is a dispute? | Was passiert im Falle von (Rechts-)Streitigkeiten? |
| Any disputes will be settled according to German law. | Alle (Rechts-)Streitigkeiten unterliegen deutschem Recht. |
| We resolve any disagreements by arbitration. | Wir regeln alle (Rechts-)Streitigkeiten über ein Schiedsgerichtsverfahren. |

## 4. Handling the offer and counter-offer

### Positive

| That's great. | Das ist hervorragend. |
| (That's a) good/excellent/great idea. | (Das ist eine) gute/ausgezeichnete/hervorragende Idee. |
| We accept/agree. | (Wir sind) einverstanden. |

LEGAL DEPARTMENT, see page 78/CONTRACT LAW, see page 121

| We can accept your payment/ delivery/discount terms. | **Wir sind mit Ihren Zahlungs-/ Liefer-/Rabattbedingungen einverstanden.** |
| We are in agreement over penalty clauses. | **Wir stimmen den Vertrags- strafeklauseln zu.** |

### Partial

| Yes, but ... | **Ja, aber ...** |
| We're on the right track. | **Wir sind auf dem richtigen Weg.** |
| We're getting there. | **Wir gehen in die richtige Richtung.** |

### Negative

| That's unacceptable. | **Das ist nicht annehmbar.** |
| That's out of the question. | **Das ist völlig ausgeschlossen.** |
| We can't accept that. | **Das ist für uns nicht annehmbar.** |
| We don't agree to that. | **Dem können wir nicht zustimmen.** |
| We don't agree to ... | **Wir sind nicht bereit, ...** |
| We are not in agreement over compensation clauses. | **Den Vertragsentschädigungs- klauseln können wir nicht zustimmen.** |

## 5. Testing the other side's case

| Have you given us all the relevant facts? | **Haben wir alle wichtigen Angaben von Ihnen erhalten?** |
| On what are those figures based? | **Worauf basieren diese Zahlen?** |
| We have heard that ... your normal prices are ... normal delivery terms are ... | **Wir haben gehört, ... Ihr üblicher Preis läge bei ... Ihre üblichen Lieferbedingungen seien ...** |
| We don't follow the logic of your argument. | **Wir können Ihrer Argumentation nicht ganz folgen.** |
| If your normal prices are ..., then we expect ... | **Wenn Ihre Preise üblicherweise bei .... liegen, erwarten wir ...** |
| Could you explain how you got to those figures? | **Könnten Sie erklären, wie Sie zu diesen Zahlen kommen?** |

GIVING OPINIONS, see page 41

## 6. Strengthening your case

If we accept your prices, then we will have to raise our prices.
**Wenn wir Ihre Preise akzeptieren, müssen wir unsere Preise erhöhen.**

That will not be good for our business.
**Das ist unserem Geschäft nicht zuträglich.**

If you can reduce your price by ..., then we will ...
**Wenn Sie Ihren Preis um ... senken könnten, würden wir ...**

If you are prepared to speed up delivery, then we will ...
**Wenn Sie bereit wären, die Lieferung etwas zu beschleunigen, würden wir ...**

If you are willing to reconsider your payment terms, then we will ...
**Wenn Sie bereit wären, Ihre Zahlungsbedingungen noch einmal zu überdenken, könnten wir...**

look at prices for our next contract.
**uns bei unserem nächsten Vertrag noch einmal über die Preise unterhalten.**

## 7. Handling stalemate

We are very far apart on this issue.
**In diesem Punkt gehen unsere Ansichten sehr weit auseinander.**

Our positions are very different on the question of ...
**Was ... anbetrifft, vertreten wir völlig unterschiedliche Positionen.**

I don't think we can resolve this matter now.
**Ich denke, daß wir diese Angelegenheit im Moment nicht lösen können.**

Shall we summarise the points of agreement ...
**Vielleicht sollten wir die Punkte zusammenfassen, in denen wir übereinstimmen ...**

and then take a short break.
**und anschließend eine kurze Pause machen.**

and then adjourn till this afternoon.
**und die Angelegenheit dann auf den Nachmittag verschieben.**

So far, we've agreed on the following points: ...
**Bis jetzt sind wir uns also in den folgenden Punkten einig: ...**

We disagree on ...
**Wir sind anderer Meinung bezüglich ...**

So we'll come back to those issues after the break.
**Wir werden also nach der Pause auf diese Fragen zurückkommen.**

## 8. Clinching the deal

| | |
|---|---|
| We have covered a lot of ground in this meeting. | **Diese Sitzung hat uns schon ein gutes Stück weitergebracht.** |
| We cannot change our offer. | **Wir können unser Angebot nicht weiter ändern.** |
| This is our final offer. | **Das ist unser letztes Angebot.** |
| We have/have not reached agreement on ... | **Wir sind uns also einig/nicht einig über ...** |
| You have accepted our terms on ... | **Sie sind also mit unseren Bedingungen hinsichtlich ... einverstanden.** |
| You cannot accept our terms on ... | **Unsere Bedingungen hinsichtlich ... sind für Sie nicht annehmbar.** |
| Let me go over all the details again. | **Lassen Sie mich noch einmal alle Einzelheiten durchgehen.** |
| Have I covered everything? | **Habe ich etwas vergessen?** |
| Do you agree? | **Stimmen Sie mir zu?** |
| Do you accept these terms? | **Sind Sie mit diesen Bedingungen einverstanden?** |

## 9. Getting it in writing

| | |
|---|---|
| I will draft an outline agreement. | **Ich werde einen Vertragsentwurf ausarbeiten.** |
| Can you prepare a draft contract? | **Könnten Sie einen Vertragsentwurf vorbereiten?** |
| I will send the agreement to you for your comments. | **Ich werde Ihnen den Vertrag zur Stellungnahme zuschicken.** |
| Please send the draft contract to me for our comments. | **Schicken Sie mir den Vertrag bitte zur Stellungnahme zu.** |
| After the contract/agreement has been signed, we can ... | **Nach der Vertragsunterzeichnung können wir ...** |
| deliver the equipment. | **die Geräte liefern.** |
| party (n) to the contract | **die Vertragspartei(en)** |
| signatory to the contract | **der Unterzeichner(-) des Vertrags** |
| terms of the contract | **die Vertragsbedingung(en)** |
| clause of the contract | **die Vertragsklausel(n)** |
| breach of contract | **der Vertragsbruch** |

CONTRACT LAW, see page 121/LEGAL JURISDICTION, see page 52

## PROJECTS AND PERFORMANCE

---

**Check-list**

To help you manage your project better, it is useful to plan it around the following stages or milestones:

| | | |
|---|---|---|
| 1. Defining objectives | ❑ | 1. Zielvorgaben |
| 2. Prioritizing and sequencing activities | ❑ | 2. Ordnen der Aktivitäten nach Wichtigkeit und Erstellen einer Reihenfolge |
| 3. Allocating resources | ❑ | 3. Zuweisung von Ressourcen |
| 4. Evaluating performance | ❑ | 4. Auswertung der Ergebnisse |
| 5. Project completion | ❑ | 5. Abschluß des Projekts |

**Project types**

| | |
|---|---|
| Company restructuring | die Umstrukturierung des Unternehmens |
| Automation project | das Automatisierungsprojekt(e) |
| IT project | das IT-Projekt(e) |
| Cost control project | das Kostenüberwachungs-projekt(e) |
| Quality project | das Qualitätsprojekt(e) |
| Research project | das Forschungsprojekt(e) |
| Installation project | das Installationsvorhaben(-) |
| Construction project | das Bauvorhaben(-) |
| Product launch | die Produkteinführung |

**The project team**

| | |
|---|---|
| The team consists of a ... | Das Team besteht aus ... |
| We have appointed a ... | Wir haben einen/eine ... ernannt. |
| project leader | Projektleiter[in] |
| project supervisor | Projektaufseher[in] |
| project manager | Projektmanager[in] |
| project assistant | Projektassistenten [-in] |
| project secretary | Projektsekretär[in] |

## 1. Defining objectives

---

| | |
|---|---|
| What exactly do we want to achieve? | Was genau wollen wir erreichen? |

| | |
|---|---|
| How exactly are we going to achieve it? | **Wie wollen wir es erreichen?** |
| Is this project really necessary? | **Ist dieses Projekt wirklich erforderlich?** |
| The aims/objectives/goals/targets of this project are to ... | **Absicht/Zweck/Ziel/Zielsetzung dieses Projekts ist ...** |
| In this project, we ... | **Im Rahmen dieses Projekts ...** |
| aim to ... | **wollen wir ...** |
| plan to ... | **planen wir ...** |
| mean to ... | **beabsichtigen wir ...** |
| propose to ... | **haben wir uns vorgenommen ...** |
| intend to ... | **versuchen wir ...** |
| reorganize the company | **das Unternehmen neu (zu) ordnen** |
| increase output | **den Ertrag (zu) steigern** |
| introduce new equipment | **neue Geräte (zu) installieren** |
| launch an updated product | **ein aktualisiertes Produkt ein(zu)führen** |

## 2. Prioritizing and sequencing activities

### The stages

| | |
|---|---|
| The project consists of 10 phases. | **Das Projekt besteht aus 10 Phasen.** |
| The project will be divided into 10 stages/activities. | **Das Projekt wird in 10 Phasen/Maßnahmen unterteilt.** |
| At the end of each stage, there is a milestone. | **Am Ende jeder Phase steht ein Meilenstein.** |
| The phases and milestones are shown on this project schedule. | **Die unterschiedlichen Phasen und Meilensteine sind im Projektplan enthalten.** |
| You can see the phases ... | **Die unterschiedlichen Phasen sind ...** |
| on the critical path analysis | **in der CPM-Methode** |
| on the flowchart | **im Ablaufdiagramm** |
| on the Gantt chart | **im Gantt-Diagramm** |

### Questions about the schedule

| | |
|---|---|
| When are we due to start the project? | **Wann sollen wir mit dem Projekt beginnen?** |

| When will the first stage be finished? | **Wann wird die erste Phase ab geschlossen sein?** |
| How long will the first activity take? | **Wie lange wird die erste Maßnahme dauern?** |
| When do we plan to complete the whole project? | **Wann soll das gesamte Projekt abgeschlossen sein?** |

### Details about the schedule

| The first stage will start on 25th July. | **Die erste Phase beginnt am 25. Juli.** |
| We will begin this activity on 25th July. | **Mit dieser Maßnahme werden wir am 25. Juli beginnen.** |
| This phase will take 3 weeks. | **Diese Phase wird 3 Wochen dauern.** |
| This stage will last until 4th August. | **Diese Phase dauert bis zum 4. August.** |
| The next stage will be to ... | **In der nächsten Phase wird ...** |
| The whole project must be completed by 15th April. | **Das gesamte Projekt muß bis zum 15. April abgeschlossen sein.** |

### Prioritising

| The most important activity is ... | **Die wichtigste Maßnahme ist ...** |
| The most critical activity is ... | **Die entscheidende Maßnahme ist ...** |
| The key stages are ... | **Die Schlüsselphasen sind ...** |
| The major stages are ... | **Die Hauptphasen sind ...** |

### Project activities

| collecting the data | **Daten erfassen** |
| interpreting the data | **Daten auswerten** |
| researching the market | **Marktforschung betreiben** |
| designing the prototype | **den Prototyp entwerfen** |
| testing the prototype | **den Prototyp testen** |
| selecting the subcontractors | **die Zulieferer auswählen** |
| recruiting the workforce | **Arbeitskräfte einstellen** |
| subcontracting the manufacture of components | **Unteraufträge für die Herstellung von Komponenten vergeben** |
| producing the equipment | **das Equipment herstellen** |
| choosing an advertising agency | **eine Werbeagentur aussuchen** |

| | |
|---|---|
| agreeing the promotion | **die Promotionsmaßnahmen abstimmen** |
| finalizing the launch date | **das Datum für die Produkteinführung festlegen** |
| installing the equipment | **die Geräte installieren** |
| starting up the plant | **die Anlage/das Werk in Betrieb nehmen** |
| handing over the plant | **die Anlage/das Werk übergeben** |

## 3. Allocating resources

### Forecasting

| | |
|---|---|
| I am sure/convinced that ... we will need more time. | **Ich bin sicher/überzeugt, daß ... wir mehr Zeit brauchen.** |
| It is likely that ... we will need more money. | **Wahrscheinlich ... werden wir mehr Geld benötigen.** |
| We may ... need more people. | **Unter Umständen ... brauchen wir mehr Personal.** |
| We are unlikely to ... need more equipment. | **Es ist unwahrscheinlich, daß ... wir zusätzliche Geräte benötigen.** |
| We definitely/certainly won't ... | **Wir brauchen bestimmt/mit Sicherheit keine ...** |
| need more materials. | **zusätzlichen Materialien.** |

### Time

| | |
|---|---|
| How much time will we need? | **Wie lange werden wir brauchen?** |
| How long do we have for the first stage? | **Wieviel Zeit haben wir für die erste Phase?** |
| We will need more/less time than budgeted. | **Wir werden mehr/weniger Zeit brauchen als vorgesehen.** |
| We'll require ... a longer time for stage 1 a shorter time for stage 2 another 3 days for stage 3 | **Wir werden ... benötigen. für Phase eins mehr Zeit für Phase 2 weniger Zeit für Phase 3 drei zusätzliche Tage** |
| We need to complete this phase in spring/summer/autumn (fall)/ winter. | **Wir müssen diese Phase im Frühjahr/im Sommer/im Herbst/ im Winter abschließen.** |

DATES, see page 15

### Budget

| How much will it cost? | Wie teuer wird das Projekt werden? |
| --- | --- |
| What is the budget? | Wie groß ist das Budget? |
| We will need more money than allocated. | Wir werden mehr Geld benötigen als vorgesehen. |
| It will cost more than budgeted. | Es wird teurer werden als vorgesehen. |
| We forecast it will cost another DM 15,000. | Wir gehen von Mehrkosten in Höhe von DM15.000 aus. |

### People

| How many people do we need? | Wieviele Mitarbeiter brauchen wir? |
| --- | --- |
| We don't have enough people. | Wir haben nicht genug Personal. |
| Should we use our people or can we subcontract some of the work out? | Sollen wir unsere Mitarbeiter einsetzen oder können wir Unterverträge für einige der Arbeiten vergeben? |
| We will need to employ/hire some extra ... | Wir müssen einige zusätzliche ... einstellen. |
| operators | Maschinenarbeiter, Bediener |
| specialists | Spezialisten, Fachleute |
| technicians | Techniker |
| workers | Arbeiter |
| We plan to subcontract some of the work out. | Für einige der Arbeiten wollen wir Unterverträge vergeben. |

### Responsibilities

| The project leader has overall responsibility for ... | Der Projektleiter[in] trägt die Gesamtverantwortung für ... |
| --- | --- |
| The project supervisor is in charge of ... | Der Projektaufseher[in] ist zuständig für ... |
| The project manager will take care of ... | Der Projektmanager[in] kümmert sich um ... |
| The project assistant is responsible for ... | Der Projektassistent[in] ist verantwortlich für ... |
| The project secretary will support/assist the project leader. | Der Projektsekretär[in] unterstützt den Projektleiter. |

FINANCE DEPARTMENT, see page 73/COMPANY POSITIONS, see page 29

| | |
|---|---|
| financial questions | **die Finanzfragen** |
| personnel matters | **die Personalfragen** |
| day-to-day administration | **die laufende Verwaltung** |
| accommodation on site | **die Unterbringung vor Ort** |
| contracts with suppliers | **die Verträge mit Lieferanten** |
| dealing with contractors | **mit Auftragnehmern verhandeln** |
| buying in materials | **Material beschaffen** |
| organizing transport | **den Transport organisieren** |

### Materials

| | |
|---|---|
| What materials do we need? | **Was brauchen wir an Material?** |
| Do we have the necessary equipment? | **Haben wir die notwendigen Geräte?** |
| We don't have enough materials/equipment. | **Wir haben nicht genug Material/ Geräte.** |
| We can produce the materials in-house. | **Wir können das Material selbst/ intern herstellen.** |
| We need to buy in the materials. | **Wir müssen das Material kaufen.** |
| What equipment do we need to hire/lease/buy? | **Welche Geräte müssen wir mieten/leasen/kaufen?** |

## 4. Evaluating performance

### The project

| | |
|---|---|
| How is the project going? | **Wie läuft das Projekt?** |
| The project is on target. | **Das Projekt läuft nach Plan.** |
| We are ahead of schedule. | **Wir sind dem Zeitplan voraus.** |
| We are behind schedule. | **Wir liegen im Zeitplan zurück.** |
| The costs are as forecast. | **Die Kosten liegen im vorgesehenen Rahmen.** |
| The costs are running above/ below budget. | **Die Kosten fallen niedriger/höher aus als vorgesehen.** |
| We have had a cost overrun. | **Es sind Mehrkosten angefallen.** |
| We can't ... recruit the right workers. | **Wir können nicht ... die nötigen Arbeiter einstellen.** |
| We need to review the situation. | **Wir müssen die Situation überdenken.** |

| | |
|---|---|
| We are facing some difficulties/ problems with … | **Wir haben Schwierigkeiten/ Probleme mit …** |
| the timing of the project. | **dem Timing des Projekts.** |
| the financing of the project. | **der Finanzierung des Projekts.** |
| the manpower for the project. | **der Personalausstattung für das Projekt.** |
| the equipment for the project. | **Maschinen für das Projekt** |
| We need to look again at … | **Wir müssen uns noch einmal mit … befassen.** |
| the schedule | **dem Zeitplan** |
| the budgets | **dem Budget** |
| our manpower needs | **unserem Personalbedarf** |
| our material requirements | **unserem Materialbedarf** |
| We must control costs. | **Wir müssen die Kosten unter Kontrolle halten.** |
| We need to … | **Wir müssen …** |
| lay off some of the workers. | **einige Arbeiter vorübergehend entlassen.** |
| fire the supervisor. | **den Aufseher[in] entlassen.** |

### Personal qualities

| | |
|---|---|
| The project leader is … | **Der Projektleiter[in] ist …** |
| efficient | **tüchtig** |
| effective | **effektiv** |
| hard-working | **fleißig** |
| competent | **kompetent** |
| conscientious | **gewissenhaft** |
| ambitious | **ehrgeizig** |
| The project supervisor is … | **Der Projektaufseher[in] …** |
| logical | **denkt logisch** |
| methodical | **geht systematisch vor** |
| analytical | **ist ein guter Analytiker** |
| rational | **denkt rational** |
| calm | **ist ruhig** |
| inflexible | **ist wenig flexibel** |
| good with facts and figures | **kann gut mit Fakten und Zahlen umgehen** |
| The project manager is … | **Der Projektmanager[in] …** |
| practical | **ist ein Praktiker** |
| energetic | **ist tatkräftig** |
| dynamic | **ist dynamisch** |

| single-minded | ist zielstrebig |
| impatient | ist ungeduldig |
| good at negotiating | hat großes Verhandlungs-geschick |

| The project designer is ... | Der Projektdesigner[in] ist ... |
| creative | kreativ |
| imaginative | einfallsreich |
| unorthodox | unorthodox |
| impractical | kein Praktiker |

| The project assistant is ... | Der Projektassistent[in] ... |
| sympathetic | ist verständnisvoll |
| perceptive | ist einfühlsam |
| communicative | ist mitteilsam |
| good at developing team relationships | versteht es, den Teamgeist zu wecken |

## Business trends

| to increase/to raise | erhöhen |
| to put up/to step up | anheben/erhöhen |
| *We have increased the budget for stage one.* | *Wir haben das Budget für Phase eins erhöht.* |
| an increase/a rise | eine Erhöhung/ein Anstieg *m* |
| *We have to budget for an increase in the cost of materials.* | *Wir müssen mit einem Anstieg/ einer Erhöhung der Material-kosten rechnen.* |
| to decrease/to cut | senken/kürzen |
| to reduce | vermindern |
| *We have decreased the budget for phase two.* | *Wir haben das Budget für Phase zwei gekürzt.* |

| dramatical(ly) | dramatisch |
| vast(ly) | gewaltig |
| huge(ly) | außerordentlich |
| enormous(ly) | enorm |
| substantial(ly) | wesentlich |
| considerable (considerably) | beträchtlich |
| significant(ly) | signifikant |
| moderate(ly) | mäßig |
| slight(ly) | leicht |
| a little | ein wenig |

| | |
|---|---|
| to fall/to drop | fallen/sinken |
| to go down/to slump | zurückgehen/stürzen |
| *The manpower costs have fallen.* | *Die Personalkosten sind gesunken.* |
| a fall/a drop | ein Fall(¨-e) *m*/eine Senkung(en) |
| a cut/a reduction | eine Kürzung/eine Verringerung |
| a slump | ein Sturz(¨-e) *m* |
| *We estimate there will be a decrease in the cost of materials.* | *Wir rechnen mit einer Senkung der Materialkosten.* |
| to hold ... stable | ... stabil halten |
| to maintain ... at the same level | ... auf dem selben Stand halten |
| *We have kept costs constant during the project.* | *Wir konnten die Kosten während des Projekts konstant halten.* |
| to remain constant | konstant bleiben |
| to stay stable | stabil bleiben |

## 5. Project completion

| | |
|---|---|
| We have finished/completed the project. | Wir haben das Projekt abgeschlossen/fertiggestellt. |
| The product is ready for launch. | Das Produkt kann auf den Markt gebracht werden. |
| We are ready to ... | Wir können jetzt ... |
| start up the new equipment. | die neuen Geräte in Betrieb nehmen. |
| We have managed to ... | Es ist uns gelungen ... |
| increase output. | den Ertrag zu steigern. |
| Congratulations. We have completed the project successfully. | Herzlichen Glückwunsch. Wir haben das Projekt erfolgreich abgeschlossen. |
| Well done. You have achieved your aim/goal/target/objective. | Gut gemacht. Sie haben die gesetzten Ziele erreicht. |
| I'd like to thank the project team for their ... | Ich möchte dem Projektteam für ... danken. |
| hard work during the project | die geleistete Arbeit |
| commitment/dedication | das Engagement/seinen Einsatz |
| collaboration | die gute Zusammenarbeit |
| participation | die Mitarbeit |

# Company Departments

## ADMINISTRATION

### Administrative staff

| | |
|---|---|
| administrator | der Verwalter(-) [-in] |
| office manager | der Büroleiter(-) [-in] |
| personal assistant | der persönliche(n) Assistent(en) [-in] |
| *she's the personal assistant to the Managing Director/CEO* | *sie ist die persönliche Assistentin des Generaldirektors* |
| secretary | der Sekretär(e) [-in] |
| typist | die Schreibkraft(-e) |

### Information organization

| | |
|---|---|
| archive (n) | das Archiv(e) |
| *we keep the old records in the archives* | *wir bewahren die alten Unterlagen in den Archiven auf* |
| file (n)/(v) | die Akte(n)/abheften, ablegen, zu den Akten nehmen |
| *have you filed that letter?* | *haben Sie den Brief abgeheftet?* |
| filing cabinet | der Aktenschrank(-e) |
| photocopier | der Kopierer |
| sort (v) | sortieren |

# CUSTOMER SERVICE

| | |
|---|---|
| agent | der Vertreter(-) [-in] |
| *he acts as agent for us in Australia* | *er vertritt uns in Australien* |
| busy | beschäftigt |
| cater for/serve | beliefern |
| *we cater for/serve a wide range of customers* | *wir beliefern eine große Anzahl von Kunden* |
| custom | die Kundschaft |
| customer | der Kunde(n) [-in] |
| customize | nach Bestellung anfertigen |
| *all our products are customized* | *Alle unsere Produkte werden nach Bestellung angefertigt* |
| deal (n)/(v) | der Geschäftsabschluß(-sse)/ handeln |
| delay (n) | die Verzögerung(en) |
| *we're sorry for the delay* | *entschuldigen Sie bitte die Verzögerung* |
| demand (n) | die Nachfrage |
| *we can't keep up with demand* | *wir können mit der Nachfrage nicht Schritt halten* |
| discontinue | auslaufen, nicht mehr herstellen |
| *I'm afraid this line has been discontinued* | *ich fürchte, dieses Produkt läuft aus/wird nicht mehr hergestellt* |
| exchange (n) | der Tausch/Austausch/Umtausch |
| exempt (v) | befreien, freistellen |
| *these products are VAT/sales tax exempt* | *diese Produkte sind von der Mehrwertsteuer befreit* |
| export (n)/(v) | der Export(e)/exportieren |
| fetch/pick up | abholen |
| *we'll fetch/pick up the order this afternoon* | *wir werden die bestellten Waren am Nachmittag abholen* |
| file (n) | die Kartei(en), die Datei(en) |
| *we keep all our customers on file* | *Alle unsere Kunden werden in einer Kartei/Datei erfaßt* |
| customer file | die Kundenkartei(en), die Kundendatei(en) |
| handle (v) | bearbeiten, Güter umschlagen |

DISTRIBUTION, see page 71

| | |
|---|---|
| import (n)/(v) | der Import(e)/importieren |
| install | installieren |
| *when would you like the equipment installed?* | *wann soll die Anlage installiert werden?* |
| item | der Posten(-) |
| *the order consisted of four items* | *die Bestellung enthielt vier Posten* |
| off-season | außerhalb der Saison |
| paperwork | die Schreibarbeit(en) |
| *there's a lot of paperwork to do* | *es liegt eine Menge Schreibarbeit an* |
| part-exchange | in Zahlung nehmen |
| quality | die Qualität |
| run out of | ausgehen |
| *I'm afraid we've run out of those items* | *ich fürchte, diese Posten sind uns ausgegangen* |
| scarce | knapp |
| schedule (n)/(v) | der Zeitplan(-̈e)/planen, vorsehen |
| *we've scheduled delivery for the end of the month* | *die Lieferung ist für Ende des Monats vorgesehen/geplant* |
| service | der Kundendienst, der Service |
| *the service is slow* | *der Kundendienst ist langsam* |
| after-sales service | der Kundendienst |
| service industry | die Dienstleistungsindustrie |
| tariff | die Gebühr(en), der Tarif(e) |
| triplicate, in | in dreifacher Ausfertigung |
| *the order form needs filling out in triplicate* | *das Auftragsformular muß in dreifacher Ausfertigung vorliegen* |

## Negotiating

| | |
|---|---|
| bargain (n)/(v) | der Geschäftsabschluß(-̈sse)/ verhandeln |
| barter (n) | das Tauschgeschäft(e) |
| conditions of sale | die Verkaufsbedingungen |
| *our conditions of sale are printed on the back of the invoice* | *unsere Verkaufsbedingungen finden Sie auf der Rückseite der Rechnung* |
| haggle | feilschen |
| negotiate | verhandeln |

NEGOTIATIONS, see page 48

| | |
|---|---|
| negotiable | **verhandelbar** |
| *these terms are not negotiable* | *diese Bedingungen sind nicht verhandelbar* |
| negotiation | **die Verhandlung(en)** |

## Complaints

| | |
|---|---|
| blame (v) | **verantwortlich machen/sein** |
| claim (n) | **die Reklamation(en), der Schadensfall(¨e), die Beanstandung(en)** |
| *the customer has made a claim for damages* | *der Kunde fordert Schadenersatz* |
| compensate | **Schadenersatz leisten, entschädigen** |
| damage | **der Schaden(¨)** |
| *the accident caused a lot of damage* | *der Unfall hat großen Schaden verursacht* |
| damages | **der Schadenersatz, die Entschädigung(en)** |
| fault/defect (n) | **der Fehler(-), der Mangel(¨)** |
| guarantee (n) | **die Garantie(n)** |
| *the guarantee lasts a year* | *es besteht eine einjährige Garantie* |
| hazard | **das Risiko(-en)** |
| insure | **versichern** |
| insurance claim | **der Versicherungsanspruch(¨e)** |
| insurance cover | **der Versicherungsschutz** |
| insurance policy | **die Versicherungspolice(n)** |
| *does your policy cover this claim?* | *wird dieser Schadensfall durch Ihre Versicherung abgedeckt?* |
| overdue | **überfällig** |
| *the delivery is overdue* | *die Lieferung ist überfällig* |
| repair (n)/(v) | **die Reparatur(en)/reparieren** |
| spoil | **verderben** |
| *the goods were spoiled in transit* | *die Ware ist während des Transports verdorben* |

## Payment

| | |
|---|---|
| credit | **der Kredit(e), die Gutschrift(e)** |
| credit note | **die Gutschrift(e)** |
| hire purchase | **der Ratenkauf(¨e)** |

PAYMENT, see also page 77

| invoice (n)/(v) | die Rechnung(en)/Rechnung ausstellen, in Rechnung stellen |
| *you'll be invoiced at the end of the month* | *Sie erhalten die Rechnung am Ende des Monats* |
| lease (n)/(v) | die Miete(n)/(ver)mieten |
| outright purchase | der Kauf mit sofortiger vollständiger Bezahlung |
| over-charged | überhöht |
| overpaid | zuviel bezahlt |
| *you've overpaid so we'll send you a credit note* | *Sie haben zuviel bezahlt, wir werden Ihnen deshalb eine Gutschrift schicken* |
| pay (n) | bezahlen |
| pay by cheque/check | mit Scheck bezahlen |
| pay in cash | bar bezahlen |
| payable | zahlbar |
| *this invoice is payable in 30 days* | *diese Rechnung ist innerhalb von 30 Tagen zahlbar* |
| payment | die Zahlung(en) |
| *we demand payment in advance* | *wir verlangen die Zahlung im voraus* |
| prepaid | frankiert |
| *please enclose a prepaid envelope* | *legen Sie bitte einen frankierten Rückumschlag bei* |
| rebate | der Rabatt(e) |
| settle | begleichen, bezahlen |
| *could you settle the bill in advance?* | *könnten Sie die Rechnung im voraus bezahlen?* |
| statement | die Abrechnung(en) |
| *we will send you a monthly statement* | *wir senden Ihnen eine monatliche Abrechnung* |

## Orders

| acknowledge | bestätigen |
| *the order was acknowledged on 30 June* | *der Auftrag wurde am 30. Juni bestätigt* |
| acknowledgment | die Bestätigung(en) |
| available | verfügbar, vorhanden, erhältlich |
| availability | die Verfügbarkeit, das Vorhandensein |

bring forward/move up
*we'd like to bring forward/move up the delivery date*

**vorverlegen**
*wir würden das Lieferdatum gerne vorverlegen*

bulk
*we offer 10% discount for bulk orders*
in bulk

**die Masse(n), die Menge(n)**
*bei Großaufträgen bieten wir Ihnen 10 Prozent Rabatt*
**in großer Menge, in großen, en gros**

cancel
cancellation

**stornieren**
**die Stornierung(en)**

confirm
*could you please confirm your order in writing?*

**bestätigen**
*könnten Sie Ihren Auftrag bitte schriftlich bestätigen?*

notify
*we'll notify you of any delay*

**benachrichtigen**
*bei Verzögerungen werden wir Sie benachrichtigen*

offer (n)/(v)

**das Angebot(e)/anbieten**

order (n)
*fulfill an order*
on order
*we've got 25 on order*
back order
place an order
*are you ready to place an order?*

**der Auftrag(¨e), die Bestellung(en)**
*einen Auftrag erfüllen/ausführen*
**bestellt**
*wir haben 25 bestellt*
**der unerledigte(n) Auftrag(¨e)**
**einen Auftrag erteilen**
*möchten Sie einen Auftrag erteilen?*

postpone

**verschieben**

quotation
quote (v)
*could you quote us for 500 units?*

**das Preisangebot(e)**
**ein Preisangebot machen**
*können Sie uns ein Preisangebot für 500 Einheiten machen?*

ready
receive

**fertig**
**erhalten**

receipt
*could you let me have a receipt?*

**die Quittung(en)**
*könnten Sie mir eine Quittung ausstellen?*

reorder
repeat order

**nachbestellen**
**die Nachbestellung(en)**

shortage
*there's a severe shortage of stock*
in stock/out of stock

**der Mangel/die Knappheit**
*die Lagerbestände sind knapp*
**vorrätig/nicht vorrätig**

# DISTRIBUTION

| | |
|---|---|
| by boat/ferry/ship/tanker | per Boot/Fähre/Schiff/Tanker |
| by post/special delivery/airmail | per Post/Eilzustellung/Luftpost |
| by truck/van/train | per Lkw/Lieferwagen/Eisenbahn |
| cargo | die Ladung(en), die Fracht |
| carriage/freight | der Transport(e) |
| *the price includes carriage* | *der Preis ist inklusive Transport* |
| cif (cost, insurance and freight) | cif |
| crate | die Lattenkiste(n) |
| deliver | liefern |
| delivery | die Lieferung(en) |
| delivery note | der Lieferschein(e) |
| *there should be a delivery note with the invoice* | *der Rechnung sollte ein Lieferschein beiliegen* |
| delivery time | die Lieferzeit(en) |
| *28 days delivery time* | *Lieferzeit 28 Tage* |
| depot | das Lager(-) |
| dispatch (v) | versenden |
| distribute | vertreiben |
| duty | der Zoll(ˉe) |
| enclose | beilegen |
| *please find enclosed our price list* | *beiliegend finden Sie unsere Preisliste* |
| envelope | der Briefumschlag(ˉe) |
| f.o.b. (free on board) | f.o.b, frei schiff |
| forward (v) | befördern |
| *could you forward the goods to the distributor?* | *könnten Sie die Waren zum Händler befördern?* |
| freight | die Fracht |
| in transit | auf dem Transport weg |
| *the order was lost in transit* | *die Bestellung ging auf dem Transport weg verloren* |
| lading, bill of | das Konnossement(e) |
| load (v) | laden |
| *the goods were loaded onto the trucks* | *die Güter wurden in die Lkws geladen* |
| mail (n)/(v) | die Postsendung(en)/mit der Post versenden |
| pack (v) | verpacken, einpacken |

| | |
|---|---|
| package (n)/(v) | das Paket(e)/verpacken |
| pallet | die Palette(n) |
| ship (v) | versenden |
| *have you shipped the goods?* | *haben Sie die Waren versandt?* |
| shipment | der Versand, die Versendung(en) |
| unload | entladen, ausladen |

## Channels

| | |
|---|---|
| branch | die Filiale(n) |
| *there is a branch in every major town* | *es gibt eine Filiale in jeder größeren Stadt* |
| bottleneck | der Engpaß(̈-sse) |
| chain | die Kette(n) |
| *this store is part of a chain* | *dieses Geschäft gehört zu einer Kette* |
| channel | der Kanal(̈-e) |
| *our main distribution channel is via the wholesaler to the retailer* | *unser Hauptvertriebskanal verläuft über den Großhändler zum Einzelhändler* |
| consignment | die Warensendung(en) [in] |
| *we're expecting a consignment later today* | *wir erwarten heute eine Warensendung* |
| dealer | der Händler(-) [in] |
| department store | das Warenhaus(̈-er), das Kaufhaus (̈-er) |
| direct export | der Direktexport(e) |
| franchise (n) | das Franchising |
| middleman | der Zwischenhändler(-) [-in] |
| network | das Netz(e) |
| *we're building a dealer network* | *wir bauen ein Händlernetz auf* |
| quota | die Quote(n) |
| retail (n) | der Einzelhandel |
| retail outlet | das (Einzelhandels-)Geschäft(e) |
| retailer | der Einzelhändler(-) [in] |
| scarce | knapp |
| sourcing | die Akquisition(en) |
| *dual sourcing* | *die Doppelakquisition(en)* |
| storage | die Lagerung |
| tariff | der Zolltarif(e) |
| warehouse | das Lagerhaus(̈-er) |
| wholesale (n) | der Großhandel |

# FINANCE

| | |
|---|---|
| accounts | der Abschluß(-̈sse) |
| *the monthly accounts show all the figures* | *der Monatsabschluß enthält alle wichtigen Zahlen* |
| accountancy | das Rechnungswesen |
| accountant | der Buchhalter(-) [-in] |
| acquire | erwerben |
| acquisition | der Erwerb |
| advance (n)/(v) | die Vorauszahlung(en)/ vorauszahlen |
| backdate | (zu)rückdatieren |
| black, in the | in den schwarzen Zahlen |
| books, keep the | die Bücher führen |
| borrow | ausleihen |
| break even (v) | die Kosten decken |
| break-even point | der Kostendeckungspunkt(e) |
| *we've reached the break-even point* | *wir arbeiten kostendeckend* |
| budget (n)/(v) | das Budget(s)/einplanen |
| *we've budgeted for a loss* | *wir haben einen Verlust eingeplant* |
| capital | das Kapital |
| cash | das Bargeld |
| cheque/check | der Scheck(s) |
| cost(s) | die Kosten *pl* |
| fixed/variable/running | festen/variablen/laufenden |
| credit (n) | der Kredit(e) |
| currency | die Währung(en) |
| debt | die Schulden |
| debtor | der Schuldner(-) |
| deduct | abziehen |
| defer | aufschieben, stunden |
| *the taxation can be deferred until next year* | *die Steuern können bis zum nächsten Jahr gestundet werden* |
| due | fällig |
| earn | verdienen |
| earnings | der Gewinn(e), der Ertrag(-̈e), die Einnahme(n) |
| *annual earnings exceeded our forecast* | *der Jahresgewinn übertraf unsere Erwartungen* |

BANKING, see page 115

| finance (n)/(v) | die Finanzierung(en)/finanzieren |
|---|---|
| *they are willing to finance the project* | *sie sind bereit, das Projekt zu finanzieren* |
| funds | die Finanzmittel *pl* |
| income | das Einkommen(-) |
| interest | der Zins(en) |
| interest rate | der Zinssatz(-e) |
| *interest rates were cut by ½%* | *die Zinssätze wurden um ein halbes Prozent gesenkt* |
| lend | Kredit gewähren |
| lender | der Kreditgeber(-) |
| liquidity | die Liquidität |
| loan | das Darlehen(-) |
| overdraw | überziehen |
| overdraft | die Überziehung(en) |
| *our overdraft facility is 50,000DM* | *unser Überziehungskredit beträgt DM50.000* |
| owe | schulden |
| petty cash | die Portokasse(n) |
| profit | der Gewinn(e), der Profit(e) |
| profitable | rentabel, gewinnbringend |
| profitability | die Rentabilität |
| rate | die Rate(n), der Satz(-e) |
| recover | sich erholen |
| red, in the | in den roten Zahlen |
| save (v) | sparen |
| savings | die Ersparnisse *pl* |
| subsidize | subventionieren |
| subsidy | die Subvention(en) |

## Investment

| base rate | der Leitzins, der Eckzinssatz(-e) |
|---|---|
| *terms are 2% above base rate* | *die Zahlungsbedingungen liegen 2 Prozent über den Eckzinssätzen* |
| bond | die Anleihe(n) |
| broker | der Börsenmakler(-) [-in] |
| *our broker advised us to sell our shares* | *unser Börsenmakler hat uns geraten, unsere Aktien zu verkaufen* |
| dealer | der Aktienhändler(-) [-in] |
| debenture | die Schuldverschreibung(en) |

| | |
|---|---|
| dividend | die Dividende(n) |
| *they announced the same dividend as last year* | *sie haben dieselbe Dividende angekündigt wie letztes Jahr* |
| earnings per share | die Gewinne *pl* pro Aktie |
| equity | das Eigenkapital |
| gross yield | die Bruttorendite(n) |
| invest | anlegen |
| investment | die Anlage(n) |
| portfolio | der Wertpapierbestand(¨-e), das Portefeuille |
| *you should have some oil shares in your portfolio* | *Sie sollten einige Ölaktien in Ihren Wertpapierbestand aufnehmen* |
| premium | das Agio(s) |
| securities | das Wertpapier(e) |
| share/stock | die Aktie(n) |
| shareholder/stockholder | der Aktionär(e) |

## Financial statements

| | |
|---|---|
| asset | der Vermögenswert(e), die Aktiva *pl* |
| current assets | das Umlaufvermögen |
| fixed assets | das Anlagevermögen |
| intangible assets | die immateriellen Vermögensgegenstände |
| audit (n)/(v) | die Abschlußprüfung(en)/ prüfen |
| auditor | der Abschlußprüfer(-) [-in] |
| balance sheet | die Bilanz(en) |
| *the balance sheet looks very sound* | *die Bilanz sieht sehr solide aus* |
| cash flow | der Cash-flow |
| negative cash flow | der negative Cash-flow |
| debit (n)/(v) | das Soll/belasten |
| depreciate | abschreiben |
| *these assets are depreciated over 3 years* | *diese Vermögenswerte werden über 3 Jahre abgeschrieben* |
| depreciation | die Abschreibung(en) |
| expenditure | die Kosten *pl*, der Aufwand, die Aufwendung(en) |

FINANCIAL PROBLEMS, see page 80

| expenses | die Kosten *pl*, die Ausgaben *pl*, der Aufwand |
| goodwill | der Geschäftswert, der Firmenwert |
| *goodwill is included under intangible assets* | *der Firmenwert wird unter den immateriellen Vermögensgegenständen aufgeführt* |
| gross (adv) | brutto |
| gross margin | die Bruttospanne(n) |
| gross profit | der Bruttogewinn(e) |
| half-yearly results | das Halbjahresergebnis(se) |
| inventory | die Vorräte |
| ledger | das Hauptbuch(-er) |
| sales/purchase ledger | das Lieferantenbuch(-er), das Debitorenbuch(-er) |
| liabilities | die Passiva *pl* |
| current liabilities | die kurzfristigen Verbindlichkeiten |
| margin | die Gewinnspanne(n), die Handelsspanne(n) |
| overheads | die Betriebskosten *pl* |
| *our overheads are too high* | *unsere Betriebskosten sind zu hoch* |
| profit and loss account/ income statement | die Gewinn- und Verlustrechnung(en) |
| quarterly | vierteljährlich |
| reserves | die Rücklagen *pl* |
| results | das Ergebnis(se) |
| retained earnings | die einbehaltenen Gewinne |
| return (n) | der Ertrag(-e), der Gewinn(e), die Rendite(n) |
| return on investment | die Kapitalrendite, die Investitionsrentabilität |
| turnover/sales | der Umsatz(-e) |
| *annual turnover/sales has doubled over 5 years* | *der Jahresumsatz hat sich in 5 Jahren verdoppelt* |
| working capital | das Nettoumlaufvermögen(-) |
| write-off (n)/(v) | die Abschreibung(en)/ abschreiben |
| *this asset has now been written off* | *dieser Vermögenswert ist nun abgeschrieben* |

PAYMENT, see also page 76

## Payment

| | |
|---|---|
| bad debt | die uneinbringliche Forderung |
| *this invoice has been posted as a bad debt* | *diese Rechnung wurde als uneinuneinbringliche Forderung verbucht* |
| bank draft/check | der Bankscheck(s) |
| bank statement | der Kontoauszug(¨e) |
| blank cheque/check | der Blankoscheck(s) |
| bounce | platzen |
| *the cheque/check bounced* | *der Scheck ist geplatzt* |
| convert (v) | umtauschen |
| credit limit | der Kreditrahmen(-) |
| credit rating | die Bonität |
| direct debit | die Abbuchung(en) |
| demand (n) | die Nachfrage |
| discount | der Preisnachlaß(¨sse) |
| invoice (n)/(v) | die Rechnung(en)/Rechnung ausstellen, in Rechnung stellen, berechnen |
| letter of credit | das Akkreditiv(e) |
| *we will pay by letter of credit* | *wir bezahlen per Akkreditiv* |
| outstanding | ausstehend |
| *$4,500 is still outstanding* | *4500 Dollar stehen noch aus* |

## Tax

| | |
|---|---|
| capital gains tax | die Kapitalertragssteuer |
| corporation tax | die Körperschaftssteuer |
| declare | erklären |
| tax declaration | die Steuererklärung(en) |
| income tax | die Einkommenssteuer |
| taxable | besteuerbar, steuerpflichtig |
| *is this purchase taxable?* | *muß dieser Kauf versteuert werden?* |
| tax allowance | der Steuerfreibetrag(¨e) |
| tax deductible | (von der Steuer) absetzbar |
| tax evasion | die Steuerhinterziehung(en) |
| tax loophole | die Lücke im Steuergetz |
| tax relief | die Steuererleichterung(en) |
| *you can get tax relief* | *Sie können Steuererleichterungen geltend machen* |
| value added tax *(sales tax)* | die Mehrwertsteuer |

## LEGAL

| | |
|---|---|
| abide by | festhalten an |
| abuse (n) | der Mißbrauch |
| abuse of power | der Machtmißbrauch |
| appeal (v) | die Berufung einlegen |
| arbitrate | ein Rechtsmittel einlegen |
| arbitration | das Schiedsgerichtsverfahren(-), die Schiedsgerichtsbarkeit |
| *the dispute has gone to arbitration* | *der Streit wurde vor ein Schiedsgericht gebracht* |
| bequest (n) | das Vermächtnis |
| *the property was left to her as a bequest* | *der Besitz wurde ihr vermacht* |
| bond | die Bürgschaft(en) |
| break the law | das Gesetz brechen |
| case | der Fall(¨e) |
| case law | das Fallrecht |
| civil law | das Zivilrecht |
| claim (n)/(v) | der Rechtsanspruch(¨e), die Forderung(en)/beanspruchen, fordern |
| *they have a claim* | *sie haben einen Anspruch* |
| claimant | der Anspruchsteller(-) [-in] |
| conflict | der Konflikt(e) |
| conflict of interest | der Interessenkonflikt(e) |
| copyright (n) | das Urheberrecht(e) |
| court | das Gericht(e) |
| *we're going to court* | *wir gehen vor Gericht* |
| damages | der Schadenersatz |
| embezzle | veruntreuen |
| embezzlement | die Veruntreuung(en) |
| fee | die Gebühr(en) |
| indemnify | entschädigen |
| indemnity | die Entschädigung(en) |
| infringe copyright | gegen das Urheberrecht verstoßen |
| infringement | der Verstoß(¨sse) |
| irrevocable letter of credit | das unwiderrufliche(n) Akkreditiv(e) |
| judicial | gerichtlich |

CONTRACT LAW, see page 121/EMPLOYMENT LAW, see page 122

| | |
|---|---|
| jurisdiction | die Gerichtsbarkeit(en) |
| *this contract comes under British jurisdiction* | *dieser Vertrag unterliegt britischem Recht* |
| law | das Gesetz(e) |
| within/outside the law | gesetzeskonform/ gesetzeswidrig |
| against the law | gegen das Gesetz |
| legal/illegal | legal/illegal |
| legal department | die Rechtsabteilung(en) |
| liability | die Haftung |
| limited liability | beschränkte Haftung |
| litigant | die Prozeßpartei(en) |
| loophole, tax | das Steuerschlupfloch(¨er) |
| misconduct | das Fehlverhalten |
| professional misconduct | das standeswidrige Verhalten |
| party | die Partei |
| third party | der Dritte(n) |
| patent | das Patent(e) |
| file a patent application | eine Patentanmeldung einreichen |
| penalty | die Geldstrafe(n) |
| penalty clause | die Strafklausel(n) |
| *the contract included a penalty clause for late completion* | *der Vertrag beinhaltete eine Strafklausel für nicht termingerechte Vertragserfüllung* |
| pledge (n) | die Zusicherung |
| precedent | der Präzedenzfall(¨e) |
| *there is no precedent for this decision* | *für diese Entscheidung gibt es keinen Präzedenzfall* |
| quorum | das Quorum |
| settlement | die Einigung(en) |
| settle out of court | sich außergerichtlich einigen |
| sue | verklagen |
| *we can sue them for non-payment* | *wir können sie wegen Nichtzahlung verklagen* |
| suit | der Prozeß(-sse) |
| trademark | das Warenzeichen(-) |
| tribunal | der Gerichtshof(¨e) |
| unjust | ungerecht |
| unlawful | ungesetzlich |

waive
*the company decided to waive its usual fee in this case*

verzichten auf
*das Unternehmen entschied sich, in diesem Fall auf seine üblichen Gebühren zu verzichten*

## People

| | |
|---|---|
| actuary | der Versicherungsmathematiker(-) [-in] |
| advocate | der Rechtsanwalt(ä-e) [-in] |
| attorney/barrister | der Rechtsanwalt(ä-e) [-in] |
| bailiff/sheriff | der Gerichtsvollzieher(-) [-in] |
| lawyer | der Rechtsanwalt(ä-e) [-in] |
| legal advisor | der Rechtsberater(-) [-in] |
| notary | der Notar(e) [-in] |
| solicitor | der Rechtsanwalt(ä-e) [-in] |

## Financial problems

bankrupt (adj)
  to go bankrupt

bankrott
in Konkurs gehen, Bankrott machen

bankruptcy
der Konkurs(e)

debt
die Schulden

foreclose

eine Forderung geltend machen, zwangsvollstrecken

*the bank foreclosed on the property*

*die Bank ließ ihre Forderungen auf den Besitz zwangsvollstrecken*

foreclosure
die Zwangsvollstreckung

insolvency
die Zahlungsunfähigkeit

insolvent
zahlungsunfähig

liquidate
abwickeln, liquidieren

liquidation
der Konkurs(e), die Abwicklung(en)

*the company has gone into liquidation*

*das Unternehmen hat Konkurs angemeldet*

liquidator
der Konkursverwalter(-) [-in]

receiver

der Konkursverwalter(-) [-in]

*a receiver has been appointed to sell off the assets*

*es wurde ein Konkursverwalter bestellt, um die Vermögenswerte zu verkaufen*

receivership
die Konkursverwaltung

## MARKETING

| | |
|---|---|
| capture market share | einen Marktanteil erobern |
| cartel | das Kartell(e) |
| client | der Kunde(n) |
| compete | konkurrieren |
| competition | die Konkurrenz |
| competitor | der Konkurrent(en) [-in] |
| competitive | konkurrenzfähig |
| competitive pricing | konkurrenzfähige Preise |
| domestic market | der Binnenmarkt(¨e) |
| down-market | billig, anspruchslos |
| end-user | der Endverbraucher(-) |
| *we sell direct to the end-user* | *wir verkaufen direkt an den Endverbraucher* |
| exhibit (v) | ausstellen |
| exhibition | die Ausstellung(en) |
| flop (n) | der Reinfall(¨e) |
| *the launch was a complete flop* | *die Produkteinführung war ein totaler Reinfall* |
| forecast (n)/(v) | die Prognose(n)/prognostizieren |
| *we forecast that we will become market leader next year* | *wir wagen die Prognose, daß wir im nächsten Jahr Marktführer sein werden* |
| goodwill | der Firmenwert |
| logo | das Logo(s), das Emblem(e) |
| market (n) | der Markt(¨e) |
| market leader | der Marktführer(-) |
| market niche | die Marktlücke(n) |
| *they have found a profitable market niche* | *sie haben eine gewinnträchtige Marktlücke gefunden* |
| market penetration | die Marktdurchdringung |
| market segmentation | die Marktsegmentierung |
| market share | der Marktanteil(e) |
| mass-market | der Massenmarkt(e) |
| outlet | das (Einzelhandels-)Geschäft(e) |
| resistance | der Widerstand(¨e) |
| *there is some price resistance* | *es gibt einigen Preiswiderstand* |
| saturate | sättigen |
| sector | der Sektor(en) |
| segment | das Segment(e) |

SALES DEPARTMENT, see page 96

| | |
|---|---|
| share (n) | der Anteil(e) |
| survey (n) | die Übersicht |
| target (n)/(v) | das Ziel(e)/abzielen |
| up-market | teuer, anspruchsvoll |
| *it's an upmarket product* | *es ist ein teures Produkt, das auf* |
| *aimed at the luxury sector* | *den Luxussektor abzielt* |

## Products

| | |
|---|---|
| benefit (n) | der Nutzen |
| brand (n) | die Marke(n) |
| brand leader | der Markenführer(-) |
| brand loyalty | die Markentreue |
| *brand loyalty will stop* | *Markentreue hält die Kunden* |
| *customers switching to* | *davon ab, zu generischen* |
| *generic products* | *Produkten zu wechseln* |
| by-product | das Nebenprodukt(e) |
| diversify | diversifizieren |
| flagship product | das Vorzeigeprodukt(e) |
| generic | generisch |
| giveaway | das Werbegeschenk(e) |
| goods | die Güter *pl* |
| label | das Etikett(e), die Bezeichnung(en) |
| *private label products are selling well* | *Hausmarken verkaufen sich gut* |
| launch(n)/(v) | die Produkteinführung(en)/ein Produkt einführen |
| life cycle | die Lebensdauer |
| positioning | das Positionieren |
| product line/range | die Produktlinie(n)/die Produktpalette(n) |
| prototype | der Prototyp(en) |
| seasonal | saisonbedingt, jahreszeitlich bedingt |
| sell-by date | das Verfallsdatum(-en) |
| *this product has passed its sell-by date* | *das Verfallsdatum dieses Produkts ist abgelaufen* |
| shelf-life | die Haltbarkeit |
| tailor-made | maßgeschneidert |
| trade mark | das Warenzeichen(-) |
| white goods | die weiße Ware |

INTRODUCING THE PRODUCT, see page 31

## Advertising

| | |
|---|---|
| account executive | der Kundenbetreuer(-) [-in] |
| advertise | werben, anzeigen |
| advertisement | die Werbung, die Anzeige(n) |
| art director | der künstlerische(n) Leiter(-) [-in] |
| artwork | die künstlerische Gestaltung |
| audience | das Publikum |
| *the ad has to reach a certain audience* | *die Anzeige soll ein bestimmtes Publikum erreichen* |
| banner | das Transparent(e) |
| body copy | der Fließtext |
| brief (n)/(v) | der Kurzbericht(e)/informieren über |
| broadsheet | die seriöse(n) Zeitung(en) |
| *we're going to advertise in the broadsheet and tabloid press* | *wir werden in der seriösen Presse und in der Boulevard- presse werben* |
| brochure | die Broschüre(n) |
| canvass | Kunden werben |
| *we have canvassed a lot of potential customers* | *wir haben eine Menge potentieller Kunden geworben* |
| caption | die Überschrift(en), der Bildtext |
| catalogue/catalog | der Katalog(e) |
| *this product is not included in our current catalogue/catalog* | *dieses Produkt ist nicht in unserem aktuellen Katalog enthalten* |
| circular | das Rundschreiben(-) |
| endorse | unterstützen |
| endorsement | die Unterstützung, die Zustimmung |
| *endorsement by a well-known actress will boost sales* | *die Unterstützung durch eine bekannte Schauspielerin wird den Umsatz ankurbeln* |
| flier | das Flugblatt(-er) |
| freesheet | das Anzeigenblatt(-er) |
| issue (n) | die Ausgabe(n) |
| jingle | das Jingle(-) |
| *the ad has a very catchy jingle* | *die Werbung hat ein sehr einprägsames Jingle* |
| layout | das Layout |

| | |
|---|---|
| magazine | die Zeitschrift(en) |
| *we'll reach our audience through magazines* | *wir erreichen unser Publikum über Zeitschriften* |
| media | das Medium(-en) |
| mass media | das Massenmedium(-en) |
| media coverage | die Medienberichterstattung |
| outdoor advertising | die Außenwerbung |
| *we've designed some posters for outdoor advertising* | *wir haben einige Plakate für die Außenwerbung entworfen* |
| pamphlet | der Handzettel(-) |
| poster | das Plakat(e) |
| prospectus | der Prospekt(e) |
| *the company issued a shareholder prospectus* | *das Unternehmen hat ein Prospekt für die Aktionäre herausgebracht* |
| publication | die Veröffentlichung(en) |
| ratings | die Quote(n) |
| weekly TV ratings | die wöchentlichen Einschaltquoten |
| readership | die Leserschaft |
| slogan | der Slogan(s), der Werbespruch |
| spot | der Fernsehspot(s) |
| TV spot | der TV-Spot(s) |
| sticker | der Anstecker(-) |
| tabloid | das Boulevardblatt(-er) |
| viewer | der Zuschauer(-) |
| voice-over | der Begleitkommentar(e) |

### Pricing

| | |
|---|---|
| bargain (n) | der Gelegenheitskauf(-e) |
| ceiling | die Obergrenze(n) |
| price ceiling | die Preisobergrenze(n) |
| cut-price rate/cut-rate price | der Billigpreis(e) |
| *cut-price deals have reduced margins* | *Billigpreise haben die Gewinnspannen verringert* |
| discount (n) | der Rabatt(e) |
| elastic | elastisch |
| going rate | üblicher/gängiger Preis |
| *we should charge the going rate* | *wir sollten den üblichen Preis berechnen* |

| | |
|---|---|
| gross margin | die Bruttospanne(n) |
| inelastic | unelastisch |
| introductory offer | das Einführungsangebot(e) |
| knockdown/mask-down price | der Mindestpreis(e) |
| margin | die Gewinnspanne(n), die Handelsspanne(n) |
| mark up (v)/(n) | heraufsetzen/die unverbindliche Preisempfehlung des Herstellers |
| *the retailer has marked up the price by 50%* | *der Händler hat den Preis um 50 Prozent heraufgesetzt* |
| MRP (Manufacturer's Recommended Price) | der empfohlene Richtpreis |
| overheads | die Gemeinkosten |
| premium | die Prämie(n) |
| rate | der Preis(e), der Tarif(e) |
| refund (n)/(v) | die Rückerstattung(en)/ rückerstatten |
| retail price | der Ladenpreis(e), der Einzelhandelspreis(e) |
| retail price index | der Einzelhandelspreisindex |
| surcharge (n)/(v) | der Aufpreis(e)/aufschlagen |
| value (v) | der Wert(e) |

## Public relations

| | |
|---|---|
| identity | die Identität |
| corporate identity | das Firmenimage, die Firmenidentität |
| image | das Image |
| corporate image | das Firmenimage |
| lobby (v) | politische Beeinflussung betreiben |
| *we are lobbying the Minister for/Secretary of Agriculture* | *wir versuchen, auf den Landwirt-schaftsminister Einfluß zu nehmen, um unsere Interessen durchzusetzen* |
| press officer | der Pressereferent(en) [-in] |
| press relations | die Pressebeziehungen |
| press release | die Pressemitteilung(en) |
| *we have issued a press release* | *wir haben eine Pressemitteilung herausgegeben* |
| sponsor (v) | sponsern, fördern |
| sponsorship | die Förderung |

## PERSONNEL

| | |
|---|---|
| absent | **abwesend** |
| absenteeism | **das Fernbleiben vom Arbeitsplatz** |
| canteen | **die Kantine(n)** |
| career | **die Karriere(n)** |
| core time | **die Kernzeit(en)** |
| *core time is between 10:00 and 15:00* | *die Kernzeit liegt zwischen 10:00 Uhr und 15:00 Uhr* |
| employ | **einstellen, beschäftigen** |
| employee | **der Arbeitnehmer(-)** |
| employer | **der Arbeitgeber(-)** |
| equal opportunity | **die Chancengleichheit** |
| *this company has an equal opportunities policy* | *dieses Unternehmen verfolgt eine Politik der Chancengleichheit* |
| flexitime | **die Gleitzeit(en)** |
| hire | **einstellen** |
| human resources | **das Personal** |
| job centre/center | **das Arbeitsamt(¨er)** |
| job sharing | **das Job-sharing, die Arbeitsplatzteilung** |
| job satisfaction | **die Zufriedenheit am Arbeitsplatz** |
| leader | **die Führungskraft(¨e)** |
| leadership | **die Führung** |
| *we are looking for leadership qualities* | *wir suchen nach Führungsqualitäten* |
| liaison | **die Verbindung(en)** |
| loyalty | **die Loyalität** |
| manpower | **die Arbeitskräfte** |
| manpower planning | **die Arbeitskräfteplanung** |
| pool | **die Schreibzentrale(n)** |
| *secretaries are drawn from a pool* | *die Sekretärinnen kommen aus der Schreibzentrale* |
| position | **die Position(en)** |
| profession | **der Beruf(e)** |
| punctuality | **die Pünktlichkeit** |
| shift | **die Schicht(en)** |
| *the first shift is from 06:00 to 14:00* | *die erste Schicht dauert von 06:00 Uhr bis 14:00 Uhr* |
| night shift | **die Nachtschicht(en)** |

| shopfloor | **die Belegschaft(en)** |
| sick note | **die Krankmeldung(en)** |
| trade union | **die Gewerkschaft(en)** |
| vacation | **der Urlaub** |
| working hours | **die Arbeitszeit(en)** |
| *working hours are currently* | *die Wochenarbeitszeit beträgt* |
| *37 per week* | *zur Zeit 37 Stunden* |
| work load | **die Arbeitsbelastung(en)** |

## Types of jobs

| blue-collar worker | **der Arbeiter(-) [-in]** |
| board of directors | **das Betriebsvorstand** |
| clerk | **der Büroangestellte(n)** |
| management | **das Management** |
| junior/middle/senior | **unteres/mittleres/oberes** |
| manager | **der Manager(-) [-in]** |
| line/staff manager | **der leitende Angestellte** |
| manual (adj) | **manuell, mit der Hand** |
| manual worker | **der Arbeiter(-) [-in]** |
| skilled | **Fach-** |
| semi-skilled/unskilled | **angelernt/ungelernt** |
| shift worker | **der Schichtarbeiter(-)** |
| staff | **die Belegschaft** |
| superior | **der Vorgesetzte(n)** |
| *his superior reports to the* | *sein Vorgesetzter untersteht* |
| *Managing Director/CEO* | *dem Geschäftsführer* |
| white-collar worker | **der Angestellte(n)** |

## Disputes

| conditions | **die Bedingungen** *pl* |
| working conditions | **die Arbeitsbedingungen** *pl* |
| conditions of employment | **die Anstellungsbedingungen** *pl* |
| grievance | **die Beschwerde(n)** |
| *their grievances include low* | *sie beschwerten sich unter* |
| *pay and long hours* | *anderem über den geringen* |
| | *Lohn und die lange Arbeitszeit* |
| industrial action | **die Arbeitskampfmaßnahmen** |
| industrial relations | **die Arbeitgeber-Arbeitnehmer-** |
| | **Beziehungen** |
| industrial unrest | **die betrieblichen Unruhen** |

COMPANY POSITIONS, see page 29/EMPLOYMENT LAW, see page 122

| | |
|---|---|
| picket (n)/(v) | **der Streikposten(-)/Streikposten aufstellen** |
| *the factory was picketed during the strike* | ***vor dem Werk wurden während des Streiks Streikposten aufgestellt*** |
| strike (n)/(v) | **der Streik(s)/streiken** |
| work to rule | **Arbeit nach Vorschrift** |

### Recruitment

| | |
|---|---|
| applicant | **der Bewerber(-) [-in]** |
| application form | **das Bewerbungsformular(e)** |
| apply for a job | **sich um eine Stelle bewerben** |
| appoint | **einstellen** |
| candidate | **der Kandidat(en) [-in]** |
| curriculum vitae/resumé | **der Lebenslauf(-e)** |
| experience | **die Erfahrung** |
| fill (a position) | **ausfüllen (eine Position)** |
| interview, to come for | **zum Einstellungsgespräch erscheinen** |
| interviewee | **der/die Befragte(n)** |
| interviewer | **der Befrager(-)** |
| job description | **die Stellenbeschreibung(en)** |
| qualifications | **die Qualifikationen** |
| qualified/unqualified | **qualifiziert/unqualifiziert** |
| *we're only interested in qualified personnel* | ***wir sind nur an qualifizierten Mitarbeitern interessiert*** |
| recruit (v) | **einstellen** |
| recruitment | **die Einstellung(en)** |
| reference | **die Referenz(en)** |
| *they followed up her references* | ***sie gingen ihre Referenzen durch*** |
| select | **auswählen** |
| vacancy | **die offene(n) Stelle(n)** |
| *I'm afraid we have no vacancies at present* | ***ich fürchte, wir haben zur Zeit keine offene Stellen*** |

### Leaving

| | |
|---|---|
| dismissal | **die Entlassung(en)** |
| fire (v) | **feuern, fristlos entlassen** |
| *he was fired for stealing* | ***er wurde wegen Diebstahls fristlos entlassen*** |

| | |
|---|---|
| hand in one's notice | **seine Kündigung einreichen** |
| lay-off (n)/(v) | **die vorübergehende(n) Entlassung(en)/vorübergehend entlassen** |
| redundant/laid off | **arbeitslos/entlassen** |
| *2,000 workers will be made redundant/laid off* | ***2.000 Arbeiter werden entlassen*** |
| resign | **zurücktreten** |
| resignation | **der Rücktritt(e)** |
| retire | **in Pension/Rente gehen** |
| retirement | **die Pensionierung(en)** |
| *he was offered early retirement* | ***sie boten ihm die vorzeitige Pensionierung/den Vorruhestand an*** |

## Assessment

| | |
|---|---|
| appraise/review | **beurteilen** |
| *all the staff are appraised/ reviewed annually* | ***Alle Mitarbeiter werden jährlich beurteilt*** |
| appraisal/review | **die Beurteilung(en)** |
| competence | **die Kompetenz** |
| grade (n)/(v) | **die Note(n)/benoten** |
| perform | **leisten, Leistung erbringen** |
| performance appraisal | **die Leistungsbeurteilung(en)** |
| probation | **die Probezeit(en)** |
| *he's on probation for 6 months* | ***er hat 6 Monate Probezeit*** |

## Training & development

| | |
|---|---|
| apprentice | **der Lehrling(e)** |
| *the company takes on 5 apprentices a year* | ***das Unternehmen stellt jährlich 5 Lehrlinge ein*** |
| apprenticeship | **die Lehrzeit(en), die Lehrstelle(n)** |
| course | **der Kurs(e)** |
| facilitate | **erleichtern** |
| *the training should facilitate decision-making* | ***durch die Schulung soll die Entscheidungsfindung erleichtert werden*** |
| mentor | **der Mentor(en) [-in]** |
| on-the-job training | **die Ausbildung am Arbeitsplatz** |
| promote | **(be)fördern** |
| progress (n)/(v) | **der Fortschritt(e)/Fortschritte machen** |

| | |
|---|---|
| seminar | das Seminar(e) |
| *we are organizing a seminar on leadership skills* | *wir organisieren ein Seminar über Führungsqualitäten* |
| train (v) | schulen |
| training | die Schulung(en) |

## Remuneration

| | |
|---|---|
| bargain (v) | verhandeln |
| collective bargaining | die Tarifverhandlungen |
| benefit (n) | die Leistung(en) |
| fringe benefit | die Gehaltsnebenleistung(en) |
| *company cars are a common fringe benefit* | *Firmenwagen sind eine übliche Gehaltsnebenleistung* |
| sickness benefit | das Krankengeld |
| compensate | abfinden |
| deduction | der Abzug(¨e) |
| *my take-home pay after all deductions is very little* | *nach allen Abzügen ist mein Nettoverdient nur sehr gering* |
| incentive | der Anreiz(e) |
| income | das Einkommen(-) |
| overtime | die Überstunde(n) |
| *you can make up the wage with overtime* | *Sie können den Lohn mit Überstunden aufbessern* |
| pay (n)/(v) | der Lohn(¨e), das Gehalt(¨er)/ bezahlen |
| pay package | die Lohntüte(n) |
| payroll | die Gehaltsliste(n) |
| pension | die Pension(en), die Rente(n) |
| perk | die Vergünstigung |
| profit-sharing | die Gewinnbeteiligung(en) |
| *the employees all benefit from a profit-sharing scheme* | *sämtliche Mitarbeiter profitieren von einem Gewinnbeteiligungsplan* |
| raise (n)/(v) | die Erhöhung(en)/erhöhen |
| *I just received a salary raise* | *ich habe gerade eine Gehaltserhöhung bekommen* |
| reward (n) | die Vergütung(en) |
| salary | das Gehalt(¨er) |
| share option | die Aktienoption(en) |
| wage | der Lohn(¨e) |

# PRODUCTION

## Quality

| | |
|---|---|
| accurate | **sorgfältig** |
| accuracy | **die Sorgfalt, die Genauigkeit** |
| assess | **beurteilen** |
| defect | **der Mangel(-)** |
| *the defect was caused by a faulty machine* | ***der Mangel wurde durch eine fehlerhafte Maschine verursacht*** |
| evaluate | **bewerten** |
| inspect | **überprüfen** |
| ISO | **ISO** |
| quality assurance/control | **die Qualitätssicherung/die Qualitätskontrolle(n)** |
| quality circle | **der Qualitätszirkel(-)** |
| *the plant has set up quality circles* | ***das Werk hat Qualitätszirkel eingerichtet*** |
| reject (n) | **der Ausschuß** |
| reject rate | **die Ausschußquote(n)** |
| scrap (n) | **der Ausschuß** |
| zero defect | **Nullfehler-** |
| *we are aiming for zero defect production* | ***unser Ziel ist eine Nullfehler-produktion*** |

## Process

| | |
|---|---|
| assemble | **montieren** |
| assembly | **die Montage** |
| assembly line | **das Fließband(-er)** |
| *the assembly line has been automated* | ***das Fließband wurde automatisiert*** |
| automate | **automatisieren** |
| automation | **die Automatisierung(en)** |
| component | **die Komponente(n)** |
| continuous process | **der Dauerbetrieb** |
| convert | **umrüsten, umwandeln** |
| efficiency | **die Effizienz** |
| efficient | **effizient** |
| finished good | **das Fertigprodukt(e)** |
| goods | **die Güter** *pl* |
| intermittent production | **die Werkstattfertigung** |

| | |
|---|---|
| line assembly | **die Fließbandmontage** |
| line worker | **der Fließbandarbeiter(-) [-in]** |
| off-the-shelf | **ab Lager** |
| produce (v) | **produzieren, fertigen** |
| production | **die Produktion, die Fertigung** |

## Planning

| | |
|---|---|
| backlog | **der Rückstand, der (Auftrags-) Bestand(-̈e)** |
| *there is a backlog of orders to deal with* | ***es besteht ein Auftragsrückstand, der aufgeholt werden muß*** |
| batch | **die Sendung(en)** |
| capacity | **die Kapazität(en)** |
| *we are working at full capacity* | ***unsere Kapazitäten sind voll ausgelastet*** |
| critical path analysis | **die CPM-Methode** |
| cycle time | **die Taktzeit(en)** |
| delivery cycle | **der Lieferzeit(en)** |
| downtime | **die Ausfallzeit(en)** |
| *machine downtime costs money* | ***Ausfallzeiten bei den Maschinen kosten Geld*** |
| flow rate | **die Förderleistung(en)** |
| idle | **stillstehend, außer Betrieb** |
| job lot | **die Partieware(n)** |
| lead time | **die Bearbeitungszeit(en)** |
| *the lead time is too long* | ***die Bearbeitungszeit ist zu lang*** |
| make-to-order | **auftragsbezogen produzieren** |
| make-to-stock | **auf Lager produzieren** |
| output | **der Ausstoß** |
| productive | **produktiv** |
| productivity | **die Produktivität** |
| *productivity levels have increased* | ***die Produktivität hat sich erhöht*** |
| prototype | **der Prototyp(en)** |
| schedule | **der Zeitplan(-̈e)** |
| set-up time | **die Rüstzeit(en)** |
| slack (adj) | **flau, schwach** |
| throughput | **der Durchsatz** |
| work-in progress | **das unfertige(n) Erzeugnis(se)** |

### Resources & stock

| | |
|---|---|
| bill of materials | die Stückliste(n) |
| equip | ausrüsten, ausstatten |
| equipment | die Ausrüstung(en), die Geräte |
| inventory | der (Lager-)Bestand(¨e) |
|   raw materials inventory |   der Rohmaterialbestand(¨e) |
| just-in-time | just-in-time, bestandslos, fertigungssynchron |
| machine | die Maschine(n) |
| machinery | die Maschinen pl |
| MRP (Materials Requirements Planning) | die Materialbedarfsplanung(en) |
| materials handling | der (innerbetriebliche) Materialtransport |
| raw material | der Rohstoff(e) |
| stock (n) | der Lagerbestand(¨e) |
| stock levels | der Lagerbestand(¨e) |
|   in stock |   auf Lager |
|   *we have just one left in stock* |   *wir haben nur noch einen/eine/ eins auf Lager* |
|   out of stock |   nicht mehr auf Lager |
| stock control | die Lagersteuerung |
| stockpile (n)/(v) | die Vorräte/bevorraten |
| store (n)/(v) | das Lager/lagern |
| storage | die Lagerung |

### Maintenance

| | |
|---|---|
| break down | ausfallen |
|   *this machine has never broken down* |   *diese Maschine ist nie ausgefallen* |
| failure | der Ausfall(¨e) |
| fault | der Mangel(¨), der Fehler(-) |
| faulty | mangelhaft, fehlerhaft |
| maintain | warten |
| maintenance | die Wartung |
| repair (n)/(v) | die Reparatur(en)/reparieren |
| reliable | zuverlässig, verläßlich |
| reliability | die Zuverlässigkeit, die Verläßlichkeit |
| shut-down (n) | die Stillegung(en) |
| shut down (v) | stillegen |

# PURCHASING

| | |
|---|---|
| auction (n) | **die Versteigerung(en)** |
| buy | **kaufen** |
| buyer, junior/senior | **der erste(n)/zweite(n) Einkäufer(-) [-in]** |
| purchaser | **der Käufer(-) [-in]** |
| source | **die Quelle(n)** |
| *you should have at least two sources* | ***man sollte mindestens zwei Quellen haben*** |
| spend (n) | **die Ausgabe(n)** |
| *a total purchasing spend of over 1 million* | ***eine Gesamtkaufkraft von über 1 Million*** |
| spend (v) | **ausgeben** |
| supply (v) | **liefern** |
| supplies | **die Zulieferungen, die Vorräte** |
| supplier | **der Zulieferer(-), der Lieferant(en)** |
| vendor | **der Lieferant(en)** |

## Functions

| | |
|---|---|
| inventory management | **die Bestandsverwaltung(en)** |
| inventory control | **die Bestandskontrolle(n)** |
| logistics | **die Logistik** |
| materials management | **die Materialwirtschaft** |
| vendor appraisal | **die Lieferantenbeurteilung(en)** |
| *the criteria for vendor appraisal include price, quality and delivery* | ***zu den Kriterien für die Lieferantenbeurteilung gehören Preis, Qualität und Lieferung*** |

## Finance

| | |
|---|---|
| bill (n) | **die Rechnung(en)** |
| billing | **die Abrechnung(en)** |
| *we prefer quarterly billing* | ***wir bevorzugen eine vierteljährliche Abrechnung*** |
| currency | **die Währung(en)** |
| currency fluctuations | **die Währungsschwankungen** |
| weak/strong currency | **starke/schwache Währung** |

## Supply & demand

| | |
|---|---|
| buyers'/sellers' market | **der Käufer-/Verkäufermarkt** |

| | |
|---|---|
| demand (n) | die Nachfrage |
| under-demand | die mangelnde Nachfrage |
| *prices are low because of under-demand* | *wegen mangelnder Nachfrage sind die Preise niedrig* |
| over-demand | die Übernachfrage |
| supply | das Angebot |
| under-supply | das Unterangebot |
| over-supply | das Überangebot |

### Tendering process

| | |
|---|---|
| accept | den Zuschlag erhalten |
| *our offer was accepted* | *unser Angebot erhielt den Zuschlag* |
| call for tenders | die Aufforderung zur Angebotsabgabe |
| *the call for tenders was published in the press* | *die Aufforderung zur Angebotsabgabe wurde in den Zeitungen ausgeschrieben* |
| open/closed tender | die offene(n)/geschlossene(n) Ausschreibung(en) |
| reject (v) | ablehnen |
| submit a tender/an offer | ein Angebot abgeben |
| tender specifications | das Lastenheft(e) |
| tender evaluation | die Angebotsbewertung(en) |

### Price negotiation and documents

| | |
|---|---|
| bottom-line | das Mindestangebot(e) |
| *our bottom-line was DM150,000* | *unser Mindestangebot betrug 150.000 DM* |
| cut (n) | die Preissenkung(en) |
| *we forced a 10% price cut on all our suppliers* | *wir setzten bei unseren Lieferanten eine Preissenkung von 10 Prozent durch* |
| letter of intent | die Absichtserklärung(en) |
| *we sent the supplier a letter of intent* | *wir haben dem Lieferanten eine Absichtserklärung geschickt* |
| margin | die Gewinnspanne(n), die Handelsspanne(n) |
| purchase order | der Auftrag(¨e) |
| target price | der Richtpreis(e) |

# SALES

| | |
|---|---|
| client/customer | der Kunde(n) [-in] |
| end-user | der Endverbraucher(-) |
| give-away | das Werbegeschenk(e) |
| *we usually supply give-aways such as pens* | *normalerweise verteilen wir Werbegeschenke wie z. B. Stifte* |
| prospect | der Interessent(en), der potentielle(n) Kunde(n) |
| sales call | der (Vertreter-)besuch(e) |
| *I've got one more sales call to make* | *ich muß noch einen weiteren Besuch machen* |
| sales conference | die Konferenz(en), Besprechung(en), die Tagung(en) |
| target | die Botschaft |
| *we have a very ambitious sales target this year* | *wir haben dieses Jahr sehr ehrgeizige Verkaufsziele* |
| sample | das Muster(-), die Auswahl |

## Selling people & organisation

| | |
|---|---|
| field sales | der Außendienst |
| *we've got a team of 3 field salespeople* | *wir haben 3 Außendienstmitarbeiter* |
| sales area | das Absatzgebiet(e) |
| *the country is divided into four sales areas* | *das Land ist in vier Absatzgebiete unterteilt* |
| sales manager | der Verkaufsleiter(-) [-in] |
| salesforce | das Verkaufspersonal |

## Types of selling

| | |
|---|---|
| door-to-door sales | der Haustürverkauf |
| direct sales | der Direktverkauf |
| hard selling | die aggressive Verkaufsmethode(n) |
| *hard selling doesn't work in this business* | *aggressive Verkaufsmethoden funktionieren in diesem Geschäft nicht* |
| soft selling | die „weiche(n)" Verkaufsmethode(n) |
| telephone sales | der Telefonverkauf |

# Industries and Professions

## CONSTRUCTION

**Materials used in construction**

| | |
|---|---|
| asphalt | **der Asphalt** |
| brick | **der Ziegelstein(e)** |
|   red brick | **der Backstein(e)** |
| cement | **der Zement** |
| clay | **der Ton** |
| concrete | **der Beton** |
|   pre-fabricated concrete | **der Fertigbeton** |
|   reinforced concrete | **der Stahlbeton** |

| | |
|---|---|
| glass | **das Glas** |
| frosted glass | **das Mattglas, das Milchglas** |
| plain glass | **das einfache Glas** |
| reinforced glass | **das Panzerglas** |
| safety glass | **das Sicherheitsglas** |
| gravel | **der Kies** |
| macadam | **der Makadam** |
| masonry | **das Mauerwerk** |
| mortar | **der Mörtel** |
| plastic | **der Kunststoff(e)** |
| slate | **der Schiefer** |
| steel | **der Stahl** |
| steel girder | **der Stahlträger(-)** |
| stone | **der Stein(e)** |
| cobble stone | **der Kopfstein(e)** |
| tarmac | **der Asphalt, der Makadam** |
| tile | **die Fliese(n), die Kachel(n)** |
| timber | **das (Bau-)Holz(-er)** |
| uPVC | **das uPVC** |
| wood | **das Holz(-er)** |
| wooden beam | **der Holzbalken(-)** |
| wooden plank | **die Holzdiele(n)** |

*Planning regulations in this area prohibit the use of prefabricated concrete.*

*Die Baubestimmungen für dieses Gebiet verbieten die Verwendung von Fertigbeton.*

### Professions in construction

| | |
|---|---|
| architect | **der Architekt(en) [-in]** |
| brick layer | **der Maurer(-) [-in]** |
| builder | **der Bauarbeiter(-) [-in]** |
| carpenter | **der Zimmermann (-leute)** |
| designer | **der Konstrukteur(e) [-in]** |
| developer | **der Bauunternehmer(-) [-in]** |
| draughtsman | **der Zeichner(-) [-in]** |
| engineer | **der Ingenieur(e) [-in]** |
| civil | **der (Tief-)Bauingenieur(e) [-in]** |
| sanitary | **der Sanitärtechniker(-) [-in]** |
| structural | **der Bauingenieur(e) [-in]** |
| glazier | **der Glaser(-) [-in]** |
| joiner | **der Tischler(-) [-in]** |
| painter | **der Maler(-) [-in]** |

PROPERTY, see page 110

| planner | der Planer(-) [-in] |
| plasterer | der Stukkateur(e) [-in] |
| plumber | der Klempner(-) [-in] |
| surveyor | der Vermessungsingenieur(e) [-in] |
| quantity surveyor | der Kalkulator(en) [-in] |

*Our on-site management team consists of an architect, responsible for drawing up the plan, a civil engineer and a surveyor.*

*Unser Bauleitungsteam vor Ort besteht aus einem Architekten, der die Pläne zeichnet, einem (Tief-)Bauingenieur und einem Vermessungsingenieur.*

### Processes in construction

| to build | bauen |
| to chart | kartographieren |
| to construct | bauen, konstruieren |
| to cool | (ab)kühlen |
| to demolish | abreißen, einreißen |
| to design | entwerfen |
| to dig | graben, ausheben |
| to draft | zeichnen, entwerfen |
| to draw | skizzieren, zeichnen |
| to erect | errichten |
| to excavate | ausheben, ausschachten |
| to heat | erhitzen |
| to install | installieren, montieren |
| to maintain | warten |
| to measure | (ver)messen |
| to plan | planen |
| to refurbish | sanieren |
| to renovate | renovieren |
| to repair | reparieren |
| to replace | ersetzen |
| to scaffold | einrüsten |
| to sketch | skizzieren |
| to ventilate | (be)lüften |
| to wire | verkabeln, verspannen |

*Our company specialises in refurbishing old houses: everything from designing the plans to carrying out the job.*

*Unser Unternehmen hat sich auf die Altbausanierung spezialisiert – von der Planung bis zur Ausführung der Arbeiten.*

# ENGINEERING

### Branches of engineering

| | |
|---|---|
| architectural engineering | **das Bauingenieurwesen** |
| chemical engineering | **die Chemotechnik** |
| civil engineering | **das (Tief-)Bauwesen** |
| drainage engineering | **der Wasserbau** |
| electrical engineering | **die Elektrotechnik** |
| electronic engineering | **die elektronische Technik** |
| fire protection engineering | **die Brandschutztechnik** |
| highway engineering | **der Straßenbau** |
| hydraulic engineering | **der Pumpen- und Rohrleitungsbau** |
| industrial engineering | **die Fertigungsorganisation** |
| marine engineering | **der Schiffsmaschinenbau** |
| mechanical engineering | **der Maschinenbau** |
| mining and metallurgical engineering | **das Bergbau- und Eisenhüttenwesen** |
| nuclear engineering | **die Kerntechnik** |
| petroleum production engineering | **die Petrochemie** |
| production engineering | **die Fertigungsplanung** |
| railway engineering | **der Eisenbahnbau** |
| safety engineering | **die Sicherheitstechnik** |
| sanitary engineering | **die Sanitärtechnik** |
| structural engineering | **das Bauwesen** |
| welding engineering | **die Schweißtechnik** |

*We plan to call in a safety engineering company to advise us on improving standards.*

**Wir beabsichtigen, einen Sicherheitsingenieur zu Rate zu ziehen, der uns bei der Verbesserung unserer Standards beraten soll.**

### Applications of engineering

| | |
|---|---|
| boiler | **der Kessel(-)** |
| boring | **die Bohrung(en)** |
| bridge | **die Brücke(n)** |
| dye (n) | **die Farbstoff(e)** |
| electricity supply | **die Stromversorgung** |
| gas manufacture | **die Gaserzeugung** |
| hydraulics | **die Hydraulik** |

| mining | der Bergbau |
| paper manufacture | die Papierherstellung |
| power generation | die Energieerzeugung |
| power transmission | die Energieübertragung |
| printing | das Druckwesen |
| shipbuilding | der Schiffbau |

## Equipment in engineering

| boiler | der Kessel(-) |
| crane | der Kran(-̈e) |
| gas engine | die Gasmaschine(n) |
| machine tools | die Werkzeugmaschine(n) |
| pump | die Pumpe(n) |
| turbine/engine | die Turbine(n) |
|   steam turbine |   die Dampfturbine |
|   water turbine |   die Wasserturbine |

*This boiler has an auxiliary safety valve to prevent a build-up of pressure.*

***Der Kessel verfügt über ein zusätzliches Sicherheitsventil, um das Entstehen von Überdruck zu verhindern.***

## Processes in treating metals

| to anneal | (aus)glühen |
| to anodize | anodisieren |
| to electroplate | galvanisieren |
| to forge | hämmern |
| to found | gießen |
| to galvanize | verzinken |
| to grind | wetzen, schleifen |
| to harden | härten |
| to mint | prägen |
| to plate | plattieren |
| to roll | walzen |
| to temper | blau anlaufen lassen/vergüten |
| to terneplate | mit Bleizinnlegierung überziehen |
| to tinplate | verzinnen |

*Some of our customers ask us to galvanize the metal in order to strengthen it.*

***Einige unserer Kunden wünschen, daß wir das Metall verzinken, um es zu verstärken.***

# FOOD AND CATERING

### The meals

| | |
|---|---|
| breakfast | **das Frühstück** |
| lunch | **das Mittagessen** |
| dinner | **das Abendessen** |
| picnic | **das Picknick** |
| snack | **der Imbiß** |

### The elements of food

| | |
|---|---|
| carbohydrates | **die Kohlenhydrate** |
| fats | **das Fett(e)** |
| proteins | **das Protein(e)** |
| vitamins | **das Vitamin(e)** |
| minerals | **die Mineralien** |

### Types of food

| | |
|---|---|
| cereals | **die Getreideflocken** |
| dairy products | **das Molkereiprodukt(e)** |
| drinks | **das Getränk(e)** |
| eggs | **das Ei(er)** |
| fats | **das Fett(e)** |
| fish | **der Fisch(e)** |
| fruit | **das Obst** |
| meat | **das Fleisch** |
| nuts | **die Nuß(-̈sse)** |
| organic food | **das Nahrungsmittel(-) aus biodynamischem Anbau** |
| preserves | **die Konserve(n)** |
| pulses/lentils | **die Hülsenfrucht(-̈e)** |
| sweets | **die Süßigkeit(en)** |
| vegetables | **das Gemüse** |

*We have changed the ingredients in many of our products, because of the danger to health caused by fats and sweets.*

**Angesichts der Gesundheitsrisiken, durch Fette und Zucker, haben wir die Zutaten in vielen unserer Produkte verändert.**

DINING OUT, see page 27

### Parts of a meal

| | |
|---|---|
| aperitif | **der Aperitif(s)** |
| starter/first course | **die Vorspeise(n)** |
| soup | **die Suppe(n)** |
| salad | **der Salat(e)** |
| main course | **das Hauptgericht(e)** |
| dessert | **die Nachspeise(n)** |
| cheese | **der Käse** |

### Growing processes in food-making

| | |
|---|---|
| to fatten | **mästen** |
| to fertilize | **düngen** |
| to germinate | **keimen** |
| to grow | **ziehen, anpflanzen** |
| to harvest | **ernten** |
| to hatch | **(aus)brüten** |
| to milk | **melken** |
| to pick | **pflücken, (ab)ernten** |
| to plough/plow | **pflügen** |
| to propagate | **vermehren** |
| to rear | **Vieh halten/aufziehen** |
| to slaughter | **schlachten** |
| to sow | **säen** |

*We guarantee that the animals have been organically reared and slaughtered in a humane way.* **Wir garantieren, daß die Tiere auf natürliche Weise aufgezogen und ohne unnötige Qualen geschlachtet wurden.**

### Food preparation

| | |
|---|---|
| to bake | **backen** |
| to boil | **kochen** |
| to chop up | **kleinschneiden** |
| to cook | **kochen** |
| to cure | **haltbar machen** |
| to cut | **schneiden** |
|   into pieces/slices | **in Stücke/in Scheiben** |
|   to cut up | **zerschneiden** |
| to fry | **braten** |
| to grill | **grillen** |

| | |
|---|---|
| to heat | heiß machen, erhitzen |
| to marinate | marinieren |
| to melt | schmelzen |
| to pickle | einlegen |
| to roast | braten, rösten |
| to salt | salzen, würzen |
| to smoke | räuchern |
| to stew | schmoren |
| to sweeten | süßen |
| to toast | toasten |

*We cut up the fruit into small pieces before we put it into cans.* — *Wir schneiden das Obst in kleine Stücke, bevor wir es in Dosen füllen.*

## The business of catering

| | |
|---|---|
| banquet hall | der Bankettsaal(-säle) |
| bar | die Bar(s) |
| buffet | das Büfett(s) |
| café | das Café(s) |
| cafeteria | die Cafeteria(s) |
| chef | der Küchenchef(s) |
| coffeeshop | das (Steh-)Café(s) |
| cook (n) | der Koch(-e) [-in] |
| diner | das Eßlokal(e) |
| fast food | das Fast-Food, das Schnellgericht |
| feast | das Fest(e), das Festessen(-) |
| meal | die Mahlzeit(en) |
| pub | die Kneipe(n) |
| refreshment | die Erfrischung(en) |
| restaurant | das Restaurant(s) |
| restaurateur | der Gastwirt(e) [-in] |
| serve | servieren, bedienen |
| snack | der Imbiß(-sse), der Snack(s) |
| teahouse | das Teehaus(-er) |
| waiter | der Kellner(-) |
| drinks waiter | der Weinkellner(-) |
| waitress | die Kellnerin(nen) |

*The conference centre/center provides three main function rooms and is able to serve buffet meals for up to 300 delegates.* — *Das Konferenzzentrum verfügt über drei große Veranstaltungsräume und bietet Büfetts für bis zu 300 Delegierte an.*

# INFORMATION TECHNOLOGY

### Source of information

| | |
|---|---|
| archive | das Archiv(e) |
| databank | die Datenbank(en) |
| database | die Datenbank(en) |
| file | die Datei(en) |
| library | die Bibliothek(en), die Bücherei(en) |

*The customer database contains the names and addresses of all our customers.*
**Unsere Kundendatenbank enthält die Namen und Adressen aller unserer Kunden.**

### The representation of information

| | |
|---|---|
| digital data | die Digitaldaten |
| digitize | digitalisieren |
| encipher | verschlüsseln |
| image | die Abbildung(en), das Bild(er) |
| message | die Meldung(en) |
| signal | das Signal(e) |
| electric signal | das elektrische(n) Signal(e) |
| electromagnetic signal | das elektomagnetische(n) Signal(e) |
| transformation | die Transformation |

*If you digitize data, you can store it in a digital form, i.e. as a series of 1s and 0s.*
**Wenn man Daten digitalisiert, kann man sie in digitaler Form, d. h. als Reihen von Einsen und Nullen speichern.**

### The storage of information

| | |
|---|---|
| bit | das Bit(s) |
| byte | das Byte(s) |
| CD/compact disk | die CD(s) |
| CD-ROM | die CD-ROM(s) |
| data | die Daten |
| data recording | die Datenaufzeichnung(en) |
| magnetic data recording | die magnetische Datenaufzeichnung |
| optical data recording | die optische Datenaufzeichnung |

| disk | die Diskette(n), die Platte(n) |
|---|---|
| floppy disk | die Floppy-Disk(s) |
| hard disk | die Festplatte(n) |
| memory | der Speicher(-) |
| random access memory | RAM, der Direktzugriffsspeicher |
| read-only memory (ROM) | ROM, der Festspeicher |

### The transmission and processing of information

| amplifier | der Verstärker(-) |
|---|---|
| computer | der Computer(-) |
| computer system | das Computersystem(e) |
| computer network | das Computernetz(e) |
| electrical impulses | der elektrische(n) Impuls(e) |
| microphone | das Mikrofon(e) |
| radio communication systems | das Funksystem(e) |
| radio transmitter | der Radiosender(-) |
| signal | das Signal(e) |
| electronic signal | das elektronische(n) Signal(e) |
| electromagnetic signal | das elektomagnetische(n) Signal(e) |
| telephone | das Telefon(e) |
| telephone network | das Telefonnetz(e) |
| teletype network | das Fernschreibnetz(e) |
| television | das Fernsehen |

*The new Pentium® chip is at the heart of the system, processing huge amounts of data at incredible speeds.*

*Der neue Pentium®-Chip ist als Herz des Systems in der Lage, enorme Datenmengen mit unglaublicher Geschwindigkeit zu verarbeiten.*

### Processes

| to convert | umwandeln |
|---|---|
| to degrade | abbauen, verschlechtern |
| to distort | verzerren |
| to receive | empfangen |
| to transmit | übertragen, senden |

*This equipment can convert the old analog signals into digital signals.*

*Dieses Gerät kann die alten analogen Signale in digitale Signale umwandeln.*

TELECOMMUNICATIONS, see page 112

# PHARMACEUTICALS AND CHEMICALS

### Chemicals and life

| | |
|---|---|
| alkaloid | das Alkaloid(e) |
| carbohydrates | die Kohlenhydrate |
| cholesterol | das Cholesterin |
| coloration | das Färbemittel(-) |
| drug | das Medikament(e), die Droge(n) |
| enzyme | das Enzym(e) |
| hormone | das Hormon(e) |
| lipid | das Lipid(e) |
| nucleic acids | die Nukleinsäuren |
|   Deoxyribonucleic acid (DNA) | die Desoxyribonukleinsäure (DNA) |
|   Ribonucleic acid (RNA) | die Ribonukleinsäure (RNA) |
| peptide | das Peptid(e) |
| pigment | der Farbstoff(e) |
|   chlorophyll | das Chlorophyll |
|   melanin | das Melanin |
| protein | das Protein(e) |
|   amino acid | die Aminosäure(n) |
|   glutamine | das Glutamin |
|   gluten | das Gluten |
|   keratin | das Keratin |
|   myoglobin | das Myoglobin |
| steroid | das Steroid(e) |
| vitamin | das Vitamin(e) |

*As the lack of any hormone may cause a major deficiency, we now synthesize most of them artificially.*

*Da das Fehlen eines Hormons zu schwerwiegenden Mangelerscheinungen führen kann, stellen wir die meisten Hormone jetzt synthetisch her.*

### Body systems

| | |
|---|---|
| autonomic nervous system | das vegetative Nervensystem |
| cardiovascular system | das Herz- und Gefäßsystem |
| central nervous system | das zentrale Nervensystem |
| digestive system | der Verdauungsapparat |
| excretory system | der Ausscheidungsapparat |
| histamine response system | das Histamin-Regulationssystem |
| immune response system | das Immunsystem |

| reproductive system | der Fortpflanzungsapparat |
| skeletal muscle system | das Knochen-Muskelsystem |

*Our new digestive tablets help with the ingestion, digestion and absorption of food.*

***Unsere neuen Verdauungstabletten erleichtern die Nahrungsaufnahme und die Verdauung.***

### Drugs

| antidepressant | das Antidepressium(-a) |
| atropin | das Atropin |
| analgesic | das Analgetikum(-a) |
| salicylic acid | die Salicylsäure |
| anaesthetic | das Narkotikum(-a) |
| chloroform | das Chloroform |
| cocaine | das Kokain |
| procaine | das Procain |
| antibiotic | das Antibiotikum(-a) |
| penicillin | das Penicillin |
| streptomycin | das Streptomycin |
| antiseptic | das Antiseptikum(-a) |
| beta blocker | der Betablocker(-) |
| chemotherapeutics | die Chemotherapie |
| quinine | das Chinin |
| sulfa drug | das Sulphonamid |
| hallucinogen | das Halluzinogen(e) |
| cannabis | das Cannabis |
| hashish | das Haschisch |
| marijuana | das Marihuana |
| mescaline | das Meskalin |
| narcotic | das Narkotikum(-a), das Rauschgift(e) |
| heroin | das Heroin |
| methadone | das Methadon |
| morphine | das Morphium |
| opium | das Opium |
| sedative | das Sedativum(-a) |
| barbiturate | das Barbiturat(e) |
| thalidomide | das Thalidomid |
| stimulant | das Stimulans (*pl* Stimulanzien) |
| amphetamine | das Amphetamin(e) |
| caffeine | das Koffein |
| tranquilliser | das Sedativum(-a) |
| diazepam | das Diazepam |

| others | sonstige |
|---|---|
| antacid | das Antacidum |
| antihistamine | das Antihistamin(e) |
| diuretic | das Diuretikum(-a) |
| ephedrine | das Ephedrin |
| laxative | das Abführmittel |

*Some anaesthetics are used before or during surgery to depress the central nervous system.* / ***Einige Narkotika werden vor oder während einer Operation zur Beruhigung des zentralen Nervensystems eingesetzt.***

### The drug business

| ethical drug | das verschreibungspflichtige(n) Arzneimittel(-) |
|---|---|
| generic drug | das Generikum(-a) |
| me-too product | die Eigenentwicklung(en) |
| prescription drug | das rezeptpflichtige(n) Medikament(e) |
| proprietary drug | das freiverkäufliche(n) Arzneimittel(-) |
| patent drug | das patentierte(n) Arzneimittel(-) |
| veterinary pharmaceutical | das tierärztliche(n) Arzneimittel(-) |

*Proprietary drugs are sold over the counter; ethical drugs may be obtained legally only with a prescription from an authorized health-care provider.* / ***Für freiverkäufliche Arzneimittel ist kein Rezept erforderlich; verschreibungspflichtige Arzneimittel sind nur gegen Rezept eines zugelassenen Arztes erhältlich.***

### Drug forms

| liquid | die Flüssigkeit(en) |
|---|---|
| capsule | die Kapsel(n) |

### Branches of medicine

| clinical medicine | die klinische Medizin |
|---|---|
| preventive medicine | die Präventivmedizin |
| fringe medicine | die Randmedizin |
| alternative medicine | die Alternativmedizin |
| complementary medicine | die Komplementärmedizin |
| holistic medicine | die Ganzheitsmedizin |
| folk medicine | die Volksmedizin |

## PROPERTY

### The types of property

| | |
|---|---|
| apartment/flat | die Wohnung(en) |
| furnished apartment | die möblierte(n) Wohnung(en) |
| studio apartment | die Einzimmerwohnung(en) |
| apartment block/block of flats | der Wohnblock(-e), das Wohnhaus(-er) |
| bungalow | der Bungalow(s) |
| chalet | das Chalet(s) |
| chateau | das Schloß(-sser) |
| consulate | das Konsulat(e) |
| duplex/two-storey house | das zweistöckige Haus(-er) |
| embassy | die Botschaft(en) |
| estate | das Landgut(-er) |
| farmhouse | das Bauernhaus(-er) |
| field | das Feld(er) |
| grounds | das Land, der Grund, der Boden |
| house | das Haus(-er) |
| country house | das Landhaus(-er) |
| ranch house | das Wohnhaus(-er) auf einer Ranch |
| tenement house | das Mietshaus(-er) |
| terraced (row) house | das Reihenhaus(-er) |
| town house | das Stadthaus(-er) |
| lodge | die Hütte(n), das Pförtnerhaus, das Gärtnerhaus |
| mansion | die Villa(-en) |
| office | das Büro(s) |
| palace | der Palast(-e) |
| park | der Park(s) |
| penthouse | das Penthouse(-häuser) |
| plot | das Stück Land |
| property | die Immobilie(n) |
| stately home | der Herrensitz(e) |
| villa | die Villa(-en), das Landhaus(-er) |

*Our client requires 350 square metres of office space, fully equipped with telecommunications connections, and in a central location.*

**Unser Kunde sucht Büroräume mit 350 Quadratmetern Fläche in zentraler Lage, die bereits mit allen Telefonanschlüssen ausgestattet sind.**

CONSTRUCTION, see page 97

### The relationship with property

| | |
|---|---|
| boarder | der Pensionsgast(¨-e) |
| homeowner | der Eigentümer(-) [-in] |
| householder | der Inhaber(-) [-in] |
| leaseholder | der Pächter(-) [-in] |
| lessee | der Mieter(-) [-in] |
| lessor | der Vermieter(-) [-in] |
| lodger | der Untermieter(-) [-in] |
| occupier | der Eigentümer(-) [-in] |
| owner | der Besitzer(-) [-in] |
| paying guest | der zahlende(n) Gast(¨-e) |
| tenant | der Mieter(-) [-in] |

*Under the terms of this lease the landlord, Mr Brown, grants possession and use of the property at this address to you as tenant or lessee for a term of 25 years.*

*Gemäß der Mietbedingungen gewährt der Vermieter, Mr. Brown, Ihnen die Nutzung der benannten Immobilie als Mieter/ Pächter für die Dauer von 25 Jahren.*

### The legal aspects of property

| | |
|---|---|
| assign | abtreten |
| convey | übertragen |
| conveyance | die Übertragung |
| freehold | das Eigentumsrecht, der Grundbesitz |
| hire | mieten |
| lease (v) | mieten, pachten |
| leasehold | der Pachtbesitz, der Mietbesitz |
| hereditament | der vererbliche Vermögensgegenstand |
| let | vermieten, verpachten |
| sublet | untervermieten |
| ownership | der Besitz |
| rent | (ver)mieten, (ver)pachten |
| rental | die Miete(n), die Pacht |
| tenure | die Pacht |
| trust, in | in treuhänderischer Verwaltung |

*As a potential buyer of the freehold, it is important to check the seller's title to the property.*

*Als potentieller Käufer des Grundbesitzes müssen Sie unbedingt die Eigentumsrechte des Verkäufers an der Immobilie überprüfen.*

# TELECOMMUNICATIONS

## Systems in telecommunications

| | |
|---|---|
| cable (n) | **das Kabel(-)** |
| cablegram | **das Kabeltelegramm(e)** |
| electronic mail | **die elektronische Post** |
| facsimile/fax | **das Fax(e)** |
| teleconferencing | **die Telekonferenz(en)** |
| telegram | **das Telegramm(e)** |
| telegraphy | **die Telegraphie** |
| telephony | **das Fernsprechen** |
| videoconferencing | **die Videokonferenz(en)** |
| wire | **der Draht(ᵉe)** |
| wireless telegraphy | **die drahtlose Telegraphie, die Funktelegraphie** |

## Technology in telecommunications

| | |
|---|---|
| asynchronous transfer mode (ATM) | **der asynchrone Übertragungsmodus** |
| bandwidth | **die Bandbreite** |
| converter | **der Umsetzer(-), der Converter(-)** |
| data | **die Daten** |
| analog data | **analoge Daten** |
| digital data | **digitale Daten** |
| transfer (v) data | **Daten übertragen** |
| modem | **das Modem(s)** |
| fax modem | **das Faxmodem(s)** |
| multiplexing | **das Multiplexen** |
| time-division multiplexing | **der Zeitmultiplexbetrieb** |
| network | **das Netz(e)** |
| Internet | **das Internet** |
| local area net (LAN) | **das LAN, das lokale(n) Netz(e)** |
| wide-area networks | **das WAN, das Weitverkehrsnetz(e)** |
| signal | **das Signal(e)** |
| switching | **die Vermittlung** |
| packet switching | **die Paketvermittlung** |

*The A44 modem enables computer data to be transmitted over a telephone line at very high speeds.*

**Mit einem A44-Modem können Computerdaten mit extrem hoher Geschwindigkeit über eine Telefonleitung übertragen werden.**

### Equipment and devices in telecommunications

| | |
|---|---|
| amplifier | der Verstärker(-) |
| antenna | die Antenne(n) |
| cable | das Kabel(-) |
| coaxial cable | das Koaxialkabel(-) |
| fibre/fiber optic cable | das Glasfaserkabel(-) |
| circuit | die Schaltung(en), der Schaltkreis(e) |
| integrated circuit | der integrierte(n) Schaltkreis(e) |
| printed circuit | die gedruckte(n) Schaltung(en) |
| communications satellite | der Fernmeldesatellit(en), der Nachrichtensatellit(en) |
| electric | elektrisch |
| electric circuit | der Stromkreis(e) |
| electric switch | der elektrische(n) Schalter(-) |
| headphone | der Kopfhörer(-) |
| headset | die Sprechgarnitur(en) |
| laser | der Laser(-) |
| loudspeaker | der Lautsprecher(-) |
| microphone | das Mikrofon(e) |
| microprocessor | der Mikroprozessor(en) |
| microwave | die Mikrowelle(n) |
| photoelectric cell | die Fotozelle(n) |
| radar | der Radar |
| receiver | der Empfänger(-) |
| semiconductor | der Halbleiter(-) |
| telephone | das Telefon(e) |
| car telephone | das Autotelefon(e) |
| cellular phone | das Zelltelefon(e) |
| radio telephone | das Funktelefon(e) |
| telephone exchange | die (Fernsprech-) Vermittlung(en) |
| videophone | das Bildtelefon(e) |
| transistor | der Transistor(en) |
| switchboard | die Vermittlung(en) |
| transmitter | der Sender(-), das Fernmeldegerät(e) |

*Standard coaxial cable can carry up to 132,000 messages simultaneously.*

*Mit einem Standard-Koaxialkabel können gleichzeitig bis zu 132.000 Meldungen übertragen werden.*

## TEXTILES AND CLOTHING

### Types of textiles

| | |
|---|---|
| canvas | das Segeltuch |
| cashmere | das Kaschmir |
| chintz | der Chintz |
| corduroy | der Kordsamt |
| cotton | die Baumwolle |
| damask | der Damast |
| denim | der Denim, der Jeansstoff |
| fibre/fiber | die Faser(n) |
| flannel | der Flanell |
| gauze | die Gaze |
| hessian | das Sackleinen |
| jute | die Jute |
| linen | das Leinen |
| mohair | das Mohair |
| satin | der Satin |
| silk | die Seide |
| synthetics | die Synthetics |
|   polyester |   das Polyester |
|   polymer |   das Polymer(e) |
|   vinyl fibre/fiber |   die Vinylfaser(n) |
| velvet | der Samt |
| wool | die Wolle |

*Synthetics such as nylon and polyester, which are stronger than silk and lower in price, have led to a tremendous reduction in silk production and consumption.*

**Synthetics wie Nylon und Polyester, die stärker und preiswerter sind als Seide, haben zu einem enormen Rückgang bei der Herstellung und beim Verbrauch von Seide geführt.**

### Processes in textile manufacture

| | |
|---|---|
| to crochet | häkeln |
| to darn | stopfen |
| to dye | färben |
| to felt | mit Filz belegen |
| to knit | stricken |
| to press | bügeln |
| to spin | spinnen |
| to weave | weben |

## BANKING

### The business of banking

| | |
|---|---|
| retail banking | **das Privatkundengeschäft** |
| wholesale/corporate banking | **das Firmenkundengeschäft** |
| universal/full-service banking | **das Universalbankgeschäft** |
| investment banking | **das Wertpapier- und Emissionsgeschäft** |
| merchant banking | **die Merchant-Bank(en), die Handelsbank(en)** |
| trustee banking | **das Sparkassengeschäft** |

*We specialize in wholesale banking for corporate and institutional investors.*

***Wir haben uns auf das Firmenkundengeschäft für Unternehmen und institutionelle Anleger spezialisiert.***

### The services provided

| | |
|---|---|
| account | **das Konto(-en)** |
| bank account | **das Bankkonto(-en)** |
| current/checking account | **das Girokonto(-en)** |
| deposit account | **das Einlagenkonto(-en)** |
| savings account | **das Sparkonto(-en)** |
| time deposit account | **das Festgeldkonto(-en)** |
| cash dispenser/automatic teller | **der Geldautomat(en)** |
| correspondent banking | **die Korrespondenzbank(en)** |
| credit | **der Kredit(e)** |
| credit card | **die Kreditkarte(n)** |
| credit limit | **der Kreditrahmen, die Kreditgrenze(n)** |
| credit line | **die Kreditlinie** |
| deposit (n)/(v) | **die Einlage(n)/eine Einlage leisten** |
| deposit account | **das Einlagenkonto(-en)** |
| deposit box | **das Schließfach(¨-er)** |
| foreign exchange/currency | **die Devisen** *pl* |
| interest | **der Zins(en)** |
| interest rate | **der Zinssatz(¨-e)** |
| fixed interest rate | **der feste(n) Zinssatz(¨-e)** |
| variable interest rate | **der variable(n) Zinssatz(¨-e)** |
| investment | **die Investition(en), die Kapitalanlage(n)** |
| investment counselling | **die Anlageberatung** |
| investment services | **die Anlagedienstleistungen** |

FINANCE DEPARTMENT, see page 73

| | |
|---|---|
| loan | das Darlehen(-) |
| short-term loan | das kurzfristige(n) Darlehen(-) |
| long-term loan | das langfristige(n) Darlehen(-) |
| lend | einen Kredit gewähren |
| letter of credit | das Akkreditiv(e) |
| mortgage | die Hypothek(en) |
| overdraft | die Überziehung(en) |
| portfolio management | die Vermögensverwaltung |
| project financing | die Projektfinanzierung(en) |
| risk analysis | die Risikoanalyse(n) |
| safe-deposit box | das Schließfach(¨er) |
| save | sparen |
| savings | die Ersparnisse |
| transfer (n)/(v) | die Überweisung(en)/überweisen |
| bank transfer | die Banküberweisung(en) |
| travellers' cheque/check | der Travellerscheck(s) |

*Our savings accounts offer very attractive rates of interest.*

**Wir können Ihnen sehr attraktive Zinssätze für Sparkonten anbieten.**

### The profession of banking

| | |
|---|---|
| bank manager | der Bankmanager(-) [-in], der Filialleiter(-) [-in] |
| cashier | der Kassierer(-) [-in] |
| customer advisor | der Kundenberater(-) [-in] |
| dealer | der Händler(-) [-in] |
| financial analyst | der Finanzanalyst(en) [-in] |
| financier | der Financier(s) |
| investment advisor/counsellor | der Anlageberater(-) [-in] |
| investor | der Anleger(-) [-in] |
| market maker | der Primärhändler [-in] |
| portfolio manager | der Vermögensverwalter(-) [-in] |
| security guard | der Wachmann |
| teller | der Kassierer(-) [-in] |
| trader | der Wertpapierhändler(-) [-in] |

*If you have money to invest, our investment advisors will be happy to discuss your needs.*

**Wenn Sie Geld anlegen wollen, werden unsere Anlageberater Sie gern beraten.**

*A portfolio manager can make day-to-day decisions about your investments.*

**Ein Vermögensverwalter kann täglich Entscheidungen über Ihre Anlagen treffen.**

# INSURANCE

## Types of insurance

| | |
|---|---|
| aviation insurance | **die Luftfahrtversicherung(en)** |
| credit insurance | **die Kreditversicherung(en)** |
| fire insurance | **die Brandversicherung(en)** |
| group insurance | **die Gruppenversicherung(en)** |
|   group life insurance | **die Gruppenlebens-versicherung(en)** |
|   group health insurance | **die Gruppenkranken-versicherung(en)** |
|   group annuities | **die Gruppenversicherung(en)** |
| health insurance | **die Krankenversicherung(en)** |
|   permanent health insurance | **die Berufsunfähigkeits-versicherung(en)** |
| liability insurance | **die Haftpflichtversicherung(en)** |
| life insurance/assurance | **die Lebensversicherung(en)** |
| marine insurance | **die Seeversicherung(en)** |
| motor/car insurance | **die Kraftfahrzeug-versicherung(en)** |
|   comprehensive | **die Vollkaskoversicherung(en)** |
|   third party, fire and theft | **die Haftpflicht-, Brand- und Diebstahlversicherung(en)** |
| re-insurance | **die Rückversicherung** |
| theft insurance | **die Diebstahlversicherung(en)** |

*Under the terms of your motor insurance, you are not covered for damage caused to your own car.*

***Gemäß den Bedingungen Ihrer Kfz- Versicherung sind Sie nicht gegen Schäden an Ihrem eigenen Fahrzeug versichert.***

## The elements of insurance

| | |
|---|---|
| accidental occurrence | **das Unfallereignis(se)** |
| agreement | **die Vereinbarung(en)** |
| claim (n) | **der Schaden(¨), der Anspruch(¨e)** |
| commission | **die Provision(en)** |
|   pay commission | **Provision zahlen** |
| contract | **der Vertrag(¨e)** |
| hazard | **das Wagnis(se)** |
| loss | **der Schaden(¨), der Verlust(e)** |
| mutuality | **die Gegenseitigkeit** |

| | |
|---|---|
| peril | das Risiko(-en) |
| insurable peril | das versicherbare Risiko |
| uninsurable peril | das nicht versicherbare Risiko |
| policy | die Police(n) |
| cancel a policy | eine Police kündigen/ aufheben |
| issue a policy | eine Police ausstellen |
| policy coverage | die Versicherungsdeckung |
| premium | der Beitrag(-e), die Prämie(n) |
| annual premium | der Jahresbeitrag(-e) |
| monthly premium | der monatliche(n) Beitrag(-e) |
| pay a premium | einen Beitrag/Beiträge zahlen |
| regular premium | die laufende Prämie |
| single premium | der Einmalbeitrag |
| rating | die Tarifierung |
| reimburse | entschädigen, rückerstatten |
| risk | das Risiko(-en) |
| insurable risk | das versicherbare Risiko |
| underwriting | die Versicherung, der Abschluß des Versicherungsvertrags |
| underwriting rates | die Versicherungstarife |

*If you want to make a claim, you must complete the form giving precise details of how the accident happened.*

**Wenn Sie einen Schaden melden wollen, müssen Sie dieses Formular unter genauer Angabe des Unfallhergangs ausfüllen.**

*You can pay for your insurance by 1 annual premium or spread it over 12 monthly premiums.*

**Sie können Ihre Versicherung mit einem Jahresbeitrag oder zwölf Monatsbeiträgen bezahlen.**

### Risks

| | |
|---|---|
| accident | der Unfall(-e) |
| accidental damage | der Unfallschaden(-) |
| accidental loss | der Unfallschaden(-) |
| breakdown | die Panne(n), der Ausfall(-e) |
| business interruption | die Betriebsunterbrechung(en) |
| death | der Tod(e) |
| explosion | die Explosion(en) |
| fire | der Brand(-e) |
| flood | die Überschwemmung(en) |
| illness | die Krankheit(en) |

| | |
|---|---|
| If you insure yourself against business interruption, then we will pay out in the event that you are prevented from carrying out your normal business activities. | *Wenn Sie eine Betriebsunterbrechungs-Versicherung abschließen, leisten wir Zahlungen für den Fall, daß Sie nicht in der Lage sind, Ihren normalen Geschäftsbetrieb aufrechtzuerhalten.* |

### The people involved in insurance

| | |
|---|---|
| actuary | der Aktuar(e/-) [-in] |
| adjuster | der Schadensregulierer(-) [-in] |
| agent | der Versicherungsvertreter(-) [-in] |
| broker | der Versicherungsmakler(-) [-in] |
| insurer | der Versicherer(-) |
| insured | der/die Versicherte(n) |
| policy holder | der Versicherungsnehmer(-) [-in] |
| underwriter | der Versicherer(-), der Unterzeichner(-) |

| | |
|---|---|
| Our actuaries apply the theories of probability and statistics and the principles of finance to problems of insurance. | *Unsere Aktuare wenden bei Versicherungsfragen sowohl Wahrscheinlichkeits- und Statistiktheorien, als auch Finanzprinzipien an.* |

### Claims

| | |
|---|---|
| cash (adv/n) | bar/das Bargeld |
| cash value | der Kapitalwert, der Marktwert |
| claim damages | Schadenersatzansprüche geltend machen |
| compensation | die Entschädigung(en) |
| damages | der Schadenersatz |
| depreciation | die Wertminderung |
| make a claim for damage/loss | einen Schaden melden, Schadenersatz fordern |
| new for old | der Ersatz |
| wear and tear | der Verschleiß, die Abnutzung |

| | |
|---|---|
| If you make a claim for damage or loss, then your compensation will be either on the basis of new for old or with a deduction for normal wear and tear. | *Wenn Sie Schadenersatz fordern, erhalten Sie eine Entschädigung auf der Grundlage der Abnutzung oder abzüglich einer Summe für den normalen Verschleiß.* |

# LAW

## General elements of law

| | |
|---|---|
| action | die Klage(n), der Prozeß(-sse) |
| bring an action against someone | jemanden verklagen |
| arbitration | die Schiedsgerichtsbarkeit |
| award (n) | die Zuerkennung(en) |
| capacity | die Rechtsfähigkeit, die Geschäftsfähigkeit |
| case | der Fall(-e), die (Rechts-)Sache(n) |
| civil case | die Zivilsache(n) |
| criminal case | die Strafsache(n) |
| claim (n) | der (Rechts-)Anspruch(-e) |
| make a claim against someone | einen Anspruch gegen jemanden erheben |
| compensation | die Entschädigung(en), der Schadenersatz |
| court | das Gericht(e) |
| take someone to court | jemanden vor Gericht bringen |
| damage | der Schaden(-) |
| damages | der Schadenersatz |
| defendant | der Angeklagte(n), die Angeklagte(n) |
| dispute | der Streitfall(-e) |
| to settle a dispute | einen Streit beilegen |
| duty | die Plicht(en), die Aufgabe(n) |
| duty of care | die Sorgfaltspflicht |
| impose a duty | eine Pflicht auferlegen |
| fine (n) | die Geldstrafe(n) |
| gross (adj) | grob |
| gross incompetence | grobe Inkompetenz |
| gross misconduct | grobes Fehlverhalten |
| gross negligence | grobe Fahrlässigkeit |
| grounds | die Begründung(en) |
| judge | der Richter(-) [-in] |
| lawyer | der Rechtsanwalt(-e) [-in] |
| liability | die Schuld, die Haftung |
| litigation | der Prozeß(-sse) |
| offence | das Delikt(e), die Straftat(en), das Vergehen |
| offend | verstoßen |
| offender | der (Straf-)Täter(-) [-in] |

LEGAL DEPARTMENT, see page 78

| party | die Partei(en) |
|---|---|
| guilty party | der/die Schuldige(n) |
| responsible party | die verantwortliche Partei |
| plaintiff | der Kläger(-) [-in] |
| prison | das Gefängnis(se), die Haftanstalt(en) |
| imprisonment | die Inhaftierung(en) |
| proceedings | der Prozeß(-sse) |
| prosecute | strafrechtlich verfolgen |
| remedy (n) | das Rechtsmittel |
| sentence (n) | das Urteil(e), die Strafe(n) |
| sue | klagen |
| term/requirement | die Bestimmung(en), die Bedingung(en) |
| title | der Rechtstitel |
| valid | gültig |
| invalid | ungültig |
| validity | die Gültigkeit |

## Contract law

| accept | annehmen, akzeptieren |
|---|---|
| acceptance | die Annahme |
| agreement | die Vereinbarung(en), der Vertrag(¨e) |
| conditions/terms of agreement | die Vertragsbedingungen |
| bid (n)/(v) | das Angebot(e)/anbieten |
| breach (n) | der Bruch, die Verletzung |
| breach of contract | der Vertragsbruch(¨e) |
| clause | die Klausel(n) |
| compensation | die Entschädigung(en), die Vergütung(en) |
| consideration | die Gegenleistung(en), die Erwägung(en) |
| contract (n) | der Vertrag(¨e) |
| break a contract | einen Vertrag brechen |
| make a/enter into a contract | einen Vertrag (ab)schließen |
| oral contract | der mündliche(n) Vertrag(¨e) |
| rescind a contract | einen Vertrag aufheben, von einem Vertrag zurücktreten |
| terminate a contract | einen Vertrag kündigen |
| written contract | der schriftliche(n) Vertrag(¨e) |
| intention to create legal relations | der Wille zur Schaffung eines Rechtsverhältnisses |

| | |
|---|---|
| offer (n) | **das Angebot(e)** |
| make an offer | **ein Angebot machen** |
| withdraw an offer | **ein Angebot zurückziehen** |
| party | **die Partei(en)** |

### Employment law

| | |
|---|---|
| discriminate | **diskriminieren** |
| discriminate against someone on the basis of sex, race or religion | **jemanden wegen seines Geschlechts, seiner Rasse oder seiner Religionszugehörigkeit diskriminieren** |
| dismiss | **entlassen** |
| dismissal | **die Entlassung(en)** |
| fire (v) | **feuern** |
| lump sum | **die Abfindung(en)** |
| misconduct | **das Fehlverhalten** |
| pension | **die Rente(n), der Ruhestand, die Pension(en)** |
| pensionable age | **das Rentenalter** |
| pension off | **pensionieren, in den Ruhestand versetzen** |
| re-engage | **wiedereinstellen** |
| re-engagement | **die Wiedereinstellung(en)** |
| redundant/laid off | **arbeitslos** |
| make someone redundant/lay someone off | **jemanden entlassen** |
| redundancy/dismissal payment | **die Entlassungsabfindung(en)** |
| reinstate | **wiedereinsetzen, wiedereinstellen** |
| reinstatement | **die Wiedereinsetzung(en), die Weiterbeschäftigung** |
| retire | **in Rente/Pension/den Ruhestand gehen** |
| retirement | **die Pensionierung(en), die Versetzung in den Ruhestand** |
| sack (v) | **fristlos entlassen** |
| strike | **der Streik(s)** |
| trade union | **die Gewerkschaft(en)** |

*If you are in breach of the terms of your contract of employment, you can be dismissed.*

*Wenn Sie gegen die Bestimmungen Ihres Arbeitsvertrags verstoßen, können Sie entlassen werden.*

PERSONNEL DEPARTMENT, see page 86

# TOURISM AND LEISURE

### Outdoor leisure activities

| | |
|---|---|
| archery | das Bogenschießen |
| bobsleighing/bobsledding | das Bobfahren |
| camping | das Camping |
| caving | die Höhlenforschung |
| curling | das Curling, das Eisstockschießen |
| cycling | das Radfahren |
| diving | das Tauchen |
|   deep-sea diving |   das Tiefseetauchen |
|   skin diving |   das Sporttauchen |
| exploring | auf Entdeckungsreise gehen |
| flying | das Fliegen |
| gliding | das Segelfliegen |
|   hang gliding |   das Drachenfliegen |
|   paragliding |   das Paragliding |
| hiking | das Wandern |
| hunting | die Jagd |
| jogging | das Jogging |
| luging | das Rodeln |
| mountaineering | das Bergsteigen |
| orienteering | das Orientierungsrennen |
| riding | das Reiten |
| rock-climbing | das (Fels-)Klettern |
| shooting | das Schießen |
| skating | das Rollschuhlaufen, das Schlittschuhlaufen |
|   ice hockey |   das Eishockey |
|   ice skating |   das Schlittschuhlaufen |
| skiing | das Skifahren |
|   downhill skiing |   der Abfahrtslauf, der alpine Skilauf |
|   cross-country skiing |   der Skilanglauf |
|   langlauf |   der Langlauf |
|   ski-jumping |   das Skispringen |
|   water skiing |   das Wasserskilaufen |
| snorkling | das Schnorcheln |
| surfing | das Surfen |
|   wind-surfing |   das Windsurfen |
| swimming | das Schwimmen |
| tobogganing | das Schlittenfahren |

| | |
|---|---|
| walking | das Spazierengehen, der Spaziergang |
| weight-training | das Krafttraining |
| weightlifting | das Gewichtheben |

*Many people now take two holidays/vacations a year: a skiing holiday/vacation in winter and a beach holiday/vacation in summer.*

*Viele Menschen fahren heute zweimal im Jahr in Urlaub: Skifahren im Winter und Strandurlaub im Sommer.*

## Travel and Tourism

| | |
|---|---|
| biking | das Motorradfahren |
| bus tour | die Busfahrt(en) |
| business trip | die Geschäftsreise(n) |
| cruise | die Kreuzfahrt(en) |
| cycling | das Radfahren |
| driving | das Fahren |
| excursion | der Ausflug(̈e) |
| expedition | die Expedition(en) |
| grand tour | die Bildungsreise(n) |
| hiking | das Wandern |
| journey | die Fahrt(en), die Reise(n) |
| joy ride | die Spritztour(en) |
| motoring | das Autofahren |
| outing | der Ausflug(̈e) |
| package tour | die Pauschalreise(n) |
| pleasure trip | die Vergnügungsfahrt(en) |
| ramble | die Wanderung(en) |
| ride | die Fahrt(en), der Ritt(e) |
| riding | das Reiten |
| safari | die Safari |
| study tour | die Studienreise(n) |
| tour | die Reise(n), die Tour(en) |
| package tour | die Pauschalreise(n) |
| trek | der Treck(s) |
| trip | die Reise(n) |
| visit | der Besuch(e) |
| voyage | die Reise(n) |
| walking | das Spazierengehen |

*Meditours are offering an autumn/fall cruise around the Mediterranean.*

*Meditours bietet im Herbst eine Mittelmeerkreuzfahrt an.*

# English–German Business Dictionary

| | |
|---|---|
| f | feminine |
| m | masculine |
| n | neuter |
| pl | plural |
| (adj) | adjective |
| (n) | noun |
| (v) | verb |
| so. | someone |
| sth. | something |

## A

**abandon an action**
eine Klage zurückziehen
**abroad** ins/im Ausland
**absent** abwesend
**accept** *(agree; take sth.)*
annehmen, akzeptieren
**accept delivery of a shipment** eine
Warensendung abnehmen
**accept liability for sth.** für etwas
Haftung übernehmen
**acceptable** akzeptabel
**acceptance** Annahme f
**account** Konto n, Rechnung f
**account for** Rechenschaft f ablegen,
sich verantworten
**account in credit**
Konto n mit Habensaldo
**account on hold** gesperrtes Konto
**account, on** als Anzahlung
**accounts department** Buchhaltung f
**accounts payable** Verbindlichkeiten fpl; Kreditoren mpl
**accounts receivable**
Außenstände mpl; Debitoren mpl
**accrue** auflaufen, anwachsen
**acknowledge receipt of a letter** den
Empfang eines Schreibens
bestätigen
**acquisition** Erwerb m; Übernahme f
**across-the-board** allgemein, generell
**act of God** höhere Gewalt
**acting manager**
stellvertretende(r) Leiter[in]
**action for damages**
Schadenersatzklage f
**actuals** Ist-Zahlen fpl

**add on 10% for service** 10% für
Bedienung aufschlagen
**additional charge** Aufpreis m
**additional premium** Beitrags-
zuschlag m, Prämienzuschlag m
**address** (n) Adresse f, Anschrift f
**address a letter** einen Brief adressieren
**address list** Adressenliste f
**adjourn a meeting**
eine Konferenz vertagen
**adjustment** Angleichung f; Korrektur f
**administration** Verwaltung f
**admission charge** Eintritt m
**ad valorem** dem Wert nach
**advance** (n) *(loan)*
Vorschuß m; Darlehen n
**advance** (v) *(lend)* vorschießen; leihen
**advance booking**
Vorbestellung f; Vorverkauf m
**advance on account** Kontokorrentkredit m; Überziehungskredit m
**advance payment**
Vorauszahlung f; Vorschußzahlung f
**advertise a new product** Werbung für
ein neues Produkt machen
**advertise a vacancy** ein Stellenangebot
inserieren/ausschreiben
**advertisement** Anzeige f, Werbung f
**advertiser**
Inserent m; Anzeigenkunde m
**advertising agency** Werbeagentur f
**advertising budget** Werbeetat m
**advertising rates**
Anzeigenkosten pl; Werbetarif m
**advertising space**
Werbefläche f; Anzeigenraum m
**advice note** Versandanzeige f, Avis m/n
**after-sales service** Kundendienst m
**after-tax profit** Gewinn m nach Steuern
**agency** Vertretung f, Agentur f
**agenda** Tagesordnung f, Programm n
**agent** Vertreter[in]
**agree** *(approve)* zustimmen, akzeptieren; *(be same as)* übereinstimmen
**agree to do sth.** sich einverstanden
erklären, etwas zu tun
**agreed price** vereinbarter Preis
**agreement** Vereinbarung f, Abkommen
n, Vertrag m
**aim** (n) Ziel n, Bestrebung f

**aim** (v) streben nach
**air freight** Luftfracht f
**airfreight** (v)
als Luftfracht befördern
**airmail** (n) Luftpost f
**airmail** (v) per Luftpost schicken
**airport** Flughafen m
**airtight packaging**
luftdichte Verpackung
**all expenses paid** Übernahme f
aller Kosten
**all-in price**
Pauschalpreis m, Gesamtpreis m
**all-risks policy**
Universalversicherung f
**allow 10% for carriage** 10% für
Transportkosten berechnen
**allowance for depreciation**
Wertberichtigung f auf
Anlagevermögen npl
**amend** abändern, ergänzen
**amendment**
Abänderung f, Ergänzung f
**amortization**
Amortisation f, Tilgung f
**amortize** amortisieren, tilgen
**amount** (money) Betrag m, Summe f
**amount owing** Forderung f,
zu zahlender Betrag m
**amount paid** bezahlter Betrag
**amount to**
sich belaufen auf, betragen
**analysis** Analyse f, Auswertung f
**annual accounts** Jahresabschluß m
**annual general meeting** ordentliche
Jahreshauptversammlung
**annual report** Jahresbericht m
**annually** jährlich
**answer** (n) Antwort f, Bescheid m
**answer** (v) antworten, beantworten
**answer the telephone**
den Hörer abnehmen
**answering machine**
Anrufbeantworter m
**appeal** (n) (against a decision)
Rechtsmittel n, Berufung f; (v)
Rechtsmittel/Berufung einlegen
**appeal to** (v) (attract)
ansprechen, reizen
**appendix** Anhang m, Zusatz m
**application** Antrag m, Gesuch n
**application form** Antragsformular n,
Bewerbungsformular n

**apply for a job** sich um eine
Stelle bewerben
**apply to** (affect) gelten, betreffen
**appoint** ernennen, berufen
**appointment** (job) Stelle f, Amt n;
(meeting) Termin m, Verabredung f
**appointments book**
Terminkalender m
**appointments vacant** Stellenangebote npl, offene Stellen fpl
**appreciate** schätzen;
(increase in value) steigen
**appreciation** Anerkennung f,
Wertschätzung f; (in value)
Wertzuwachs m; Aufwertung f
**approval, on**
auf Probe, versuchsweise
**approve the terms of a contract** die
Vertragsbedingungen akzeptieren
**approximate** ungefähr, annähernd
**approximately** etwa, annähernd
**arbitrate in a dispute** in einem
Streitfall vermitteln
**arbitration board/tribunal**
Schlichtungskommission f,
Schiedskommission f
**area code** Vorwahl f,
Ortsnetzkennzahl f
**area manager**
Bezirksleiter[in], Gebietsleiter[in]
**arrange** (meeting)
vereinbaren, einrichten
**arrears** Rückstände mpl
**article** (clause) Paragraph m,
Absatz m; (item) Artikel m
**as per advice**
laut Versandanzeige/Avis
**as per invoice** laut Rechnung
**as per sample** gemäß dem Muster
**ask** (so. to do sth.)
bitten; verlangen
**ask for a refund** eine
Rückerstattung fordern
**ask for further details** weitere
Details/Einzelheiten erfragen
**assess damages**
die Schäden schätzen
**assessment of damages**
Schadenfeststellung f;
Schadenberechnung f
**asset** Aktiva pl; Vermögenswert m
**asset value** Substanzwert m
**assist** helfen, unterstützen

**assistant**
Assistent[in], Mitarbeiter[in]
**assistant manager**
stellvertretende(r) Leiter[in]
**associate** *(adj)* verbunden
**associate** *(n)*
Teilhaber[in], Gesellschafter[in]
**assurance** Versicherung *f*
**assurance policy**
Lebensversicherungspolice *f*
**assure so.'s life** eine Lebensversicherung für jdn abschließen
**attend** *(meeting)*
anwesend sein, teilnehmen (an)
**attention**
Aufmerksamkeit *f*, Beachtung *f*
**auction** *(n)*
Auktion *f*, Versteigerung *f*
**auction** *(v)* versteigern
**audit** *(n)* Buchprüfung *f*, Revision *f*
**audit the accounts**
die Bücher prüfen
**auditor** Revisor[in];
Wirtschafts-prüfer[in]
**authority** Befugnis *f*, Ermächtigung *f*
**authorization** Genehmigung *f*,
Bevollmächtigung *f*
**authorize payment**
Zahlung anweisen
**availability**
Verfügbarkeit *f*, Disponibilität *f*
**available** erhältlich, verfügbar
**average** *(adj)* durchschnittlich
**average price** Durchschnitts preis *m*
**award a contract to so.** einen
Auftrag an jdn vergeben

## B

**back orders**
unerledigte Aufträge *mpl*
**back tax** Steuerschuld *f*
**back up** *(v)* *(computer file)* sichern;
*(support)* unterstützen
**backdate** rückdatieren
**backlog** Rückstand *m*
**backup copy** Sicherungskopie *f*
**bad debt** uneinbringliche
Forderung; nicht einziehbare
Außenstände *pl*
**balance** *(n)* Restbetrag *m*, Saldo *m*
**balance** *(v)* *(a budget)* ausgleichen

**balance brought down/forward**
vorgetragener Saldo
**balance carried down/forward**
übertragener Saldo
**balance due to us**
fälliger Rechnungsbetrag
**balance of payments**
Zahlungsbilanz *f*
**balance sheet** Bilanz *f*
**bank** *(n)* Bank *f*
**bank** *(v)*
(auf ein Bankkonto) einzahlen
**bank account** Bankkonto *n*
**bank balance** Kontostand *m*
**bank base rate**
Eckzins *m*, Leitzins *m*
**bank charges** Bankgebühren *fpl*
**bank draft**
Bankwechsel *m*, Banktratte *f*
**bank holiday** gesetzlicher Feiertag
**bank statement** Kontoauszug *m*
**bank transfer** Banküberweisung *f*
**banker's order** Dauerauftrag *m*
**banknote** Banknote *f*, Schein *m*
**bankrupt** *(adj)*
bankrott, zahlungsunfähig
**bankrupt** *(n)* Konkursschuldner[in]
**bankrupt** *(v)* ruinieren, in den
Konkurs treiben
**bankruptcy** Bankrott *m*, Konkurs *m*
**bar chart** Balkendiagramm *n*,
Stabdiagramm *n*
**bar code** Strichkode *m*
**bargain** *(n)* Schnäppchen *n*,
Gelegenheitskauf *m*; *(deal)*
Handel *m*, Geschäft *n*
**bargain** *(v)* aushandeln, handeln
**bargaining position**
Verhandlungsposition *f*
**barter** *(n)* Kompensationsgeschäft *n*,
Tauschgeschäft *n*
**barter** *(v)* Tauschhandel treiben,
Kompensationsgeschäfte machen
**basic** *(adj)* *(most important)*
hauptsächlich, Haupt-
**basic discount** Grundrabatt *m*
**basic tax** Eingangssteuer *f*
**batch** *(n)* *(of products)* Los *n*, Serie *f*
**batch** *(v)* stapeln
**batch number** Seriennummer *f*,
Auflagennummer *f*
**bear** *(v)* *(interest)* bringen
**bearer** Überbringer[in], Inhaber[in]

**begin** anfangen, beginnen
**behalf of, on** im Namen von
**benchmark** Eckwert m, Maßstab m
**beneficiary**
 Begünstigte(r); Nutznießer[in]
**benefit from** (v) profitieren von
**berth** (v) anlegen
**bid** (n) *(offer to buy)* Angebot n
**bilateral** bilateral, zweiseitig
**bill** (n) Rechnung f
**bill** (v) in Rechnung stellen
**billion** Milliarde f
**bill of exchange** Wechsel m, Tratte f
**bill of lading**
 Frachtbrief m, Konnossement n
**bill of sale** Kaufvertrag m
**bills payable**
 Wechselverbindlichkeiten fpl
**bills receivable**
 Wechselforderungen fpl
**blacklist** (v)
 auf die schwarze Liste setzen
**blank cheque/check** Blankoscheck m
**block** (v) blockieren, stoppen
**block booking** Gruppenbuchung f
**board** (n) *(people)* Ausschuß m
**board meeting** Vorstandssitzung f
**board of directors** Vorstand m
**bond** *(borrowing by government)*
 Schuldverschreibung f, Obligation f
**bonus** Prämie f, Zulage f
**book** (v) bestellen;
 buchen; reservieren
**book value** Buchwert m
**bookkeeper** Buchhalter[in]
**bookkeeping** Buchführung f
**border** Grenze f
**borrow** leihen, Kredit aufnehmen
**borrower**
 Kreditnehmer[in], Entleiher[in]
**boss** *(informal)* Boß m, Chef[in]
**bottleneck** Engpaß m
**bought ledger** Einkaufsbuch n
**bounce** *(cheque/check)* platzen
**box number** Chiffre f, Postfach n
**branch** Filiale f, Zweigstelle f
**brand** Marke f
**brand loyalty** Markentreue f
**brand name** Markenname m
**breach of contract** Vertragsbruch m
**break an agreement** ein Abkommen/
 einen Vertrag brechen

**break down** (v) *(itemize)* aufschlüsseln, aufgliedern; *(machine)*
 ausfallen, kaputtgehen
**break even** (v)
 kostendeckend arbeiten
**break off negotiations**
 Verhandlungen abbrechen
**break the law** das Gesetz brechen
**breakdown** (n) *(items)* Aufschlüsselung f, Aufgliederung f;
 *(machine)* Betriebsstörung f;
 Ausfall m
**breakeven point** Kostendeckungspunkt m, Break-Even-Punkt m
**bribe** (n)
 Bestechungsgeld n, Schmiergeld n
**bribe** (v) bestechen, schmieren
**briefcase** Aktentasche f
**brochure** Prospekt m, Broschüre f
**budget** (n) Finanzplan m, Budget n
**budget** (v) (im Budget) einplanen/
 veranschlagen
**budget account** Haushaltskonto n
**budgetary control** Budgetkontrolle f,
 Haushaltskontrolle f
**built-in** eingebaut
**bulk buying**
 Mengeneinkauf m, Großeinkauf m
**bureau de change** Wechselstube f
**business** *(commerce)* Geschäft n;
 Gewerbe n; *(company)* Unternehmen n, Betrieb m; *(matter)*
 Angelegenheit f, Sache f
**business, on** geschäftlich, dienstlich
**business address** Geschäftsadresse f
**business class** Business Class f
**business hours**
 Geschäftsstunden pl, Geschäftszeit f
**business lunch** Geschäftsessen n
**business premises**
 Geschäftsräume mpl, gewerbliche
 Räumlichkeiten fpl
**business strategy** Geschäfts-
 strategie f
**businessman/-woman**
 Geschäftsmann m/Geschäftsfrau f
**busy** beschäftigt
**buy** (v) kaufen, aufkaufen
**buy forward** auf Termin kaufen
**buyer** *(person)* Käufer[in]
**buying department**
 Einkauf m, Einkaufsabteilung f

# C

**calculate** berechnen, kalkulieren
**calculation** Berechnung f
**calculator** Rechner m, Rechenhilfe f
**calendar month** Kalendermonat m
**calendar year** Kalenderjahr n
**call** (n) *(phone)* Anruf m, Gespräch n; *(visit)* Besuch m
**call** (v) *(phone)* anrufen
**call off a deal** ein Abkommen/ein Geschäft rückgängig machen
**cancel** absagen; annullieren; stornieren
**cancel a contract** einen Vertrag aufheben
**cancellation clause** Rücktrittsklausel f
**cancellation of an appointment** Terminabsage f
**capacity** *(ability)* Befähigung f, Eignung f; *(production)* Kapazität f; *(space)* Fassungsvermögen n
**capital** Kapital n; Aktienkapital n
**capital expenditure** Investitionsausgabe f, Investitionen fpl
**capital gains** Veräußerungsgewinn m
**capitalization** Kapitalisierung f
**capitalize** kapitalisieren, aktivieren
**capitalize on** Kapital schlagen aus
**captive market** monopolistischer Absatzmarkt
**capture** erobern, an sich bringen
**card, business** Visitenkarte f
**card phone** Kartentelefon n
**cardboard box** Pappkarton m
**care of (c/o)** bei, c/o
**cargo** Fracht f, Ladung f
**carriage** Transport m, Transportkosten pl
**carriage forward** Frachtkosten per Nachnahme
**carriage free** frachtfrei
**carriage paid** frachtfrei, frei Haus
**carrier** *(company)* Spedition f, Transportunternehmen n
**carry** annehmen; *(have in stock)* führen, auf Lager haben; *(transport)* befördern
**carry forward** übertragen
**carton** *(box)* Karton m, Stange f
**case** (n) *(box)* Kiste f
**cash** (adj) bar

**cash** (n) *(money)* Bargeld n
**cash a cheque/check** einen Scheck einlösen
**cash advance** Barvorschuß m
**cash balance** Kassenbestand m, Bankguthaben n
**cash book** Kassenbuch n
**cash card** Geldautomatenkarte f
**cash discount** Barzahlungsrabatt m, Skonto m/n
**cash dispenser** Geldautomat m
**cash flow** Cash-flow m
**cash flow forecast** Cash-flow-Prognose f
**cash offer** Barzahlungsangebot n
**cash on delivery** per Nachnahme
**cash price** Barzahlungspreis m, Barpreis m
**cash purchase** Barkauf m
**cash sale** Barverkauf m, Kassageschäft n
**cash terms** Barzahlungsbedingungen fpl
**casting vote** ausschlaggebende Stimme
**casual work** Gelegenheitsarbeit f
**catalogue/catalog** Katalog m
**cater for** eingestellt sein auf
**caveat emptor** Ausschluß m der Gewährleistung, auf Risiko (des) Käufers
**ceiling price** Höchstpreis m
**cellular telephone** Funktelefon n
**central bank** Zentralbank f, Notenbank f
**central purchasing** Zentraleinkauf m
**centralize** zentralisieren
**certificate of approval** Zulassungsbescheinigung f
**certificate of origin** Herkunftsbescheinigung f; Provenienzzertifikat n
**certified cheque/check** bestätigter Scheck
**certified copy** beglaubigte Kopie
**certify** bescheinigen, beglaubigen
**chain store** Filialgeschäft n, Kettenladen m
**chairman** Vorsitzende(r)
**chairman and managing director** Vorsitzende(r) und Geschäftsführer[in]

**Chamber of Commerce**
Handelskammer f
**change** (n) *(difference)* Änderung f,
Wechsel m; *(cash)* Wechselgeld n
**change** (v) *(become different)* sich
ändern; *(money)* wechseln
**change hands** in andere Hände
übergehen, den Besitzer
wechseln
**channels of distribution** Vertriebswege mpl, Distributionskanäle mpl
**charge** (n) *(money)*
Gebühr f, Kosten pl
**charge** (v) *(money)*
berechnen, in Rechnung stellen
**charge a purchase** einen Kauf in
Rechnung stellen
**charge card** Kundenkarte f
**charter flight** Charterflug m
**chase** *(an order)*
antreiben, vorantreiben
**cheap** billig, preiswert
**cheap rate** niedriger Tarif
**check** (n) *(examination)*
Überprüfung f, Kontrolle f
**check** (v) *(examine)*
überprüfen, kontrollieren
**check in** *(airport)* einchecken; *(hotel)*
sich anmelden
**check-in counter**
Abfertigungsschalter m
**check-in time** Eincheckzeit f
**check out** *(hotel)* abreisen
**checkout** *(in supermarket)* Kasse f
**cheque/check** Scheck m
**cheque/check book** Scheckheft n
**chief** (adj) erste(r,s), Haupt-
**chief executive officer (CEO)**
Generaldirektor[in]
**choice** (n) *(of items)*
Auswahl f, Sortiment n
**choose** wählen, auswählen
**Christmas bonus** Weihnachtsgeld n
**circular** (n)
Rundschreiben n, Umlauf m
**circular letter of credit**
Zirkularkreditbrief m
**claim** (n) Forderung f, Anspruch m
**claim** (v) *(insurance)* fordern,
Ansprüche mpl geltend machen
**claims department**
Schadenabteilung f

**classified advertisements**
Kleinanzeigen fpl
**classified directory**
Branchenverzeichnis n
**classify** klassifizieren, einstufen
**clause** Klausel f, Absatz m
**clear** (adj) *(understandable)*
klar, verständlich
**clear** (v) *(stock)* räumen
**clear a cheque/check**
einen Scheck verrechnen
**clear profit**
Reingewinn m, Nettogewinn m
**clearing bank**
Clearingbank f, Geschäftsbank f
**clerical error** Schreibfehler m
**clerk**
Büroangestellte(r),
Sachbearbeiter[in]
**client** Kunde[-in], Auftraggeber[in]
**clientele** Kundschaft f,
Kundenkreis m
**clinch** (v) abschließen
**close a meeting**
eine Sitzung schließen
**close an account** ein Konto auflösen
**close down** schließen; stillegen
**closed** geschlossen
**closing balance**
Endsaldo m, Schlußsaldo m
**closing date**
Schlußtag m, letzter Termin
**closing price** Schlußnotierung f
**closing stock** Schlußbestand m
**closing time**
Geschäftsschluß m, Ladenschluß m
**co-operate** kooperieren,
zusammenarbeiten
**co-operation**
Zusammenarbeit f, Mitarbeit f
**co-opt so.** jdn kooptieren
**code of practice** Verfahrensregeln fpl
**coin** Münze f, Geldstück n
**cold call** unangemeldeter
Vertreterbesuch, unangemeldetes
Verkaufsgespräch
**cold store** Kühlhaus n
**collaborate** zusammenarbeiten
**collaboration** Zusammenarbeit f
**collapse** (n)
Sturz m, Zusammenbruch m
**collapse** (v) zusammenbrechen
**collateral** (n) Sicherheit f, Deckung f

**collect** (v) *(fetch)* abholen
**collect a debt**
Schulden *fpl* einziehen/eintreiben
**collect call** R-Gespräch *n*
**collection** *(of goods)* Abholung *f*
**collective ownership**
Gemeineigentum *n*
**collector** *(of debts)*
Inkassobeauftragte(r);
Einziehungsbeamte(r)/-beamtin
**commerce**
Handel *m*, Handelsverkehr *m*
**commercial** (adj) kommerziell,
Handels-, Geschäfts-
**commercial** (n) *(TV)*
Werbespot *m*, Werbung *f*
**commercial law** Handelsrecht *n*
**commission** *(money)*
Provision *f*, Maklergebühr *f*
**commission rep**
Provisionsvertreter[in]
**commit funds to a project** Geldmittel
für ein Projekt einsetzen
**commitments** Verpflichtungen *fpl*
**commodity** Handelsware *f*,
Gebrauchsartikel *m*
**commodity exchange/market**
Warenbörse *f*
**common pricing** Preisabsprache *f*
**communicate** sich verständigen, in
Verbindung stehen
**communications** Verbindungen *fpl*;
*(travel)* Verkehrsverbindungen *fpl*
**commute** *(travel)* pendeln
**commuter** Pendler[in]
**company** Firma *f*, Unternehmen *n*
**company director**
Direktor[in], Firmenchef[in]
**comparable**
vergleichbar, Vergleichs-
**compare (with)** vergleichen (mit)
**comparison** Vergleich *m*
**compensate** entschädigen
**compensation for damage**
Schadenersatz *m*
**competition** *(contest)*
Wettbewerb *m*; *(commercial)*
Konkurrenz *f*
**competitive price** wettbewerbs-
fähiger/konkurrenzfähiger Preis
**competitiveness**
Wettbewerbsfähigkeit *f*,
Konkurrenzfähigkeit *f*

**competitor** Konkurrent[in],
Mitbewerber[in]
**complain** *(about)*
sich beschweren; beanstanden
**complaint**
Beschwerde *f*, Reklamation *f*
**complaints department**
Reklamationsabteilung *f*
**complete** (adj) komplett, vollständig
**complete** (v) beenden, fertigstellen
**comply with** entsprechen; befolgen
**compound interest** Zinseszins *m*
**comprehensive insurance**
kombinierte Haftpflicht- und
Vollkaskoversicherung
**compromise** (n) Kompromiß *m*
**compromise** (v)
einen Kompromiß schließen
**compulsory** obligatorisch,
verbindlich, Pflicht-
**compulsory purchase** Enteignung *f*
**computer** Computer *m*, Rechner *m*
**computer error** Computerfehler *m*
**computer file** Computerdatei *f*
**computer program**
Computerprogramm *n*
**computer services** EDV-Service *m*
**computer system** Rechnersystem *n*
**computerize** auf Datenverarbeitung,
auf EDV umstellen
**concern** (n) *(worry)*
Besorgnis *f*, Sorge *f*
**concern** (v) *(deal with)*
betreffen, angehen
**conclude** *(agreement)* abschließen
**condition** *(state)* Zustand *m*
**condition** *(terms)* Bedingung *f*,
Kondition *f*, Auflage *f*
**condition that, on** unter der
Bedingung, daß
**conditional** mit Auflagen,
unter Vorbehalt
**conditions of employment**
Arbeitsvertragsbedingungen *fpl*
**conditions of sale**
Verkaufsbedingungen *fpl*
**conduct negotiations**
Verhandlungen führen
**conference room** Besprechungszimmer *n*, Konferenzraum *m*
**confidential** vertraulich
**confirm a booking**
eine Buchung bestätigen

**confirmation** Bestätigung f
**conflict of interest**
Interessenkonflikt m
**connecting flight** Anschlußflug m
**connection**
Zusammenhang m, Verbindung f
**consignment** (sending) Versand m;
(things sent) Sendung f, Lieferung f
**consignment note** Avis m/n
**consist of** bestehen aus, sich
zusammensetzen aus
**consolidate** (shipments)
zusammenlegen
**consortium** Konsortium n
**constant** konstant, gleichbleibend
**consult** konsultieren, zu Rate ziehen
**consultancy firm** Beratungsfirma f
**consultant** Berater[in]
**consumer**
Verbraucher[in], Konsument[in]
**consumer goods**
Verbrauchsgüter npl,
Konsumgüter npl
**consumer price index**
Verbraucherpreisindex m
**consumer research**
Verbraucherforschung f
**contact** (n) (person) Kontaktperson f
**contact** (v) sich in Verbindung setzen
mit, Kontakt aufnehmen zu
**contain** enthalten
**container** (box, tin) Behälter m
**container** (for shipping) Container m
**container terminal**
Containerterminal m
**contents** Inhalt m
**contested takeover**
angefochtene Übernahme
**contingency plan** Krisenplan m
**continual(ly)** wiederholt; ständig
**continue** andauern; fortsetzen
**continuous** kontinuierlich, stetig
**contra account** Gegenkonto n
**contra an entry** (v) einen Eintrag
gegenbuchen/stornieren
**contra entry** (v) Gegenbuchung f
**contract** (n) Vertrag m
**contract** (v) sich vertraglich verpflichten, einen Vertrag abschließen
**contract note** Ausführungsanzeige f
**contract of employment**
Arbeitsvertrag m
**contractor** Auftragnehmer[in]

**contractual liability**
Vertragshaftung f
**contractually** vertraglich,
durch Vertrag
**contrary, on the** im Gegenteil
**control** (n) (check) Kontrolle f,
Überwachung f; (power) Leitung f,
Beherrschung f
**convene** einberufen; zusammenrufen
**convenient** geeignet;
praktisch, günstig
**conversion price/rate**
Umrechnungskurs m
**convert** tauschen, umtauschen
**convertible loan stock**
Wandelanleihe f
**copy** (n) (of document)
Kopie f, Durchschlag m
**copy** (v) kopieren; einen
Durchschlag/eine Abschrift machen
**corner the market** monopolisieren
**corporate image** Firmenimage n
**corporate plan** Unternehmensplan m
**corporate profits**
Unternehmensgewinne mpl
**corporation** Unternehmen n,
Kapitalgesellschaft f
**corporation tax**
Körperschaftssteuer f
**correspond with so.**
mit jdm korrespondieren, in
Briefwechsel stehen
**correspondence**
Korrespondenz f, Schriftverkehr m
**cost** (n) Kosten pl, Preis m
**cost** (v) kosten
**cost analysis** Kostenanalyse f
**cost centre/center** Kostenstelle f
**cost of living**
Lebenshaltungskosten pl
**cost of sales**
Absatzkosten pl, Vertriebskosten pl
**cost plus** Ist-Kosten pl plus
prozentualer Gewinnaufschlag
**cost price** Selbstkostenpreis m,
Einstandspreis m
**cost, insurance and freight (c.i.f.)**
Kosten, Versicherung, Fracht (cif)
**cost-effective**
rentabel; kostenwirksam
**cost-effectiveness** Kostenrentabilität f, Kostenwirksamkeit f

**cost-of-living allowance**
Lebenshaltungskostenzuschuß m
**cost-of-living index**
Lebenshaltungskostenindex m
**counter** Ladentisch m, Tresen m
**counter-claim** (n) eine Gegen-
forderung f, Widerklage f
**counter-claim** (v) eine Gegen-
forderung/Widerklage erheben
**counter-offer** Gegengebot n
**counterfoil** Kontrollabschnitt m
**countermand** widerrufen
**countersign** gegenzeichnen
**country of origin** Ursprungsland n
**coupon ad** Couponanzeige f
**courier** *(guide)* Reiseleiter[in];
*(messenger)* Kurier m, Eilbote m
**court** Gericht n
**covenant** (n)
Vertrag m, Abkommen n
**cover** (n) *(insurance)*
Versicherungsschutz m
**cover** (n) *(top)* Schutz m, Hülle f
**cover a risk** ein Risiko absichern
**cover charge** Gedeck n
**cover costs** die Kosten decken
**cover note** vorläufiger
Versicherungsschein m;
Deckungszusage f
**covering letter** Begleitbrief m
**credit** (n) Kredit m, Darlehen n
**credit** (v) gutschreiben; kreditieren
**credit account** Kundenkonto n
**credit balance**
Habensaldo m, Guthaben n
**credit control** Kreditüberwachung f,
Kreditkontrolle f
**credit entry**
Habenbuchung f, Gutschrift f
**credit freeze**
Einfrieren n von Krediten mpl
**credit limit** Kreditlimit n
**credit note** Gutschriftanzeige f
**credit, on** auf Kredit
**creditor** Gläubiger m
**cross a cheque/check** einen Scheck
zur Verrechnung ausstellen
**cumulative** kumulativ, anhäufend
**cumulative interest**
Zins und Zinseszins m
**currency** Währung f
**current account**
laufendes Konto, Girokonto n

**current assets** Umlaufvermögen n
**current liabilities**
kurzfristige Verbindlichkeiten fpl
**current rate of exchange**
Tageskurs m
**curriculum vitae (CV)** Lebenslauf m
**customer** Kunde[-in];
Auftraggeber[in]
**customer satisfaction**
Zufriedenstellung f der Kunden
**customer service department**
Kundendienst m
**customs** Zoll m, Zollbehörde f
**customs clearance** Zollabfertigung f
**customs declaration form**
Zollerklärungsformular n
**customs entry point**
Zollanmeldestelle f
**customs examination**
Zollkontrolle f
**customs official** Zollbeamte(r) [-in]
**cut** (n) Senkung f, Kürzung f
**cut** (v) streichen;
reduzieren; kürzen
**cut down on expenses**
die Kosten verringern
**cut price** (n) Niedrigpreis m,
herabgesetzer Preis
**cut-price goods** herabgesetzte
Waren fpl, Billigwaren fpl
**cycle** Zyklus m, Kreislauf m
**cyclical** zyklisch, konjunkturbedingt

# D

**damage** (n)
Schaden m, Beschädigung f
**damage** (v) beschädigen
**damages**
Schadenersatz m, Entschädigung f
**data** Daten pl
**database** Datenbank f
**date** (n) Datum n
**date** (v) datieren
**date stamp** Datumsstempel m
**day** *(working day)* Arbeitstag m
**dead account** umsatzloses Konto
**deadline** (letzter) Termin; Stichtag m
**deadlock** (n) Stillstand m
**deadlock** (v) zum Stillstand bringen
**deal** (n) Abkommen n, Geschäft n
**deal in** (v) handeln, Handel treiben

**deal with an order** einen Auftrag
  ausführen/bearbeiten
**dealer** Händler[in]
**dear** teuer, kostspielig
**debenture**
  Obligation f, Schuldverschreibung f
**debit** (n) Soll n
**debit an account** ein Konto belasten
**debit entry**
  Sollbuchung f, Belastung f
**debit note** Belastungsanzeige f,
  Lastschriftanzeige f
**debt** Schuld f
**debt collection**
  Schuldeneintreibung f
**debt collection agency** Inkassobüro n
**debtor**
  Schuldner[in]; Kreditnehmer[in]
**decide on a course of action** über die
  Vorgehensweise entscheiden
**deciding factor**
  entscheidender Faktor
**decimal point** Komma n
**declare goods to customs** Waren
  beim Zoll deklarieren
**declared value** angegebener Wert
**decrease** (n) Abnahme f,
  Verminderung f, Fall m
**decrease** (v) abnehmen, fallen,
  sich vermindern
**decrease in value** Wertminderung f
**decreasing** abnehmend
**deduct** abziehen
**deductible** abziehbar
**deduction** Abzug m, Abziehen n
**deed** Urkunde f
**default** (n)
  Nichterfüllung f, Versäumnis n
**default** (v) **on payments** mit
  Zahlungen in Verzug geraten;
  Zahlungen nicht leisten
**defaulter** säumige(r) Schuldner[in]
**defect** Defekt m, Störung f
**defective** (faulty) defekt, schadhaft
**defer payment**
  die Zahlung aufschieben
**deferment of payment**
  Zahlungsaufschub m
**deficit** Defizit n, Minusbetrag m
**defray** (costs) tragen, übernehmen
**delay** (n) Verzögerung f, Verzug m
**delay** (v) verzögern; aufhalten
**delete** streichen

**deliver** liefern, zustellen
**delivered price** Lieferpreis m
**delivery** (goods) Lieferung f
**delivery date** Liefertermin m
**delivery note** Lieferschein m
**delivery time** Lieferzeit f
**demand** (n) (for payment)
  Forderung f; (need) Nachfrage f,
  Bedarf m
**demand** (v) fordern, verlangen
**demonstrate** vorführen
**demonstration model**
  Vorführmodell n
**department** (office, shop) Abteilung f
**depend on** angewiesen sein auf
**depending on** abhängig von, je nach
**deposit** (n) (in bank) Einzahlung f,
  Einlage f; (paid in advance)
  Anzahlung f
**deposit** (v) einzahlen; in Verwahrung
  geben/deponieren
**deposit account** Sparkonto n
**deposit slip** Einzahlungsbeleg m
**depositor** Einzahler[in], Einleger[in]
**depreciate** (lose value) fallen, an
  Wert verlieren
**depreciation** (loss of value)
  Wertminderung f, Abwertung f
**depreciation rate**
  Abschreibungssatz m
**deputize for so.** jdn vertreten, als jds
  Vertreter fungieren
**deputy** Stellvertreter[in]
**deputy managing director**
  stellvertretende(r) geschäfts-
  führende(r) Direktor[in]
**design** (n) Design n, Entwurf m
**design** (v) entwerfen, entwickeln
**design department** Konstruktionsabteilung f, Designabteilung f
**desk** Schreibtisch m
**destination** Bestimmungsort m
**detail** (n) Detail n, Einzelheit f
**detailed account** spezifizierte
  Rechnung; eingehender Bericht
**Deutschmark** (Deutsche) Mark f
**devaluation** Abwertung f
**devalue** abwerten
**diagram** Diagramm n,
  graphische Darstellung f
**dial a number** eine Nummer wählen
**dialling code**
  Vorwahl f, Ortsnetzkennzahl f

**differ** sich unterscheiden; *(disagree)* anderer Meinung sein

**differences in price** Preisunterschiede *mpl*

**direct** (adj) direkt, unmittelbar

**direct** (v) leiten, führen

**direct debit, pay** (v) **by** per Einzugsauftrag bezahlen

**direct mail** Direktversand *m*, Postwurfsendung *f*

**direct tax** direkte Steuer

**direct-mail advertising** Werbung *f* durch Postwurfsendung

**directions for use** Gebrauchsanweisung *f*, Benutzerhinweise *mpl*

**director** Direktor[in]; Mitglied (n) eines Board of Directors

**directory** Verzeichnis *n*

**disclaimer** Haftungsablehnungserklärung *f*; Verzichterklärung *f*

**discontinue** auslaufen lassen, die Produktion einstellen

**discount** (n) Rabatt *m*, Preisnachlaß *m*

**discount** (v) Rabatt gewähren

**discount price** Preis *m* nach Abzug des Rabatts

**discounted cash flow (DCF)** diskontierter Cash-flow

**discrepancy** Diskrepanz *f*

**discuss** diskutieren, besprechen

**discussion** Diskussion *f*; Besprechung *f*; Debatte *f*

**disk** Platte *f*; Diskette *f*

**disk drive** Diskettenlaufwerk *n*

**dismiss an employee** einen Arbeitnehmer entlassen

**dismissal** Entlassung *f*

**dispatch** (n) *(sending)* Versand *m*; Beförderung *f*

**dispatch** (v) versenden, schicken

**dispatch note** Versandschein *m*; Avis *m/n*

**display** (n) Auslage *f*, Vorführung *f*

**display** (v) ausstellen; zeigen, vorführen

**display material** Auslagematerial *n*

**display stand** Auslagenstand *m*, Präsentationsstand *m*

**disposable** Wegwerf-, Einweg-

**disposal** Veräußerung *f*; Verfügung *f*

**dispose of excess stock** überschüssige Warenbestände veräußern

**distribute** vertreiben

**distribution** Vertrieb *m*, Verteilung *f*

**distribution costs** Vertriebskosten *pl*

**distribution manager** Vertriebsleiter[in]

**distributor** Verteiler *m*, Vertragshändler[in]

**diversification** Diversifikation *f*, Diversifizierung *f*

**diversify** diversifizieren, ausweiten

**dividend** Dividende *f*

**dividend yield** Dividendenertrag *m*

**division** *(part of a company)* Abteilung *f*; Unternehmensbereich *m*

**dock** (n) Dock *n*

**dock** (v) *(ship)* docken, eindocken

**documentation** Dokumentation *f*, Unterlagen *pl*

**dollar** Dollar *m*, US-Dollar *m*

**dollar balance** Dollarbilanz *f*

**domestic market** Binnenmarkt *m*, Inlandsmarkt *m*

**domestic production** Inlandsproduktion *f*

**domestic sales** Inlandsabsatz *m*

**door-to-door selling** Direktverkauf *m*, Haustürverkauf *m*

**dossier** Dossier *n*

**double** (v) verdoppeln

**double taxation** Doppelbesteuerung *f*

**down payment** Anzahlung *f*

**down-market** billig, auf den Massenmarkt ausgerichtet

**downside factor** Verlustfaktor *m*

**downturn** Rückgang *m*, Abflauen *n*

**dozen** Dutzend *n*

**draft** (n) *(money)* Wechsel *m*, Tratte *f*; *(plan)* Entwurf *m*, Konzept *n*

**draft a contract** einen Vertrag entwerfen

**draft plan** Planskizze *f*

**draw** *(a cheque/check)* ausstellen

**draw** *(money)* abheben

**draw** *(salary)* beziehen

**draw up a contract** einen Vertrag aufsetzen/entwerfen

**drawee** Bezogene(r), Trassat *m*

**drawer** Aussteller[in], Trassant *m*

**drop** (n) Rückgang *m*

**drop** (v) zurückgehen, fallen

**drop in sales** Umsatzrückgang m,
Absatzrückgang m
**due** *(awaited)* erwartet;
*(owing)* fällig
**dues** *(orders)* Vorbestellungen fpl
**dummy** Attrappe f; Blindband m
**dummy pack**
Schaupackung f, Leerpackung f
**dumping** Dumping n
**duplicate** (n)
Duplikat n, Zweitschrift f
**duplicate** (v) kopieren
**duplicate (of a) receipt**
Quittungsduplikat n
**duty** *(tax)* Steuer f, Zoll m
**duty-free** zollfrei

# E

**earn** *(interest)* bringen, einbringen;
*(money)* verdienen
**earnings** *(profit)* Gewinn m,
Ertrag m; *(salary)* Einkommen n,
Einkünfte pl
**easy terms**
günstige Bedingungen fpl,
Zahlungserleichterungen fpl
**economic cycle** Konjunkturzyklus m
**economic development**
wirtschaftliche Entwicklung
**economic growth**
Wirtschaftswachstum n
**economic indicators**
Konjunkturindikatoren fpl
**economic trends**
konjunkturelle Entwicklung f;
Wirtschaftsentwicklung f
**economical** sparsam, rationell
**economies of scale** Größenvorteile
mpl, Größendegression f
**economize** einsparen,
sparsam wirtschaften
**economy** *(saving)* Sparsamkeit f,
Wirtschaftlichkeit f
**economy class** Touristenklasse f,
Economy-Klasse f
**ecu/ECU (European currency unit)**
Ecu/ECU m/f
**effect** (n) Auswirkung f, Effekt m
**effect** (v) ausführen, durchführen
**effective** effektiv, Effektiv-
**effective yield**
Effektivertrag m, Effektivrendite f

**effectiveness** Wirksamkeit f,
Leistungsfähigkeit f
**efficiency** Fähigkeit f, Effizienz f
**efficient** leistungsfähig, tüchtig
**electronic mail**
elektronische Post, E-Mail f
**electronic point of sale (EPOS)**
elektronisches Kassenterminal n,
Datenkasse f
**embargo** (n)
Embargo n, Handelssperre f
**embargo** (v) ein Embargo verhängen
**embark** (sich) einschiffen
**embark on** mit etwas neu beginnen
**employ** beschäftigen, einstellen
**employee**
Arbeitnehmer[in]; Angestellte(r)
**employer** Arbeitgeber[in]
**employment** Beschäftigung f;
Anstellung f; Stelle f
**empty** (adj) leer
**enclose** beilegen, beifügen
**enclosure** Anlage f, Beilage f
**end** (n) Ende n, Beendigung f
**end** (v) enden; beenden
**end of season sale** Sommerschlußverkauf m, Winterschlußverkauf m
**end product** Endprodukt n
**end user**
Endverbraucher m, Endbenutzer m
**endorse a cheque/check**
einen Scheck girieren
**endorsement** *(action)* Indossierung f;
Indossament n; *(on insurance)*
Nachtrag m (zu einer Police)
**energy-saving** (adj) energiesparend
**engaged** *(telephone)* besetzt
**engaged tone** Besetztzeichen n
**enter** *(go in)* eintreten, einsteigen
**enter** *(write in)* eintragen
**enter into** *(discussion)*
aufnehmen, eingehen
**enterprise** Unternehmertum n;
Unternehmen n
**entitle** berechtigen
**entitlement**
Anspruch m, Berechtigung f
**entrepreneur** Unternehmer[in]
**entrepreneurial** unternehmerisch
**entry** *(going in)* Eintritt m,
Eingang m; *(writing)* Eintrag m
**entry visa** Einreisevisum n
**equip** ausrüsten, ausstatten

**equipment**
Ausstattung f, Einrichtung f

**equities** Stammaktien fpl

**equity capital** Aktienkapital n

**error** Fehler m

**errors and omissions excepted (e. & o.e.)** Irrtümer und Auslassungen vorbehalten

**escape clause** Befreiungsklausel f, Rücktrittsklausel f

**establish** gründen, schaffen, bilden

**establishment** *(business)* Geschäft n, Betrieb m

**estimate** (n) *(calculation)* Schätzung f, Überschlag m; *(quote)* Kostenvoranschlag m

**estimate** (v) schätzen

**estimated sales** geschätzter Absatz

**European Union (EU)** Europäische Union (EU)

**evaluate costs** Kosten berechnen

**evaluation** Abschätzung f, Berechnung f

**exact** genau, exakt

**examination** *(inspection)* Untersuchung f, Prüfung f; *(test)* Prüfung f, Examen f

**examine** untersuchen, prüfen

**exceed** überschreiten, hinausgehen über

**excellent** ausgezeichnet, hervorragend

**excess capacity** Überkapazität f

**excessive** übermäßig

**exchange** (n) *(currency)* Devisen pl

**exchange** (v) *(currency)* wechseln, tauschen; *(one thing for another)* tauschen, umtauschen

**exchange rate** Wechselkurs m

**excise duty** Verbrauchssteuer f

**excluding** außer, ausgenommen

**exclusion clause** Ausschlußklausel f, Freizeichnungsklausel f

**exclusive agreement** Exklusivvertrag m

**exclusive of tax** ohne Steuer

**exclusivity** Exklusivrecht n

**executive** (adj) exekutiv, Exekutiv-

**executive** (n) Führungskraft f; leitende(r) Angestellte(r)

**exempt** (adj) befreit

**exempt** (v) befreien, freistellen

**exempt from tax** steuerfrei, von der Steuer befreit

**exemption from tax** Steuerbefreiung f

**exercise an option** ein Optionsrecht ausüben

**exercise of an option** Ausübung f eines Optionsrechts

**exhibit** (v) ausstellen

**exhibition** Ausstellung f

**exhibitor** Aussteller[in]

**expand** vergrößern; expandieren; ausbauen

**expenditure** Ausgaben fpl, Aufwendungen fpl

**expense** Ausgabe f, Kosten pl

**expense account** Spesenkonto n, Spesenrechnung f

**expensive** teuer

**experienced** erfahren, sachkundig

**expire** ablaufen, erlöschen

**expiry/expiration** Ablauf m, Erlöschen n

**expiry date** Ablauftermin m, Verfallsdatum n

**export** (n) Export m, Ausfuhr f

**export** (v) exportieren, ausführen

**export department** Exportabteilung f

**export licence/permit** Ausfuhrgenehmigung f

**export manager** Exportleiter[in]

**exporter** Exporteur m, Exportfirma f

**exports** Exporte mpl

**exposure** Risiko n

**express** (adj) *(fast)* per Expreß, Eil-

**express delivery** Eilzustellung f

**extend** verlängern, prolongieren

**extended credit** verlängerter Kredit

**extension** *(making longer)* Verlängerung f, Prolongation f; *(tel.)* Anschluß m; Apparat m

**external audit** außerbetriebliche/ unabhängige Revision

**external auditor** externe(r) / außerbetriebliche(r) Revisor[in]

**external trade** Außenhandel m

**extra charges** Nebenkosten pl

**extras** Nebenausgaben fpl, Sonderausgaben fpl

**F**

**face value**
 Nominalwert *m*, Nennwert *m*
**facilities** Einrichtungen *fpl*
**facility** *(credit)* Fazilität *f*, Kredit *m*
**factor** (n) *(person, company)*
 Factor *m*; *(influence)* Faktor *m*
**factoring charges** Factoring-
 Gebühren *fpl*
**factory** Fabrik *f*, Werk *n*
**factory price** Fabrikpreis *m*,
 Preis ab Werk
**fail** *(go bust)* bankrott gehen; *(not to
 succeed)* scheitern
**failing that** sonst, widrigenfalls
**failure** Scheitern *n*, Versagen *n*
**fair** (adj) gerecht, fair
**fair price** angemessener Preis
**fair wear and tear**
 normale Abnutzungs- und
 Verschleißerscheinungen *fpl*
**fall behind** *(worse position)*
 zurückfallen hinter; *(late)* in
 Rückstand/Verzug geraten
**fall due** fällig sein/werden
**fall through** fehlschlagen, mißlingen
**false pretences** Vorspiegelung *f*
 falscher Tatsachen
**fare** Fahrpreis *m*, Flugpreis *m*
**farm out work**
 Arbeit/Aufträge weitervergeben
**fast-selling items** schnell verkäu-
 fliche Artikel *mpl*, Selbstläufer *mpl*
**fax** (n) Fax *n*, Telefax *n*; (v) faxen
**feasibility report**
 Durchführbarkeitsbericht *m*
**fee** *(admission)* Gebühr *f*;
 *(for services)* Honorar *n*
**field sales manager**
 Außendienstleiter[in]
**figure** Zahl *f*, Ziffer *f*
**file** (n) *(documents)* Akte *f*,
 Aktenordner *m*; *(computer)* Datei *f*
**file** (v) **documents**
 Dokumente abheften
**filing cabinet** Aktenschrank *m*
**filing card** Karteikarte *f*
**fill a gap** eine Lücke schließen
**final demand** letzte Mahnung/
 Zahlungsaufforderung
**final dividend**
 Schlußdividende *f*, Restdividende *f*

**finalize** endgültig festlegen, zum
 Abschluß bringen
**finance** (n) Finanzierung *f*;
 finanzielle Mittel *pl*
**finance** (v) finanzieren
**finance director**
 Leiter[in] der Finanzabteilung
**finances** Finanzen *pl*; Finanzlage *f*
**financial** finanziell, Finanz-
**financial institution**
 Finanzinstitut *n*, Kreditinstitut *n*
**financial position** Finanzlage *f*
**financial resources** Finanzmittel *pl*,
 finanzielle Mittel *pl*
**financial risk** finanzielles Risiko
**financial year** Finanzjahr *n*,
 Geschäftsjahr *n*, Rechnungsjahr *n*
**financing** Finanzierung *f*
**fine** (n) Geldstrafe *f*,
 gebührenpflichtige Verwarnung
**fine** (v) zu einer Geldstrafe
 verurteilen, eine gebührenpflichtige
 Verwarnung erteilen
**fire damage**
 Brandschaden *m*, Feuerschaden *m*
**fire insurance** Feuerversicherung *f*
**firm** (n) Firma *f*, Unternehmen *n*
**firm price** Festpreis *m*
**first in first out (FIFO)** *(accounting)*
 FIFO-Abschreibungsmethode *f*
**first option** Vorhand *f*
**first-class** erstklassig, Spitzen-
**fiscal measures**
 finanzpolitische Maßnahmen *fpl*
**fix** *(mend)*
 in Ordnung bringen, reparieren
**fix a meeting for 3 p.m.** eine Ver-
 sammlung für 15 Uhr anberaumen
**fixed costs**
 Fixkosten *pl*, Gemeinkosten *pl*
**fixed income** festes Einkommen,
 feste Einkünfte *pl*
**fixed scale of charges**
 verbindliche Gebührenordnung *f*
**fixed-price agreement**
 Festpreisvereinbarung *f*
**flat rate**
 Grundgebühr *f*, Einheitstarif *m*
**flexibility** Flexibilität *f*
**flexible** flexibel
**flight information** Fluginformation *f*
**flip chart** Flip-Chart *f*

**float** (n) *(money)* Wechselgeld n; kleine Kasse f
**floor** *(level)* Stock m, Etage f
**floor plan** Grundriß m, Raumverteilungsplan m
**floor space** Grundfläche f, Bodenfläche f
**flop** (n) Reinfall m, Pleite f
**flop** (v) ein Reinfall, eine Pleite sein
**flotation** Gesellschaftsgründung f (an der Börse)
**flourishing** florierend, gutgehend
**flow chart** Arbeitsablaufdiagramm n, Flußdiagramm n
**fluctuate** fluktuieren, schwanken
**fluctuation** Fluktuation f, Schwankung f
**follow up** aufgreifen, nachgehen
**follow-up letter** Erinnerungsschreiben n
**for sale** zu verkaufen
**force majeure** höhere Gewalt
**forced sale** Zwangsverkauf m, Notverkauf m
**forecast** (n) Prognose f, Vorhersage f
**forecast** (v) voraussagen, prognostizieren
**foreign currency** Devisen pl, Fremdwährung f
**foreign money order** Auslandszahlungsanweisung f
**forfeit a deposit** eine Anzahlung verwirken
**forfeiture** Verwirkung f, Verfall m
**form** (n) Formular n, Vordruck m
**form of words** Formulierung f
**formal** offiziell; formell; förmlich
**forward buying** Terminkauf m
**forward market** Terminmarkt m
**forward rate** Terminkurs m
**forwarding address** Nachsendeadresse f
**forwarding instructions** Versandanweisungen fpl
**franc** Franc m, (Schweizer) Franken m
**franchise** (n) Franchise f
**franchise** (v) auf Franchise-Basis vergeben
**franchisee** Franchise-Nehmer[in]
**franchiser** Franchise-Geber[in]
**franchising** Franchising n
**franking machine** Frankiermaschine f

**fraud** Betrug m
**free** (adj) *(not busy)* frei, unbesetzt; *(no payment)* kostenlos, Frei-; *(no restrictions)* frei, unabhängig
**free** (adv) *(no payment)* kostenlos, gratis
**free delivery** Lieferung frei Haus/ Bestimmungsort
**free of tax** steuerfrei
**free on board** frei an Bord (f.o.b.)
**free sample** Gratisprobe f
**free trade zone** Freihandelszone f
**freeze** (v) *(prices)* einfrieren
**freight** *(carriage)* Fracht f
**freight costs** Transportkosten pl, Frachtkosten pl
**freight forward** Fracht gegen Nachnahme
**freight plane** Transportflugzeug n
**frequent** oft, häufig
**frozen account** gesperrtes Konto
**frozen assets** eingefrorene Vermögenswerte mpl, eingefrorenes Guthaben n
**fulfil/fulfill an order** einen Auftrag ausführen
**full** völlig, vollständig
**full price** voller Preis
**full refund** Erstattung f in voller Höhe
**full-time** ganztags, Ganztags-, hauptberuflich
**fund** (n) Fonds m; zweckgebundene Mittel pl
**fund** (v) finanzieren
**further to** im Nachtrag, über ... hinaus
**future delivery** Terminlieferung f

# G

**gain** (n) *(size)* Zuwachs m, Zunahme f; *(value)* Gewinn m, Wertzuwachs m
**gap in the market** Marktlücke f
**gearing** Verhältnis (n) Fremdkapital/Eigenkapital; Verschuldungsgrad m
**general** allgemein, generell
**general manager** geschäftsführende(r) Direktor[in]
**gentleman's agreement** Vereinbarung f auf Treu und Glauben

**genuine purchaser**
ernsthafte(r) Käufer[in]
**gift** Geschenk n
**gift voucher** Geschenkgutschein m
**give** (as gift)
schenken; überreichen
**glut** (n) Schwemme f, Überhang m
**going rate** üblicher/gängiger Satz
**gold card** goldene Kreditkarte
**good buy** guter Kauf
**good quality** gute Qualität
**good value** (for money)
preiswert, preisgünstig
**goods** Waren fpl
**goodwill** Goodwill m,
(ideeller) Firmenwert m
**government bonds**
Staatsanleihen fpl
**government contractor** Betrieb m
mit Staatsaufträgen mpl
**graduate trainee** Hochschulab-
gänger[in] in der Berufsausbildung
**graduated income tax**
gestaffelte Einkommensteuer
**gram/gramme** Gramm n
**grand total**
Gesamtsumme f, Endbetrag m
**gratis** gratis, umsonst
**gross** (n) (144) Gros n
**gross** (v) brutto verdienen;
brutto einnehmen
**gross domestic product (GDP)**
Bruttoinlandsprodukt (BIP) n
**gross national product (GNP)**
Bruttosozialprodukt (BSP) n
**gross profit**
Bruttogewinn m, Rohgewinn m
**gross salary** Bruttogehalt n
**gross weight**
Bruttogewicht n, Rohgewicht n
**growth** Wachstum n, Zunahme f
**growth rate** Wachstumsrate f
**guarantee** (n) Garantie f
**guarantee** (v)
garantieren; sich verbürgen
**guidelines** Richtlinien fpl

# H

**half** (n) Hälfte f
**half-price sale**
Verkauf m zum halben Preis
**half-year** Halbjahr n

**hand luggage** Handgepäck n
**hand over** übergeben
**handle** (v) (deal with) handhaben,
sich befassen mit
**handle** (v) (sell) führen, handeln mit
**handling charge**
Bearbeitungsgebühr f
**handwritten** von Hand geschrieben,
handgeschrieben
**harbour/harbor** Hafen m
**hard bargain, drive a** hart ver-
handeln/harte Bedingungen stellen
**hard currency** harte Währung
**hard disk** Festplatte f
**haulage costs/haulage rates**
Transportkosten pl
**head of department**
Abteilungs-leiter[in]
**head office**
Hauptgeschäftsstelle f, Zentrale f
**headquarters (HQ)**
Hauptsitz m, Zentrale f
**heavy costs/heavy expenditure** hohe
Kosten pl, hohe Ausgaben fpl
**heavy equipment**
Schwermaschinen fpl
**heavy goods vehicle (HGV)**
Schwertransporter m
**hidden asset**
unterbewerteter Vermögenswert
**hidden reserves** stille Reserven fpl
**high interest** hohe Zinsen pl
**high rent** hohe Miete
**high-quality** Qualitäts-/hochwertig
**highly-paid** hochbezahlt
**highly-priced** teuer
**hire a car** einen Wagen mieten
**hire purchase (HP)**
Teilzahlungskauf m, Mietkauf m
**hire staff** Personal n einstellen
**historical figures**
historische Zahlen fpl
**hold** (v) (contain) enthalten, fassen
**hold a meeting/a discussion** eine
Sitzung/eine Diskussion abhalten
**hold over** vertagen, verschieben
**hold up** (v) (delay)
verzögern, aufhalten
**hold-up** (n) (delay)
Verzögerung f, Stockung f
**holding company** Holdinggesellschaft f, Dachgesellschaft f
**home address** Privatadresse f

**home sales** Inlandsabsatz m
**honour/honor a bill**
  einen Wechsel einlösen
**hourly rate** Stundensatz m
**hourly wage** Stundenlohn m
**hourly-paid workers** stundenweise
  bezahlte Arbeiter mpl
**house** (company) Haus n
**house-to-house selling**
  Direktverkauf m an der Haustür
**hurry up**
  vorantreiben, beschleunigen

# I

**illegal** illegal, ungesetzlich
**illegally** illegal
**immediate** umgehend, sofortig
**immediately**
  umgehend, gleich, sofort
**imperfect** fehlerhaft
**implement** (n) Gerät n, Werkzeug n
**implement an agreement** einen
  Vertrag erfüllen
**implementation**
  Erfüllung f, Durchführung f
**import** (n) Import m
**import** (v) importieren, einführen
**import duty** Einfuhrzoll m
**import licence/import permit** Import-
  lizenz f, Importgenehmigung f
**import quota**
  Einfuhrkontingent n, Importquote f
**importer** Importeur m, Importfirma f
**imports** Importe mpl, Einfuhren fpl
**impulse buyer** Spontankäufer[in]
**in-house**
  betriebsintern, innerbetrieblich
**incentive** Anreiz m
**incidental expenses**
  Nebenausgaben fpl,
  Nebenkosten pl
**include** einschließen, enthalten
**inclusive** inklusive, einschließlich
**inclusive charge**
  Inklusivpreis m, Pauschale f
**inclusive of tax** inklusive Steuer
**income** Einkommen n, Einkünfte pl
**income tax** Einkommensteuer f und
  Lohnsteuer f
**incoming call**
  eingehendes Telefongespräch

**incorporate** (a company)
  eine Kapitalgesellschaft
  gründen/amtlich eintragen
**incorrect(ly)** ungenau, fehlerhaft
**increase** (n) Erhöhung f, Zunahme f
**increase** (v) (sich) erhöhen,
  zunehmen, (an)steigen
**increase** (v) **in price** teurer werden
**incur** (costs)
  auf sich nehmen, eingehen
**incur debts** Schulden machen
**indebted** verschuldet
**indemnification**
  Entschädigung f, Schadenersatz m
**indemnify so. for a loss** jdn für einen
  Verlust entschädigen
**indemnity**
  Entschädigung f, Vergütung f
**index** (n) (of prices) Index m
**index-linked** indexgebunden, der
  Inflationsrate angeglichen
**indicator** Indikator m
**indirect taxation**
  indirekte Besteuerung
**induction courses/induction training**
  Einführungskurse mpl,
  Einführungslehrgang m
**industrial accident**
  Betriebsunfall m, Arbeitsunfall m
**industrial relations** Arbeitgeber-
  Arbeitnehmer-Beziehungen fpl
**industrial tribunal** Arbeitsgericht n
**industrialist** Industrielle(r)
**industry** (companies)
  Branche f, Wirtschaftszweig m
**inefficiency**
  Ineffizienz f, Inkompetenz f
**inefficient** ineffizient, unfähig
**inflation** Inflation f
**inflationary** inflationär, Inflations-
**influence** (n) Einfluß m, Auswirkung f
**influence** (v) beeinflussen
**information** Information f
**infrastructure** Infrastruktur f
**infringe a patent**
  das Patentrecht verletzen
**infringement of patent**
  Patentverletzung f
**initial** (v) abzeichnen, paraphieren
**initial capital**
  Startkapital n, Gründungskapital n
**initiate discussions**
  Diskussionen einleiten

**input information** Daten *pl* eingeben
**inquire** sich erkundigen,
Erkundigungen einziehen
**inquiry** Anfrage *f*
**insolvent** zahlungsunfähig, insolvent
**inspect** prüfen, kontrollieren
**inspection** Prüfung *f*, Kontrolle *f*
**instalment** Rate *f*
**instant credit** Sofortkredit *m*
**institution** Institut *n*; Gesellschaft *f*
**institutional investors**
institutionelle Anleger *mpl*;
Kapitalsammelstellen *fpl*
**instrument** *(document)*
Urkunde *f*, Dokument *n*
**insurance** Versicherung *f*
**insurance broker**
Versicherungsmakler[in]
**insure**
versichern, Versicherung *f*
abschließen
**intangible assets**
immaterielle Vermögenswerte *mpl*
**interest** (n) *(on investment)*
Zinsen *mpl*, Kapitalertrag *m*
**interest** (v)
interessieren, Interesse hervorrufen
**interest charges**
Zinsbelastung *f*, Sollzinsen *mpl*
**interest rate** Zinssatz *m*
**interface** (n) Schnittstelle *f*
**interim payment** Abschlagszahlung *f*, Interimszahlung *f*
**intermediary** Vermittler[in]
**internal audit**
interne Revision, Innenrevision *f*
**international trade** internationaler
Handel; Welthandel *m*
**interpret** dolmetschen
**interpreter** Dolmetscher[in]
**intervention price** Interventions-
preis *m*, garantierter Mindestpreis
**interview** (n) *(for a job)*
Vorstellungsgespräch *n*
**interview** (v) *(for a job)*
ein Vorstellungsgespräch führen
**introduce** vorstellen, einführen
**introductory offer**
Einführungsangebot *n*
**inventory** (n) *(list of contents)*
Inventarverzeichnis *n*,
Inventarliste *f*; *(stock)*
Warenbestand *m*

**inventory control**
Lagerhaltungskontrolle *f*
**invest** investieren, (Geld) anlegen
**investment**
Investition *f*, Kapitalanlage *f*
**investment income**
Kapitalerträge *mpl*; Erträge *mpl*
aus Beteiligungen
**invisible earnings** unsichtbare
Einkünfte *pl*, Einkünfte aus
unsichtbaren Leistungen
**invisible trade** unsichtbarer Handel
**invite** einladen, auffordern
**invoice** (n) Rechnung *f*
**invoice** (v) Rechnung ausstellen
**invoice number** Rechnungsnummer *f*
**invoice value** Rechnungsbetrag *m*
**irrecoverable debt**
uneinbringliche Forderung
**irredeemable bond**
unkündbare Anleihe
**irregularities** Unregelmäßigkeiten *fpl*, Vorschriftswidrigkeit *f*
**irrevocable letter of credit**
unwiderrufliches Akkreditiv
**issue a letter of credit**
ein Akkreditiv ausstellen
**issue instructions**
Anweisungen *fpl* geben
**item** *(on agenda)* Punkt *m*;
*(thing for sale)* Artikel *m*
**itemized account**
aufgegliederte Abrechnung

## J

**job** *(employment)* Job *m*, Arbeit *f*,
Stelle *f*; *(piece of work)* Arbeit *f*;
Aufgabe *f*
**job description** Stellenbeschreibung *f*
**job security**
Sicherheit *f* des Arbeitsplatzes
**job title** Berufsbezeichnung *f*;
Bezeichnung *f* der Tätigkeit
**join** verbinden, anfügen
**joint account** gemeinsames Konto,
Gemeinschaftskonto *n*
**joint managing director** geschäfts-
führende(r) Mitdirektor[in]
**joint signatory** Mitunterzeichner[in]
**joint venture** Joint-venture *n*,
Gemeinschaftsunternehmen *n*
**journal** *(accounts book)* Journal *n*

**junior clerk** untere(r) Angestellte(r)
**junk mail** Reklamesendungen *fpl*; Papierkorb-Werbung *f*
**jurisdiction** Zuständigkeit *f*

# K

**keen competition** scharfer Wettbewerb *m*, harte Konkurrenz *f*
**keen prices** günstige Preise *mpl*
**keep a promise** ein Versprechen halten
**keep up with the demand** mit der Nachfrage Schritt halten
**key** *(on keyboard)* Taste *f*
**kilo/kilogram** Kilo *n*, Kilogramm *n*
**knock down** (v) *(price)* herunterhandeln; nachlassen
**knock off** *(reduce price)* nachlassen, ablassen; *(stop work)* Feierabend machen

# L

**label** (n) Etikett *n*, Anhängeschild *n*
**label** (v) etikettieren; auszeichnen
**labour/labor costs** Arbeitskosten *pl*, Lohnkosten *pl*
**labour/labor disputes** Arbeitskämpfe *mpl*
**lack of funds** fehlende Geldmittel *pl*
**land goods at a port** Güter in einem Hafen löschen
**landed costs** Fracht- und Löschungskosten *pl*
**landing charges** Löschungskosten *pl* und Löschungszölle *mpl*
**landlord** Vermieter *m*
**lapse** (v) verfallen; ablaufen
**late** *(adv)* spät, verspätet
**latest** letzte(r,s), neuste(r,s)
**lawful trade** erlaubter Handel
**lawsuit** Prozeß *m*, Klage *f*
**lawyer** Rechtsanwalt[-in]
**lay off workers** (vorübergehend) Arbeiter entlassen
**lease** (n) Pachtvertrag *m*; Mietvertrag *m*
**lease** (v) *(of landlord)* verpachten; vermieten; *(of tenant)* pachten; mieten
**lease equipment** Anlagen/ Ausrüstung vermieten

**leasing** Leasing *n*
**ledger** Hauptbuch *n*
**legal** *(referring to law)* juristisch, rechtlich, Rechts-
**legal advice** Rechtsberatung *f*
**legal costs/legal charges** Anwaltskosten *pl*
**legal proceedings** Gerichtsverfahren *n*, Prozeß *m*
**legal status** rechtliche Stellung, Rechtsposition *f*
**lend** verleihen, ausleihen
**lender** Gläubiger *m*; Verleiher *m*
**lending limit** Kreditlimit *n*
**lessee** Pächter[in]; Mieter[in]; Leasingnehmer[in]
**lessor** Verpächter[in]; Vermieter[in]; Leasinggeber[in]
**letter of complaint** Beschwerdebrief *m*
**letter of credit (L/C)** Akkreditiv *n*
**letter of reference** Zeugnis *n*, Referenz *f*
**level** Stand *m*, Niveau *n*, Ebene *f*
**level off/level out** sich ausgleichen, einpendeln
**leverage** Leverage *n*
**levy** (n) Abgabe *f*, Steuer *f*
**levy** (v) erheben; einziehen
**liabilities** Verbindlichkeiten *fpl*; Schulden *fpl*
**liable for** haften für, haftbar sein für
**liable to** unterliegen, unterworfen
**licence/license** (n) Genehmigung *f*; Konzession *f*; Lizenz *f*
**license** (v) amtlich genehmigen; eine Konzession/Lizenz erteilen
**lien** Pfandrecht *n*; Zurückbehaltungsrecht *n*
**life assurance** Lebensversicherung *f*
**lift an embargo** ein Embargo aufheben
**limit** (n) Grenze *f*, Limit *n*
**limit** (v) beschränken, einschränken
**limited (liability) company (Ltd)** Gesellschaft *f* mit beschränkter Haftung (GmbH)
**limited liability** beschränkte Haftung
**liquid assets** flüssiges Vermögen
**liquidate a company** ein Unternehmen liquidieren/auflösen
**liquidate stock** Lagerbestände *mpl* flüssigmachen

**liquidation** Liquidation f;
  Abwicklung f; Konkurs m
**liquidator** Liquidator m;
  Abwickler m; Konkursverwalter m
**liquidity** Liquidität f
**list** (n) *(catalogue/catalog)*
  Verzeichnis n, Liste f
**list price** Listenpreis m
**load** (v) *(computer program)* laden
**load a ship** ein Schiff beladen
**loan** (n) Kredit m, Darlehen n
**loan** (v) ausleihen, leihen, verleihen
**loan capital**
  Fremdkapital n, Anleihekapital n
**local labour/labor**
  ortsansässige Arbeitskräfte fpl
**lock** (n) Schloß n
**lock** (v) abschließen
**lock up capital**
  Kapital festlegen/ binden
**logo** Logo n; Firmenzeichen n
**long credit** langfristiger Kredit,
  Kredit m mit langer Laufzeit
**long-dated bill** langfristiger Wechsel
**long-haul flight** Fernflug m
**long-standing agreement**
  seit langem bestehender Vertrag
**long-term** langfristig
**long-term debts**
  langfristige Verbindlichkeiten fpl
**long-term planning**
  langfristige Planung
**loose** lose, unverpackt
**lose an order** einen Auftrag verlieren
**lose money** Geld verlieren, einbüßen
**loss** *(not profit)* Verlust m, Einbuße f
**loss** *(of sth.)* Verlust m
**loss-leader** Lockartikel m
**low sales** geringer Absatz
**lower prices** (v) Preise senken
**luggage** Gepäck n
**lump sum** einmalige Summe f;
  Pauschalbetrag m

# M

**magazine** Zeitschrift f, Magazin n
**magazine insert** Werbebeilage f
**mail** Post f
**mail** (v)
  (mit der Post) verschicken/aufgeben
**mail shot** Rundschreiben n,
  Briefwerbeaktion f

**mail-order** Postversand m
**mail-order catalogue/catalog**
  Versandhauskatalog m
**mailing list** Adressenliste f
**main office**
  Hauptgeschäftsstelle f, Zentrale f
**maintain** *(keep going)*
  aufrechterhalten, erhalten
**maintenance** *(keeping in working
  order)* Wartung f, Instandhaltung f
**major shareholder/stockholder**
  Hauptaktionär[in]
**majority** Mehrheit f, Majorität f
**majority shareholder/stockholder**
  Mehrheitsaktionär[in]
**make good** wettmachen
**make money** Geld verdienen
**make out** *(invoice)* ausstellen
**make up for**
  wiedergutmachen, ausgleichen
**man** (v) besetzen
**man-hour** Arbeitsstunde f
**manage property**
  Immobilienbesitz verwalten
**manage to**
  es schaffen, es fertigbringen
**management** *(action)* Leitung f,
  Führung f; *(managers)*
  Unternehmensleitung f,
  Management n
**management trainee**
  Führungsnachwuchs m
**manager** *(of branch/shop)*
  Geschäftsführer[in], Manager[in]
**managerial staff** leitendes Personal
**managing director (MD)**
  Geschäftsführer[in]
**manning levels** Personalstärke f
**manpower** Personalbestand m
**manpower shortage**
  Arbeitskräftemangel m
**manual** (adj) handgemacht, manuell
**manual** (n) Handbuch n
**manual work** körperliche Arbeit
**manual worker** manueller
  Arbeiter/Handarbeiter m
**manufacture** (v) (maschinell)
  herstellen, fertigen
**manufactured goods** Industrie-
  güter npl, Fertigwaren fpl
**manufacturer** Hersteller m
**manufacturing costs**
  Herstellungskosten pl

**margin** *(profit)*
Gewinnspanne f, Marge f
**marginal pricing**
Grenzkostenkalkulation f
**maritime trade** Seehandel m
**mark** (n) Markierung f, Zeichen n
**mark** (n) *(German currency)*
D-Mark f, Mark f
**mark** (v) beschriften, auszeichnen
**mark down** herabsetzen, senken
**mark up** (v) heraufsetzen, erhöhen
**mark-up** *(profit margin)*
Gewinnaufschlag m
**market** (n) *(possible sales)*
Markt m; Nachfrage f
**market** (v) vertreiben,
auf den Markt bringen
**market analysis** Marktanalyse f
**market forces** Marktkräfte fpl
**market leader** Marktführer m
**market opportunities**
Marktchancen fpl, neue
Absatzmöglichkeiten fpl
**market penetration**
Marktdurchdringung f
**market research** Marktforschung f
**market share** Marktanteil m
**marketing**
Marketing n, Vermarktung f
**marketing department**
Marketing-abteilung f
**marketing manager** Marketing-
direktor[in], Vertriebsleiter[in]
**mass media** Massenmedien pl
**mass production**
Massenproduktion f, serienmäßige
Herstellung
**maternity leave**
Mutterschaftsurlaub m
**matter** (n) *(to be discussed)*
Thema n, Frage f
**matter** (v) von Bedeutung sein
**maturity date** Fälligkeitstermin m
**maximum** (adj) maximal, Höchst-;
(n) Maximum n
**mean** (n)
Mittelwert m, Durchschnitt m
**mean annual increase**
durchschnittlicher Jahreszuwachs
**means** *(money)* Mittel pl
**measurement of profitability**
Rentabilitätsmessung f

**medium-sized**
mittelgroß, mittelständisch
**medium-term** mittelfristig
**meet** *(be satisfactory)*
erfüllen, entsprechen
**meet** *(so.)* (sich) treffen (mit)
**meet a deadline** einen Termin/eine
Frist einhalten
**meet a demand** den Bedarf/die
Nachfrage decken
**meet a target** ein Ziel erreichen
**meeting** Besprechung f, Sitzung f
**memo** Mitteilung f, Notiz f
**merchandise** (n) Handelsware f
**merchandize a product**
ein Produkt vermarkten
**merchandizing**
Merchandising n,
Verkaufsförderung f
**merge** fusionieren,
zusammen-schließen
**merger** Fusion f, Unternehmenszusammenschluß m
**message** Mitteilung f, Nachricht f
**middle management**
mittleres Management
**middle-sized company**
Unternehmen n mittlerer Größe,
Mittelständler m
**middleman** Zwischenhändler m
**minimum** (adj) Mindest-
**minimum** (n) Minimum n
**minimum payment** Mindestbetrag m
**minimum wage** (garantierter)
Mindestlohn
**minority** Minorität f, Minderheit f
**minority shareholder/stockholder**
Minderheitsaktionär[in]
**minus factor**
Negativfaktor m, Minus n
**minute** (v) protokollieren, zu
Protokoll nehmen
**minutes** (n) *(of meeting)* Protokoll n
**miscalculate** falsch berechnen, falsch
kalkulieren
**miscalculation** Fehlkalkulation f
**miscellaneous**
verschieden; gemischt
**miss** *(not to hit)* verfehlen; nicht
erreichen; *(not to meet)* verpassen
**mistake** Fehler m
**misunderstanding** Mißverständnis n,
Meinungsverschiedenheit f

**mixed economy** Mischwirtschaft f
**mobilize capital**
  Gelder flüssigmachen
**mock-up** Attrappe f
**mode of payment** Zahlungsweise f
**model** (n) Modell n
**model agreement** Mustervertrag m
**modem** Modem n
**moderate** (adj) gemäßigt, mäßig
**monetary**
  monetär, Geld-, Währungs-
**money** Geld n
**money order** Postanweisung f,
  Zahlungsanweisung f
**money supply** Geldmenge f
**money up front** Vorauszahlung f
**monitor** (n) *(screen)*
  Monitor m, Bildschirm m
**monitor** (v) überwachen
**monopoly** Monopol n
**month-end accounts**
  Ultimoabrechnung f
**monthly** (adj) monatlich
**monthly statement**
  monatlicher Kontoauszug
**mortgage** (n) Hypothek f
**mortgage** (v) hypothekarisch
  belasten; eine Hypothek
  aufnehmen
**multilateral agreement**
  multilaterales Abkommen
**multinational** (n)
  multinationaler Konzern
**multiple** (adj) mehrfach, vielfach
**multiple entry visa** Visum (n) zur
  mehrmaligen Einreise
**multiply** multiplizieren

# N

**nationalized industry**
  verstaatlichte Industrie
**nationwide** landesweit
**natural resources** Naturschätze pl,
  natürliche Ressourcen fpl
**natural wastage** natürlicher
  Arbeitskräfteabgang
**negotiable** (frei)
  übertragbar, verkäuflich
**negotiable instrument** übertrag-
  bares/begebbares Wertpapier
**negotiate** verhandeln
**negotiation** Verhandlung f

**negotiator** Verhandlungsführer[in];
  Unterhändler[in]
**net** (adj) netto, Netto-
**net assets/net worth**
  Reinvermögen n
**net income/net salary**
  Nettoverdienst m, Nettogehalt n
**net margin** Nettomarge f,
  Nettogewinnspanne f
**net price** Nettopreis m
**net profit**
  Nettogewinn m, Reingewinn m
**net weight** Nettogewicht n
**net yield**
  Nettoertrag m, Reinertrag m
**network** (v) *(computers)* vernetzen
**niche** Nische f
**nil return** keinerlei Erträge mpl
**no-claims bonus**
  Schadenfreiheitsrabatt m
**nominal value** Nennwert m,
  Nominalwert m
**nominee** Nominierte(r), Kandidat[in]
**non profit-making** gemeinnützig,
  nicht auf Gewinn ausgerichtet
**non-negotiable instrument**
  nicht begebbares Wertpapier;
  Namenspapier n
**non-payment** *(of a debt)* Nichtbezahlen (n) einer Verbindlichkeit
**non-refundable deposit** nicht
  zurückerstattbare Kaution
**non-returnable packing** Einweg-
  packung f, Einwegverpackung f
**note** (n) Mitteilung f, Bescheid m
**notice** *(time allowed)* Frist f
**notification**
  Benachrichtigung f, Mitteilung f
**notify** mitteilen
**null** nichtig, ungültig
**number** (n) *(figure)* Nummer f, Zahl f
**number** (v) numerieren

# O

**objective** (n) Ziel n
**obligation** *(duty)* Verpflichtung f
**obsolete** veraltet, obsolet
**obtain** erhalten, beziehen
**obtainable** erhältlich, zu bekommen
**off** *(away from work)* frei; *(cancelled)*
  abgesagt, ausgefallen

**off-peak** außerhalb der Hauptzeiten/ Stoßzeiten

**off-season** Nebensaison f

**offer** (n) Angebot n

**offer** (v) (to buy) bieten

**office** Büro n, Geschäftsstelle f

**office hours**
Bürozeit f, Dienststunden fpl

**office staff** Büropersonal n

**official** (adj) amtlich, Amts-; dienstlich, Dienst-

**official** (n) Beamte(r)/Beamtin

**oil** (petroleum) Erdöl n; Mineralöl n

**oil price** Ölpreis m

**old-fashioned** altmodisch

**on account** als Anzahlung

**on approval**
auf Probe, versuchsweise

**on behalf of**
im Namen von; im Auftrag von

**on business** geschäftlich, dienstlich

**on order** bestellt

**on sale** zu verkaufen; im Angebot

**on time** pünktlich

**one-off** einmalig

**open** (adj) (not closed) geöffnet

**open** (v) (bank account, line of credit, meeting; start new business) eröffnen

**open credit** Blankokredit m, offener Kredit

**open market** freier Markt

**open-plan office** Großraumbüro n

**opening balance** Eröffnungsbilanz f

**opening hours**
Öffnungszeit f, Geschäftszeit f

**opening stock** Eröffnungsbestand m

**opening time** Öffnungszeit f

**operate** gelten, wirksam werden

**operating costs/operating expenses**
Betriebskosten pl

**operating manual** Benutzerhandbuch n; Bedienungsanleitung f

**operating profit** Betriebsgewinn m, operativer Gewinn

**operation**
Geschäftsbereich m; Betrieb m

**operational costs** Betriebskosten pl

**operator** Maschinist[in]

**option to purchase** Kaufoption f

**optional extras**
Extras npl, Sonderzubehör npl

**order** (n) (for goods) Auftrag m, Bestellung f; (instruction) Anweisung f, Anordnung f

**order** (n) (money) Orderpapier n

**order** (v) (goods) bestellen

**order fulfilment**
Auftragsausführung f

**order number** Auftragsnummer f

**order processing**
Auftragsabwicklung f

**order, on** bestellt

**ordinary shares** Stammaktien fpl

**organization chart** Organisationsplan m, Organigramm n

**organize** organisieren, aufbauen

**origin** Herkunft f; Provenienz f

**original** (adj) original, Original-

**out of date** veraltet, unzeitgemäß

**out of stock** nicht vorrätig

**out of work** arbeitslos

**outgoings**
Ausgaben fpl, Ausgänge mpl

**outlay** Auslagen fpl, Ausgaben fpl

**output** (n) (goods) Produktion f; Produktionsleistung f

**outsize (OS)** Übergröße f

**outstanding** (exceptional)
überragend, hervorragend; (unpaid) ausstehend, unbezahlt

**outstanding debts** Außenstände pl

**outstanding orders**
unerledigte Aufträge mpl

**overbook** überbuchen, überbelegen

**overbooking**
Überbuchung f, Überbelegung f

**overcapacity** Überkapazität f

**overcharge** (n)
zuviel berechneter Betrag

**overcharge** (v) zu viel berechnen

**overdraft** Überziehungskredit m

**overdrawn account**
überzogenes Konto

**overdue** überfällig

**overhead costs/expenses/overheads**
Gemeinkosten pl

**overproduction** Überproduktion f

**overseas trade** Überseehandel m, Auslandshandel m

**overspend one's budget** seine Budgetgrenze überschreiten

**overstocks** Überbestand m

**overtime** Überstunden fpl

**overtime pay** Überstundenlohn *m*
**owe** schulden
**owing to** wegen
**own label goods**
Eigenmarkenwaren *fpl*
**owner** Eigentümer[in]
**ownership** Eigentum *n*

# P

**pack** (n) Warenpackung *f*
**pack** (v) verpacken, einpacken
**package** Paket *n*
**package deal** Gesamtvereinbarung *f*,
Pauschalangebot *n*
**packaging material**
Verpackungsmaterial *n*
**packer** Packer[in]
**packing** *(material)*
Verpackungsmaterial *n*
**packing list/packing slip** Packliste *f*
**paid** *(invoice)* bezahlt, beglichen
**paper loss**
nicht realisierter Verlust
**paper profit** Buchgewinn *m*, noch
nicht realisierter Gewinn
**paperwork**
Schreibarbeit *f*, Papierkram *m*
**par value** Nennwert *m*
**parcel** (n) Paket *n*
**parcel post** Paketpost *f*
**parent company** Muttergesellschaft *f*
**part exchange** Inzahlungnahme *f*
**part-time work/employment** Teilzeitarbeit *f*, Teilzeitbeschäftigung *f*
**partial payment**
Teilzahlung *f*, Abschlagzahlung *f*
**particulars** Einzelheiten *fpl*,
nähere Angaben *fpl*
**partner** Teilhaber[in],
Partner[in], Sozius *m*
**party** Partei *f*
**patent applied for/patent pending**
zum Patent angemeldet
**pay** (n) *(salary, wage)*
Gehalt *n*, Lohn *m*
**pay a bill/an invoice**
eine Rechnung bezahlen
**pay back** zurückzahlen
**pay by credit card**
mit (einer) Kreditkarte bezahlen
**pay cash** bar bezahlen

**pay cheque/check**
Gehaltsscheck *m*, Lohnscheck *m*
**pay in advance** im voraus bezahlen
**pay out** auszahlen, ausgeben
**pay rise**
Gehaltserhöhung *f*, Lohnerhöhung *f*
**payable in advance**
im voraus zahlbar
**payable on delivery**
zahlbar bei Lieferung
**payable on demand** zahlbar bei
Aufforderung/Sicht
**payee** Zahlungsempfänger[in]
**payer** Zahler *m*
**paying-in slip** Einzahlungsbeleg *m*
**payment** Zahlung *f*,
Bezahlung *f*, Begleichung *f*
**payment by cheque/check** Zahlung *f*
durch Scheck
**payment in cash** Barzahlung *f*
**payment on account** Abschlagszahlung *f*, Akontozahlung *f*
**peak period** Hauptverkehrszeit *f*,
Stoßzeit *f*, Hauptbelastungszeit *f*
**peg prices**
Preise stützen/ stabilisieren
**penalize** bestrafen, mit einer
Strafe belegen
**penalty clause** Strafklausel *f*
**pending** schwebend, anstehend
**penetrate a market**
in einen Markt eindringen
**pension**
Rente *f*, Pension *f*, Ruhegehalt *n*
**per hour/day/week/annum** pro
Stunde/Tag/Woche/Jahr
**percentage** Prozentsatz *m*, Prozent *n*
**percentage discount**
prozentualer Rabatt
**period** Zeit *f*, Zeitraum *m*
**perishable goods/cargo** verderbliche
Waren *fpl*, verderbliche Fracht *f*
**permission**
Erlaubnis *f*, Genehmigung *f*
**permit** (n)
Genehmigung *f*, Erlaubnis *f*
**permit** (v) genehmigen, erlauben
**personal assistant (PA)**
persönliche(r) Assistent[in]
**personal computer (PC)**
Personalcomputer (PC) *m*
**personnel** Personal *n*, Belegschaft *f*

**personnel manager** Personalchef[in], Personalleiter[in]
**petty cash** Nebenkasse f, Portokasse f
**petty expenses** geringfügige Ausgaben fpl
**phase in** schrittweise einführen
**phase out** auslaufen lassen, allmählich einstellen
**phone** (v) anrufen
**phone call** Telefongespräch n, Anruf m
**phone card** Telefonkarte f
**photocopier** Fotokopierer m, Kopierer m
**photocopy** (n) Fotokopie f
**photocopy** (v) fotokopieren
**pie chart** Kreisdiagramm n
**piece rate** Akkordlohnsatz m, Stücklohnsatz m
**piecework** Akkordarbeit f
**pilot scheme** Versuchsprojekt n
**place an order** einen Auftrag erteilen, eine Bestellung aufgeben
**place of work** Arbeitsplatz m
**plaintiff** Kläger[in]
**plan** (n) (drawing) Plan m, Entwurf m; (project) Plan m
**plan** (v) einplanen, planen
**plane** Flugzeug n
**plant** (n) (machinery) Maschinen fpl, Anlage f
**plug** (n) (electric) Stecker m
**plug** (v) (publicize) anpreisen, Reklame machen
**plus factor** positiver Faktor
**point of sale (p.o.s./POS)** Verkaufsstelle f, Verkaufsort m
**policy** Politik f, Kurs m, Linie f
**poor quality** minderwertige Qualität
**poor service** schlechter Service
**popular prices** populäre Preise mpl
**port** (computer) Anschluß m, Port m; (harbour/harbor) Hafen m
**port of call** Anlaufhafen m
**port of embarkation** Einschiffungshafen m
**portable** tragbar
**porter** (luggage) Gepäckträger; (hotel) Portier m
**portfolio** Aktienportefeuille n
**POS material** Werbematerial n an der Verkaufsstelle
**position** (job) Stelle f, Position f

**positive** bejahend, positiv
**possess** besitzen
**post** (n) (job) Stelle f, Posten m; (letters) Post f
**post** (v) aufgeben, abschicken
**post free** portofrei
**postage** Porto n, Postgebühren fpl
**postage and packing (p&p)** Porto n und Verpackung f
**postage paid** Porto n bezahlt, gebührenfrei
**postal charges/postal rates** Postgebühren fpl, Posttarife mpl
**postcode** Postleitzahl f
**poste restante** postlagernd
**postpaid** Gebühr bezahlt
**postpone** aufschieben, vertagen
**postponement** Aufschub m, Vertagung f
**potential market** potentieller Markt
**pound** (money) Pfund n; (weight, 0.45kg) Pfund n
**power of attorney** Handlungsvollmacht f
**premises** Grundstück n, Räumlichkeiten fpl
**premium** (insurance) Versicherungsbeitrag m, Versicherungsprämie f
**premium offer** Werbegeschenk n, Zugabe f
**prepack/prepackage** (v) abpacken, fertig packen
**prepaid** vorausbezahlt
**prepayment** Vorauszahlung f
**present** (adj) (being there) anwesend; (now) gegenwärtig, derzeitig, jetzig
**present** (n) (gift) Geschenk n
**presentation** (exhibition) Präsentation f, Vorstellung f; (showing a document) Vorlage f
**press conference** Pressekonferenz f
**press release** Pressemitteilung f, Presseverlautbarung f
**pretax profit** Gewinn m vor Steuern
**prevention** Verhinderung f, Vorbeugung f
**price** (n) Preis m
**price** (v) einen Preis festsetzen
**price ceiling** oberste Preisgrenze f
**price controls** Preisbindung f, Preiskontrolle f
**price ex warehouse** Preis ab Lager

**price ex works** Preis ab Werk
**price label/price tag** Preisschild n
**price list** Preisliste f
**price war** Preiskrieg m
**price/earnings ratio (P/E ratio)** Kurs-Gewinn-Verhältnis n
**pricing policy** Preispolitik f
**prime cost** Gestehungskosten pl, Herstellungskosten pl
**principal** (adj) Haupt-, wichtigste(r/s)
**principal** (n) (money) Kapitalsumme f, Darlehensbetrag m; (person) Auftraggeber[in]
**principle** Prinzip n
**print out** ausdrucken, drucken
**printer** (person, machine) Drucker m
**printout** Ausdruck m, Computerausdruck m
**private enterprise** Privatunternehmen n
**private property** Privatgrundstück n; Privatbesitz m
**private sector** Privatsektor m
**privatization** Privatisierung f
**privatize** privatisieren
**pro forma (invoice)** Pro-forma-Rechnung f
**pro rata** anteilig, anteilsmäßig
**problem area** Problembereich m
**problem solver** Problemlöser m
**process** (v) (deal with) bearbeiten
**processing of information** Auswertung f von Informationen
**product** Produkt n, Erzeugnis n
**product design** Produktgestaltung f
**product line** Produktgruppe f, Produktlinie f
**product mix** Produktmix m, Produktpalette f
**production** (making) Produktion f
**production department** Produktionsabteilung f
**production target** Produktionsziel n
**productive discussions** produktive Gespräche npl
**productivity** Produktivität f
**productivity agreement** Produktivitätsvereinbarung f
**professional** (n) (expert) Fachmann m, Profi m
**professional qualifications** berufliche Qualifikationen fpl
**profit** Gewinn m, Profit m, Ertrag m

**profit and loss account** Gewinn- und Verlustrechnung f
**profit before/after tax** Gewinn m vor/nach Steuern
**profit centre/center** Ertragszentrum n, Profit-Center n
**profit margin** Gewinnspanne f
**profitability** Ertragskraft f, Rentabilität f
**profitable** gewinnbringend, einträglich, rentabel
**program a computer** einen Computer programmieren
**programme/program** Programm n
**progress chaser** Terminjäger m
**progress report** Lagebericht m
**project** (plan) Projekt n, Plan m
**project manager** Projektleiter[in]
**projected sales** Absatzprognose f, erwarteter Umsatz m
**promissory note** Schuldschein m
**promote** (advertise) werben, Reklame machen; (give better job) befördern
**promote a new product** für ein neues Produkt werben
**promotion** (publicity) Werbung f; (to better job) Beförderung f
**promotional budget** Werbeetat m
**prompt payment** pünktliche Zahlung
**prompt service** prompter Service m, prompte Bedienung f
**proportion** Teil m, Anteil m
**proportional** proportional
**propose to** (do sth.) vorhaben, beabsichtigen
**proprietor (-tress)** Eigentümer[in], Besitzer[in], Inhaber[in]
**prosecution** (legal action) Anklage f, strafrechtliche Verfolgung
**prospective buyer** potentieller Käufer
**prospects** Aussichten fpl
**prospectus** Prospekt m
**provided that/providing** vorausgesetzt, daß
**provision** (condition) Klausel f, Bestimmung f
**provisional budget** vorläufiger Etat
**proviso** Vorbehalt m, Bedingung f
**proxy** (person) Bevollmächtigte(r), Stellvertreter[in]
**proxy vote** stellvertretend abgegebene Stimme

**public finance** Staatsfinanzen pl
**public holiday** öffentlicher Feiertag
**Public Limited Company (Plc)**
Aktiengesellschaft f (AG)
**public relations (PR)** Public
Relations pl, Öffentlichkeitsarbeit f
**public sector** öffentlicher Sektor
**public transport**
öffentliche Verkehrsmittel npl
**publicity** Werbung f, Reklame f
**publicity budget** Werbeetat m
**publicity department**
Werbeabteilung f
**publicity manager** Werbeleiter[in]
**publicize** werben; Werbung machen
**purchase** (n) Kauf m
**purchase** (v) kaufen, erwerben
**purchase tax** Verbrauchssteuer f
**purchaser** Käufer[in]; Erwerber[in]
**purchasing**
Einkauf m, Warenbeschaffung f
**purchasing power** Kaufkraft f
**put in writing** schriftlich abfassen

## Q

**qualified** (skilled)
ausgebildet, qualifiziert
**qualify as**
seine Ausbildung zum ...
abschließen
**quality control** Qualitätskontrolle f
**quantity**
Menge f, Quantität f, Anzahl f
**quantity discount** Mengenrabatt m
**quarter** (25%) Viertel n; (three
months) Quartal n, Vierteljahr n
**quarterly** (adj)
vierteljährlich, quartalsweise
**quay** Kai m
**quorum** beschlußfähige Anzahl
**quota** Quote f, Kontingent n
**quotation/quote** (n) (estimate
of cost) Preisangebot n,
Kostenvoranschlag m
**quote** (v) (estimate costs) (einen
Preis) angeben, ein Preisangebot
machen

## R

**rail/railway** Bahn f
**railway station** Bahnhof m

**raise** (v) (increase) erhöhen,
heraufsetzen; (obtain money)
beschaffen, aufbringen
**raise an invoice**
eine Rechung ausstellen
**random check** Stichprobe f
**random error** Zufallsfehler m
**rate** (n) (amount) Rate f; (price)
Satz m, Gebühr f, Preis m
**rate of exchange** Wechselkurs m
**rate of inflation** Inflationsrate f
**rating** Veranlagung f, Schätzung f
**ratio** Verhältnis n
**rationalize** rationalisieren
**raw materials** Rohstoffe mpl
**reach a decision** zu einer
Entscheidung kommen
**reach an agreement** zu einer
Vereinbarung kommen
**ready** fertig, bereit
**ready cash** Bargeld n
**real estate**
Grundbesitz m, Immobilien pl
**real income/real wages**
Realeinkommen n, Reallohn m
**realizable assets** realisierbare
Vermögenswerte mpl
**realize** (sell for money) realisieren,
verkaufen; einbringen
**realize property/assets**
Vermögen-swerte
realisieren/veräußern
**reapply** erneut bewerben
**reassess** neu bewerten; neu
veranlagen; neu schätzen
**rebate** Rückvergütung f, Erstattung f
**receipt** (paper) Quittung f,
Empfangsbestätigung f; (receiving)
Eingang m, Erhalt m
**receipts** Einnahmen fpl
**receivables**
Außenstände pl, Forderungen fpl
**receive** erhalten, empfangen
**receiver** (liquidator)
Konkursverwalter[in]
**reception** (desk)
Empfang m, Rezeption f
**receptionist**
Herr m/Dame f am Empfang
**recession** Rezession f
**recommend** (say sth. is good)
empfehlen; (suggest action)
empfehlen, raten zu

**reconcile** abstimmen, in Einklang bringen
**reconciliation** Abstimmung f
**record** (v) aufzeichnen, protokollieren
**record sales/record losses/record profits** Spitzenumsätze mpl, Rekordverluste mpl, Höchstgewinne mpl
**records** (documents) Unterlagen fpl, Aufzeichnungen fpl
**recover** (get better) sich erholen, einen Aufschwung nehmen; (get sth. back) zurückbekommen, (wieder) hereinholen
**recovery** (getting sth. back) Wiedergewinnung f, Wiedererlangung; (getting better) Aufschwung m, Wiederbelebung f
**red tape** Bürokratismus m, Papierkrieg m
**redeem** tilgen
**redemption** (of a loan) Tilgung f
**redemption date** Tilgungstermin m
**reduce** reduzieren, verringern, senken
**reduce a price** einen Preis herabsetzen
**reduced rate** ermäßigter Tarif
**redundancy** Arbeitslosigkeit f, Entlassung f
**redundant** überflüssig, überzählig; arbeitslos
**refer** (pass to so.) weiterleiten; (to item) erwähnen; sich beziehen auf
**reference** (person who reports) Referenz f; (report on person) Referenz f, Zeugnis n
**reference number** Aktenzeichen n, Geschäftszeichen n
**refund** (n) Erstattung f, Rückerstattung f
**refund** (v) erstatten, zurückzahlen
**refundable deposit** zurückerstattbare Kaution
**refusal** Ablehnung f, Verweigerung f
**refuse** (v) ablehnen, verweigern
**regarding** bezüglich, betreffend
**regardless of** ungeachtet
**register** (n) (official list) Verzeichnis n, Register n

**register** (v) (in official list) eintragen, registrieren; (letter) als/per Einschreiben schicken
**register a company** ein Unternehmen in das Gesellschaftsregister eintragen
**registered office** eingetragener Sitz
**registered trademark** eingetragenes Warenzeichen
**Registrar of Companies** Führer m des Handelsregisters
**registration** Eintragung f, Registrierung f
**registration fee** Eintragungsgebühr f, Anmeldegebühr f
**registry** Registratur f
**regular** (always at same time) regelmäßig, regulär; (ordinary) normal, regulär
**regular customer** Stammkunde[-in]
**regulate** (by law) regeln
**regulations** Vorschriften fpl, Verordnungen fpl
**reimport** (n) Wiedereinfuhr f
**reimport** (v) wiedereinführen
**reinvest** reinvestieren, neu anlegen
**reinvestment** Wiederanlage f, Reinvestition f
**reject** (n) Ausschuß m; Ausschußware f
**reject** (v) ablehnen
**relating to** zusammenhängend mit, bezüglich
**relations** Beziehungen pl
**release dues** überfällige Bestellungen abwickeln
**reliability** Zuverlässigkeit f, Sicherheit f
**reliable** zuverlässig, seriös
**remain** (be left) bleiben, übrigbleiben
**remainder** (things left) Rest m
**remit by cheque/check** per Scheck bezahlen
**remittance** Überweisung f, Geldsendung f
**remunerate** bezahlen, vergüten
**remuneration** Bezahlung f, Vergütung f
**render an account** eine Abrechnung vorlegen
**renew a bill of exchange** einen Wechsel prolongieren

**renew a lease** einen Mietvertrag/ einen Pachtvertrag verlängern
**renewal of a lease/of a subscription/of a bill** Mietvertragsverlängerung f/ Abonnementsverlängerung f/ Wechselprolongation f
**rent** (n) Miete f, Pacht f
**rent** (v) mieten, pachten
**rental** Miete f, Pacht f; Leihgebühr f
**reorder** (n) Nachbestellung f
**reorder** (v) nachbestellen
**reorder level** Mindestnachbestellung f
**reorganization** Umstrukturierung f, Neuordnung f
**reorganize** neu organisieren, umstrukturieren
**repay** zurückzahlen; erstatten
**repayable** rückzahlbar
**repeat an order** eine Nachbestellung aufgeben, etwas nachbestellen
**repeat order** Nachbestellung f
**replacement** (item) Ersatz m
**replacement value** Wiederbeschaffungswert m
**reply** (n) Antwort f
**reply** (v) antworten
**report** (n) Bericht m
**report** (v) berichten, melden
**report to so.** jdm unterstehen
**represent** vertreten
**representative** (person) Stellvertreter[in], Vertreter[in]
**request** (n) Gesuch m, Antrag m
**request** (v) ersuchen, beantragen, anfordern
**request, on** auf Wunsch, auf Anforderung
**requirements** Bedarf m, Anforderungen fpl, Bedingungen fpl
**resale** Wiederverkauf m, Weiterverkauf m
**research and development (R&D)** Forschung und Entwicklung (F&E) f
**researcher** Forscher[in]
**reservation** Reservierung f
**reserve** (n) (money) Reserve f, Rücklage f; (supplies) Reserve f, Vorrat m
**reserve a room/a table** ein Zimmer/einen Tisch reservieren
**resident** (adj) wohnhaft, ansässig

**resign** zurücktreten, kündigen
**resources** Ressourcen fpl; Rohstoffe mpl
**response** Antwort f, Reaktion f
**responsibility** Verantwortung f, Verantwortlichkeit f
**responsible (for)** verantwortlich/zuständig (für)
**responsible to so., be** jdm unterstellt sein
**restock** wieder auffüllen
**restrict** beschränken, einschränken
**restrictive practices** restriktive Praktiken fpl
**restructure** umstrukturieren, reorganisieren
**restructuring of a loan** Kreditumschuldung f
**result from** sich ergeben aus
**result in** führen zu/zur Folge haben
**results** (company's) Jahresergebnis n
**resume negotiations** Verhandlungen wiederaufnehmen
**retail** (v) (goods) Waren im Einzelhandel verkaufen; (sell for a price) im Einzelhandel kosten
**retail goods** Waren im Einzelhandel
**retail price** Einzelhandelspreis m, Ladenpreis m
**retailer** Einzelhändler[in]
**retire** (from job) in Pension/Rente gehen, in den Ruhestand treten
**retirement age** Rentenalter n; Pensionsalter n
**retrain** umschulen
**retrenchment** Kürzung f, Abbau m
**retroactive** rückwirkend
**return** (n) (declaration) Bericht m, Erklärung f; (profit) Ertrag m, Rendite f; (sending back) Rückgabe f, Rücksendung f
**return address** Absender m
**return on investment (ROI)** Ertrag m aus Kapitalanlage
**returns** (unsold goods) Retourwaren fpl, Rücksendungen fpl
**revenue** Einnahmen pl, Einkommen n
**reverse** (adj) umgekehrt, entgegengesetzt
**reverse charge call** R-Gespräch n
**reverse the charges** ein R-Gespräch führen

**revoke** aufheben, rückgängig machen
**revolving credit** Revolvingkredit m,
revolvierender Kredit
**right** (adj) *(not wrong)* richtig
**right** (n) *(legal title)* Recht n,
Anrecht n, Anspruch m
**right of way** Wegerecht n
**rightful owner**
rechtmäßige(r) Besitzer[in]
**rights issue** Bezugsrechtsemission f
**rise** (n) *(increase)* Anstieg m,
Zunahme f; *(pay)* Lohnerhöhung f,
Gehaltserhöhung f
**rise** (v) ansteigen, zunehmen
**risk** (n) Risiko n
**risk** (v) *(money)* riskieren
**risk capital** Risikokapital n
**risky** gewagt, riskant
**rival company**
Konkurrenzunternehmen n
**road** Straße f
**road transport** Straßentransport m
**rock-bottom prices**
Niedrigstpreise mpl,
Schleuderpreise mpl
**roll over** *(a debt)* umschulden
**room** *(hotel)* Zimmer n;
*(space)* Platz m
**room service** Zimmerservice m
**rough calculation** grobe Kalkulation
**rough estimate** grobe Schätzung
**round down/up** abrunden/aufrunden
**routine work** Routinearbeit f
**royalty** Tantiemen fpl, Honorar n
**rule** (v) *(give decision)*
entscheiden, anordnen
**ruling** (n)
Entscheidung f, Anordnung f
**run** (v) *(be in force)* gelten, laufen;
*(manage)* betreiben, leiten
**run into debt** in Schulden geraten
**run out of** kein(e/n) ... mehr haben
**running costs/running expenses** Betriebskosten pl, laufende Kosten pl
**running total** laufende Summe
**rush hour** Hauptverkehrszeit f
**rush order**
Eilbestellung f, Eilauftrag m

# S

**sack so.** jdn rauswerfen/entlassen
**safe** (n) Safe m, Tresor m

**safe investment**
sichere Kapitalanlage
**safeguard** schützen, sichern
**safety precautions**
Sicherheitsvorkehrungen fpl
**safety regulations**
Sicherheitsvorschriften fpl
**salaried** festangestellt
**salary** Gehalt n
**salary review** Gehaltsaufbesserung f
**sale** (n) *(at a low price)* Ausverkauf m, Räumungsverkauf m
**sale** (n) *(selling)* Verkauf m
**sales** Absatz m; Umsatz m
**sales budget** Absatzplan m
**sales campaign** Verkaufsaktion f,
Verkaufskampagne f
**sales conference** Verkaufskonferenz f
**sales department** Verkaufs-
abteilung f, Vertriebsabteilung f
**sales figures**
Verkaufszahlen fpl, Absatzzahlen fpl
**sales forecast** Absatzprognose f
**sales manager**
Verkaufsleiter[in], Vertriebsleiter[in]
**sales people** Verkaufspersonal n
**sales target** Verkaufsziel n
**sales tax** Warenumsatzsteuer f
**salesman** *(in shop)* Verkäufer m; *(rep)*
Handelsvertreter m, Vertreter m
**salvage** (n) *(action)* Bergung f
**salvage** (v) bergen
**sample** (n) *(part)*
Muster n, Warenprobe f
**satisfy** *(customer)* zufriedenstellen
**satisfy a demand** Nachfrage
stillen/befriedigen
**saturate the market**
den Markt sättigen
**save** (v) *(money)* sparen;
*(on computer)* sichern
**savings account** Sparkonto n
**scale down/scale up**
verringern; erhöhen
**scale of charges**
Gebührenordnung f, Preisliste f
**scheduled flight** Linienflug m
**sealed tenders**
verschlossene Angebote npl
**season** *(time of year)* Jahreszeit f
**season ticket** Zeitkarte f, Dauerkarte f
**seasonal**
**seasonal demand**
saisonbedingte Nachfrage

**seasonal variations** saisonbedingte Abweichungen *fpl*

**secondhand** gebraucht, Gebraucht-, Secondhand-

**seconds** Waren *fpl* zweiter Wahl, B-Sortiment *n*

**secretary** Sekretär[in]

**sector** Sektor *m*, Bereich *m*

**secure** (v) *funds* sich finanzielle Mittel sichern

**secured creditor** Vorzugsgläubiger *m*

**secured loan** gesichertes Darlehen

**securities** Wertpapiere *npl*, Effekten *pl*

**security guard** Wachmann *m*

**security of employment** Arbeitsplatzsicherheit *f*

**seize** einziehen, beschlagnahmen

**seizure** Einziehung *f*, Beschlagnahmung *f*

**self-employed** selbständig, freiberuflich

**self-financing** (adj) selbstfinanzierend

**sell** verkaufen, absetzen

**sell forward** auf Termin verkaufen

**sell-by date** Haltbarkeitsdatum *n*

**selling** (n) Verkauf *m*

**semi-skilled workers** angelernte Arbeitskräfte *fpl*

**sender** Absender *m*

**senior manager/senior executive** höhere Führungskraft, leitende(r) Angestellte(r)

**separate** (adj) getrennt, gesondert

**serial number** Fabrikationsnummer *f*; Seriennummer *f*

**serve a customer** einen Kunden bedienen

**service** (n) *(customers)* Bedienung *f*; *(of machine)* Wartung *f*

**service** (v) *(a machine)* warten

**service charge** Bedienung *f*

**service department** Kundendienstabteilung *f*

**service manual** Wartungshandbuch *n*

**set** (adj) festgelegt, Fix-

**set price** Fixpreis *m*, festgesetzter Preis

**set up a company** eine Firma gründen

**setback** Rückschlag *m*

**settle** *(an invoice)* begleichen

**settle an account** eine Rechnung begleichen; ein Konto abschließen

**settlement** *(payment)* Begleichung *f*, Bezahlung *f*

**share** (n) *(in company)* Aktie *f*

**share** (v) *(divide among)* (sich) teilen, aufteilen; *(use with so.)* sich teilen

**share certificate** Aktienzertifikat *n*

**shareholder** Aktionär[in]

**shareholding** Beteiligung *f*, Anteil *m*, Aktienbesitz *m*

**sheet of paper** Blatt *n* Papier

**shelf life of a product** Lagerfähigkeit *f* eines Produktes

**shelve** aufschieben, auf Eis legen

**shelving** *(shelves)* Regale *npl*

**shift** (n) *(team of workers)* Schicht *f*

**shift work** Schichtarbeit *f*

**ship** (n) Schiff *n*

**ship** (v) versenden, befördern; verschiffen

**shipment** Ladung *f*; Versand *m*

**shipper** Spediteur *m*, Befrachter *m*

**shipping** Versand *m*, Verschiffung *f*

**shipping charges/shipping costs** Verladekosten *pl*, Versandkosten *pl*

**shipping instructions** Versandanweisungen *fpl*

**shop** Laden *m*, Geschäft *n*

**shop around** sich umsehen

**shopper** Käufer[in]

**shopping centre/center** Einkaufszentrum *n*

**short credit** kurzfristiger Kredit, Kredit *m* mit kurzer Laufzeit

**short of** knapp an, fehlen an

**short-term** (adj) kurzfristig

**short-term contract** Vertrag *m* mit kurzer Laufzeit

**short-term loan** kurzfristiges Darlehen

**shortage** Mangel *m*

**shortlist** (n) Auswahlliste *f*

**shortlist** (v) in die engere Wahl ziehen

**show a profit** einen Gewinn verzeichnen

**sideline** Nebenbeschäftigung *f*

**sight draft** Sichtwechsel *m*, Sichttratte *f*

**sign** (n) Schild *n*

**sign** *(cheque/check, contract)* unterschreiben

**signatory** Unterzeichner m;
Zeichnungsberechtigte(r)
**signature** Unterschrift f
**simple interest** einfache Zinsen pl
**site** Gelände n, Standort m
**site engineer** Bauleiter[in]
**situation** (state of affairs)
Situation f, Lage f
**situations vacant** Stellenangebote npl
**skeleton staff** Rumpfbelegschaft f
**skill** Kenntnisse pl, Fertigkeit f
**skilled labour/labor** Facharbeiter mpl
**slack** flau, ruhig
**slash prices/credit terms** Preise/
Kreditbedingungen stark
herabsetzen
**sleeping partner** stille(r) Teilhaber[in]
**slip** (n) (mistake) Versehen n,
Schnitzer m; (piece of paper)
Zettel m, Beleg m
**slow payer** säumiger Zahler
**slump in sales** Absatzeinbruch m
**small businesses** Kleinbetriebe mpl
**small-scale**
in begrenztem Umfang/ Rahmen
**social costs**
Kosten pl für die Allgemeinheit
**social security** Sozialhilfe f
**socio-economic groups** sozial-
ökonomische Gruppierungen fpl
**soft currency** weiche Währung
**software** Software f
**sole** alleinig, Allein-
**sole agent** Alleinvertreter[in]
**sole owner** Alleineigentümer[in]
**solicit orders**
sich um Aufträge bemühen
**solution** Lösung f
**solve a problem** ein Problem lösen
**solvency**
Zahlungsfähigkeit f, Solvenz f
**solvent** (adj) zahlungsfähig, solvent
**source of income** Einnahmequelle f
**spare part** Ersatzteil n
**special offer** Sonderangebot n
**specification**
genaue Angabe, Spezifikation f
**specify**
einzeln aufführen, spezifizieren
**spend** (money) ausgeben,
investieren; (time) verbringen
**spinoff**
Nebenprodukt n, Abfallprodukt n

**sponsor** (n)
Sponsor[in], Geldgeber[in]
**sponsor** (v) sponsern, fördern
**sponsorship** Sponsern n, Förderung f
**spot cash** sofortige Bezahlung,
Sofortliquidität f
**spot price** Lokopreis m
**spot purchase** Kassakauf m
**spread a risk** das Risiko
verteilen/streuen
**stability** Stabilität f, Beständigkeit f
**stabilize** (sich) stabilisieren, festigen
**stable prices** stabile Preise pl
**staff meeting** Personalversammlung f
**staged payments** Zahlungen fpl in
Stufen fpl/Etappen fpl
**stagger** staffeln, stufen
**stamp** (v) (letter) frankieren
**stand** (n) (at exhibition) Stand m
**standard** (adj)
handelsüblich, Standard-
**standard** (n) Standard m, Norm f
**standard rate** (of tax)
Einheits-steuersatz m
**standardize** standardisieren, normen
**standing** Ansehen n; Bonität f
**start-up costs** Anlaufkosten pl
**starting date**
Anfangsdatum n, Anlauftermin m
**starting salary** Anfangsgehalt n
**state** (n) (condition) Zustand m
**state-of-the-art** technisch auf dem
neusten Stand, hochmodern
**statement of account** Abrechnung f
**statistical analysis**
statistische Analyse
**statistics** Statistik f
**status** Status m, Stellung f
**status inquiry** Kreditauskunft f
**statute of limitations**
Verjährungsfrist f
**statutory holiday/vacation**
gesetzlicher Feiertag
**sterling** Sterling m
**stipulate**
(vertraglich) vereinbaren, festlegen
**stock** (n) (goods) Lagerbestand m,
Warenbestand m; (share in
company) Aktie f
**stock** (v) führen, auf Lager halten
**stock control** Lagersteuerung f
**stock exchange/market** Börse f
**stock list** Kursblatt n; Bestandsliste f

**stock size** Standardgröße f
**stock up** einen Vorrat anlegen, ein Lager auffüllen
**stockbroker** Börsenmakler[in], Wertpapiermakler[in]
**stockholder** Aktionär[in]
**stockist** Fachhändler m, Fachgeschäft n
**stocktaking** Inventur f, Bestandsaufnahme f
**stocktaking sale** Inventurausverkauf m
**stop** (v) *(doing sth.)* anhalten, stoppen; aufhören, einstellen
**stop a cheque/check** einen Scheck sperren (lassen)
**stop payments** die Zahlungen einstellen
**storage** (n) *(computer)* Speicher m; *(cost)* Lagerkosten pl
**storage** (n) *(in warehouse)* Lagerung f, Aufbewahrung f
**storage capacity** Lagerkapazität f
**storage facilities** Lagerungseinrichtungen fpl, Lagermöglichkeiten fpl
**store** (n) *(large shop)* Kaufhaus n, Warenhaus n; *(where goods are kept)* Lager n, Magazin n; **store** (v) *(in warehouse)* einlagern, lagern
**strategic planning** strategische Planung
**strategy** Strategie f
**strike** (n) Streik m
**strike** (v) streiken
**striker** Streikende(r)
**strong currency** starke Währung
**subcontract** (n) Subunternehmervertrag m, Untervertrag m
**subcontract** (v) einen Unterauftrag abschließen, einen Auftrag weitervergeben
**subcontractor** Subunternehmer m
**subject to** abhängig von
**sublease** (n) Untervermietung f; Unterverpachtung f
**sublease** (v) in Untermiete/Unterpacht haben
**subsidiary** (adj) nebensächlich, Neben-
**subsidiary** *(company)* Tochtergesellschaft f
**subsidize** subventionieren
**subsidy** Subvention f, Zuwendung f

**subtotal** Zwischensumme f
**succeed** *(do well)* Erfolg haben
**success** Erfolg m
**successful** erfolgreich
**sue** klagen, verklagen
**sum** *(of money)* Betrag m, Summe f
**sundries** Verschiedenes, Diverses
**supervise** überwachen, beaufsichtigen
**supervision** Aufsicht f, Kontrolle f
**supervisor** Aufsicht f, Aufseher[in], Kontrolleur m
**supervisory** Aufsichts-, Überwachungs-
**supplementary** Zusatz-, zusätzlich, ergänzend
**supplier** Lieferant m, Zulieferer m
**supply** (n) *(action)* Versorgung f, Angebot n
**supply** (v) liefern, versorgen
**supply price** Angebotspreis m, Lieferpreis m
**surcharge** Aufschlag m, Aufpreis m
**surplus** Überschuß m
**surrender** (n) *(insurance)* frühzeitiges Einlösen
**surrender value** Rückkaufswert m
**survey** (n) *(examination)* Begutachtung f
**survey** (v) *(inspect)* begutachten, untersuchen
**surveyor** Gutachter[in], Sachverständige(r)
**suspend** zeitweilig einstellen
**suspension of payments** Zahlungseinstellung f
**swap** (n) Tausch m
**swap** (v) tauschen
**switch over to** überwechseln, umstellen
**switchboard** Telefonzentrale f
**synergy** Synergie f
**system** System n
**systems analyst** Systemanalytiker[in], Systemberater[in]

# T

**tacit approval** stillschweigende Genehmigung
**take a call** ein Gespräch annehmen
**take action** etwas unternehmen, tätig werden

**take legal advice** sich juristisch beraten lassen

**take off** *(deduct)* wegnehmen; abziehen, nachlassen

**take off** *(plane)* abfliegen

**take on more staff** mehr Personal einstellen

**take out a policy** eine Versicherung abschließen

**take over** *(from so.)* übernehmen, ablösen

**take place** stattfinden

**take so. to court** jdn vor Gericht bringen

**take stock** Inventur f machen, den Warenbestand aufnehmen

**take the initiative** die Initiative ergreifen

**takeover** Übernahme f

**takeover bid** Übernahmeangebot n

**takings** Einnahmen fpl

**tangible assets** materielle Vermögenswerte mpl, Sachanlagen fpl

**target market** Zielmarkt m

**tariff** *(price)* Tarif m

**tariff barriers** Zollschranken fpl

**tax** (n) Steuer f

**tax** (v) besteuern, mit einer Steuer belegen

**tax assessment** *(action)* Steuerveranlagung f; *(result)* Steuerbescheid m

**tax consultant** Steuerberater[in]

**tax deducted at source** Quellensteuer f

**tax exemption** Steuerbefreiung f

**tax paid** versteuert

**tax rate** Steuersatz m

**tax return/tax declaration** Steuererklärung f

**tax year** Steuerjahr n

**tax-deductible** steuerlich absetzbar, steuerlich abzugsfähig

**tax-free** steuerfrei

**taxable income** steuerpflichtiges Einkommen

**taxpayer** Steuerzahler m

**telephone** (n) Telefon n

**telephone** (v) anrufen

**telephone directory** Telefonbuch n

**telephonist** Telefonist[in]

**temp** (n) Zeitarbeiter[in], Aushilfskraft f

**temporary staff** Zeitarbeitskräfte fpl

**tenancy** *(agreement)* Mietverhältnis n; Pachtverhältnis n

**tenant** Mieter[in]; Pächter[in]

**tender** (n) *(offer to work)* Angebot n

**term** *(of validity)* Frist f, Laufzeit f

**term loan** befristeter Kredit

**terminal** (adj) *(at the end)* End-, Abschluß-

**terminate an agreement** einen Vertrag kündigen/lösen

**termination clause** Kündigungsklausel f

**terms** Bedingungen fpl

**terms of employment** Einstellungsbedingungen fpl

**terms of payment** Zahlungsbedingungen fpl

**territory** *(of salesman)* Bezirk m, Gebiet n

**tertiary industry** Dienstleistungs-gewerbe n

**test** (n) Test m, Prüfung f

**test** (v) testen, prüfen

**theft** Diebstahl m

**third party** Dritte(r)

**threshold price** Schwellenpreis m

**throughput** Durchsatz m

**tie-up** *(link)* Verbindung f, Zusammenschluß m

**time scale** zeitlicher Rahmen

**time, on** pünktlich

**timetable** (n) *(appointments)* Terminkalender m, Programm n

**timetable** (n) *(trains, etc.)* Fahrplan m; *(flights)* Flugplan m

**timetable** (v) einen Zeitplan aufstellen

**tip** (n) *(money)* Trinkgeld n

**token charge** nominelle Gebühr

**toll** Benutzungsgebühr f, Maut f

**toll free** gebührenfrei

**ton** Tonne f

**tonnage** Tonnage f

**top management** Unternehmens-spitze f, Topmanagement n

**top quality** Spitzenqualität f

**total** (adj) gesamt, völlig

**total** (n) Summe f, Endbetrag m

**total** (v) ergeben, sich belaufen auf

**total amount** Gesamtbetrag m

**total cost** Gesamtkosten pl
**total invoice value**
  voller Rechnungsbetrag
**track record** Erfolgs- und
  Leistungsnachweis m
**trade** (n) (business)
  Handel m; Gewerbe n
**trade** (v) handeln, Handel treiben
**trade directory** Branchenverzeichnis n
**trade discount** Händlerrabatt m
**trade fair** Handelsmesse f
**trade journal**
  Fachzeitschrift f, Fachblatt n
**trade price** Großhandelspreis m
**trade terms** Händlerrabatt m
**trade union** Gewerkschaft f
**trade-in price**
  Preis m bei Inzahlungnahme
**trademark/trade name**
  Warenzeichen n, Handelsmarke f
**trader** Händler[in]
**trading loss** Betriebsverlust m
**trading partner** Handelspartner m
**trading profit** Betriebsgewinn m,
  Geschäftsgewinn m
**train** (v) (learn) Ausbildung machen;
  (teach) ausbilden
**trainee** Auszubildende(r), Lehrling m
**transact business** Geschäfte tätigen
**transaction** Geschäft n
**transfer** (n) Transfer m; Versetzung f;
  Überweisung f
**transfer of funds** Geldüberweisung f
**transferred charge call** R-Gespräch n
**transit** Beförderung f, Transport m
**transit visa** Transitvisum n
**translation** Übersetzung f
**transport** (n) Beförderung f
**transport** (v) befördern
**trial sample** Muster n, Probestück n
**triplicate, in**
  in dreifacher Ausfertigung
**true copy** gleichlautende Kopie
**turn down** ablehnen
**turn over** (v) (make sales) umsetzen
**turnkey operation**
  schlüsselfertiges Projekt
**turnover** (sales) Umsatz m

# U

**unaudited accounts**
  ungeprüfte Geschäftsbücher npl

**unauthorized expenditure** nicht
  genehmigte Ausgaben fpl
**unavailable** nicht erhältlich,
  nicht verfügbar
**unconditional** vorbehaltlos
**undated** nicht datiert
**under** (according to) gemäß, laut;
  (less than) unter
**under contract**
  vertraglich verpflichtet
**under new management**
  unter neuer Leitung
**undercut a rival**
  einen Konkurrenten unterbieten
**undersell**
  unterbieten; unter Preis verkaufen
**undersigned** Unterzeichnete(r)
**understanding** Übereinkunft f
**undertaking** (company) Unternehmen n; (promise) Zusicherung f
**underwrite** (guarantee)
  bürgen für; haften
**unemployed** arbeitslos
**unemployment** Arbeitslosigkeit f
**unfair competition**
  unlauterer Wettbewerb
**unfulfilled order**
  nicht ausgeführter Auftrag
**unilateral** unilateral, einseitig
**union** (trade union) Gewerkschaft f
**unique selling point/proposition**
  einzigartiges Verkaufsargument
**unit cost** Stückkosten pl
**unit price** Stückpreis m
**unload** (goods) entladen, ausladen
**unobtainable** nicht erhältlich
**unpaid invoices**
  unbezahlte Rechnungen fpl
**unsecured creditor**
  Gläubiger m ohne Sicherheiten
**unsuccessful** erfolglos
**up front** im voraus
**up to date**
  auf dem neusten Stand, aktuell
**up-market** anspruchsvoll, exklusiv
**update** (v) aktualisieren, auf den
  neuesten Stand bringen
**urgent** dringend, Eil-, eilig
**use** (n) Benutzung f, Gebrauch m
**use** (v) benutzen, einsetzen
**user-friendly** benutzerfreundlich,
  bedienerfreundlich
**utilization** Verwendung f, Nutzung f

# V

**vacancy** *(for job)* freie Stelle
**valid** gültig, rechtsgültig
**valuation** Schätzung f; Beurteilung f
**value** (n) Wert m
**value** (v) schätzen
**value added tax (VAT)**
  Mehrwertsteuer (MwSt.) f
**variable costs** variable Kosten pl
**VAT invoice**
  Mehrwertsteuerrechnung f
**vendor** Verkäufer[in]
**venture capital**
  Risikokapital n, Wagniskapital n
**verbal agreement**
  mündliche Vereinbarung
**verification**
  Überprüfung f, Bestätigung f
**verify** überprüfen, bestätigen
**vested interest** persönliches/
  wirtschaftliches Interesse
**veto a decision** ein Veto gegen eine
  Entscheidung einlegen
**visible trade**
  sichtbarer Handel/ Warenhandel m
**void** (adj) *(not valid)*
  ungültig, nichtig
**volume discount** Mengenrabatt m
**volume of trade/business**
  Handelsvolumen n
**voluntary liquidation**
  freiwillige Liquidation
**vote of thanks** Dankesworte pl
**voucher** Gutschein m, Bon m

# W

**wage** Lohn m, Arbeitslohn m
**wage negotiations**
  Lohnverhandlungen fpl;
  Tarifverhandlungen fpl
**waive** verzichten auf
**waiver clause** Verzichtklausel f
**warehouse** (n) Lager n
**warehouse** (v) lagern
**warehousing**
  Lagerung f; Lagerhaltung f
**warrant** (n) *(document)*
  (dienstlicher) Befehl
**warrant** (v) *(guarantee)* garantieren
**warranty** (n) Garantie f
**wastage** Schwund m

**waste** (n) Abfall m
**waste** (v) verschwenden
**waybill** Frachtbrief m
**wear and tear**
  Abnutzung f, Verschleiß m
**weekly** wöchentlich
**weigh** abwiegen, wiegen
**weight** Gewicht n
**weighted index** gewogener Index
**wholesale** *(adv)* (im) Großhandel,
  Großhandels-
**wholesale discount**
  Großhandelsrabatt m
**wholesaler** Großhändler[in]
**win a contract**
  einen Auftrag erhalten
**window display** Auslage f,
  Schaufensterdekoration f
**withdraw** *(an offer)*
  zurückziehen, widerrufen
**witness** (n) Zeuge[-in]
**witness** (v) *(a document)*
  bestätigen, bezeugen
**word-processing** Textverarbeitung f
**work** (n) Arbeit f; (v) arbeiten
**work in progress** Halbfabrikate npl
**work permit** Arbeitserlaubnis f
**working conditions**
  Arbeitsbedingungen pl
**worldwide** (adj) weltweit
**worth, be** wert sein
**wrap up** *(deal)* festmachen; *(goods)*
  einwickeln, einschlagen
**writ** gerichtliche Verfügung
**write down** *(assets)*
  abschreiben, teilabschreiben
**write off** *(debt)* voll abschreiben
**write out a cheque/check**
  einen Scheck ausstellen
**write-off** *(loss)* Vollabschreibung f
**written agreement**
  schriftliche Vereinbarung

# X, Y, Z

**yearly payment** jährliche Zahlung
**yellow pages** Gelbe Seiten pl,
  Branchenverzeichnis n
**yield** (n) *(on investment)*
  Ertrag m, Rendite f
**yield** (v) *(interest)*
  einbringen, abwerfen
**zip code** Postleitzahl f

# German–English Business Dictionary

| | |
|---|---|
| f | feminine |
| m | masculine |
| n | neuter |
| pl | plural |
| (adj) | adjective |
| (cpd) | in compounds |
| (v) | verb |
| so. | someone |
| sth. | something |

## A

**Abbau** m cutback
**Abfall** m waste
**Abfallprodukt** n by-product, spinoff
**Abfertigungsschalter** m check-in counter/desk
**Abflug** m departure(s)
**Abgabe** f levy
**abgesagt** cancelled
**abhalten, eine Sitzung** hold a meeting
**abhängig von** subject to, depending on
**abheben** withdraw *(money)*
**abheften, Dokumente** file documents
**abholen** collect, fetch
**Abholung** f collection *(of goods)*
**Abkommen** n agreement, deal
**Ablauf** m expiry, expiration
**ablaufen** expire, lapse
**Ablauftermin** m expiry date
**ablehnen** reject, turn down, refuse
**Ablehnung** f refusal
**ablösen** take over *(from so.)*
**Abnahme** f decrease, acceptance
**abnehmen** decrease
**abnehmen, den Hörer** answer the telephone
**abnehmen, eine Warensendung** accept delivery of a shipment
**abnehmend** decreasing
**Abonnement** n subscription
**abpacken** prepack, prepackage
**Abrechnung** f statement of account, settlement
**abreisen** depart/check out *(of hotel)*

**abrunden** round down
**absagen** cancel
**Absatz** m sales; article, clause
**Absatzeinbruch** m slump in sales
**Abschätzung** f evaluation
**abschicken** post
**Abschlagszahlung** f payment on account, interim payment
**abschließen** conclude/clinch *(an agreement)*; lock up *(a shop/an office)*; settle *(an account)*
**abschließen, eine Versicherung** take out an insurance policy
**abschließen, einen Unterauftrag** subcontract
**abschließen, seine Ausbildung zum ...** qualify as
**Abschluß bringen, zum** finalize
**abschreiben** write down *(assets)*
**abschreiben, voll** write off *(debt)*
**Abschreibungssatz** m depreciation rate
**Absender** m sender; return address
**absetzen** deduct, set against
**abstimmen** ballot, vote
**abstimmen, die Konten** reconcile the accounts
**Abteilung** f department *(in shop, office)*
**Abteilungsleiter[in]** head of department
**abwerfen** yield *(interest)*
**abwerten** devalue
**Abwertung** f devaluation
**abwesend** absent
**Abwicklung** f handling, liquidation, completion
**abzeichnen** initial (v)
**abziehbar** deductible
**abziehen** take off, deduct
**Abzug** m deduction
**AG (Aktiengesellschaft)** PLC, plc (Public Limited Company)
**Agentur** f agency
**Akkordarbeit** f piecework
**Akkordlohnsatz** m piece rate
**Akkreditiv** n letter of credit
**Akontozahlung** f payment on account
**Akte** f; **Aktenordner** m file *(of documents)*
**Aktenschrank** m filing cabinet

## Aktentasche

**Aktentasche** f briefcase
**Aktenzeichen** n reference
**Aktie** f share/stock (in a company)
**Aktiengesellschaft** f **(AG)** Public Limited Company
**Aktienkapital** n equity capital
**Aktienportefeuille** n portfolio
**Aktienzertifikat** n share/stock certificate
**Aktionär[in]** shareholder/stockholder
**Aktiva** pl assets
**aktualisieren** update
**aktuell** up to date (modern)
**Alleineigentümer[in]** sole owner
**Alleinvertreter[in]** sole agent
**allgemein** across-the-board, general
**Amt** n appointment, job
**amtlich** official (adj)
**anberaumen** schedule (a meeting)
**andauern** continue
**ändern, sich** change
**Änderung** f change (difference)
**Anerkennung** f appreciation (how good)
**anfangen** begin
**Anfangs-** (cpd) starting
**anfordern** request
**Anforderung, auf** on request
**Anforderungen** fpl requirements
**Anfrage** f inquiry
**Angaben** fpl, **nähere** particulars
**angeben, (einen Preis)** quote, estimate costs
**Angebot** n bid, offer, tender
**Angebot, im** on (special) offer
**Angebotspreis** m supply price, asking price
**angefochtene Übernahme** contested takeover
**angegebener Wert** declared value
**Angeklagte(r)** defendant
**angelernte Arbeitskräfte** fpl semi-skilled workers
**angemessener Preis** fair price
**Angestellte(r)** employee
**angewiesen sein auf** depend on
**Angleichung** f adjustment
**Anhang** m appendix
**Anhängeschild** n label
**anhäufend** cumulative
**ankommen** arrive
**Ankunft** f arrival(s)

**Anlage** f enclosure (with a letter); plant (factory)
**Anlaufhafen** m port of call
**Anlaufkosten** fpl start-up costs
**Anlauftermin** m starting date
**Anleihekapital** n loan capital
**anmelden, sich** check in (at hotel)
**annähernd** approximate(ly)
**Annahme** f acceptance
**annehmen** accept; carry/approve in a vote
**annehmen, ein Gespräch** take a phone call
**annullieren** annul, cancel
**anordnen** rule, give decision
**Anrecht** n right (legal title)
**Anreiz** m incentive
**Anruf** m (telephone) call
**Anrufbeantworter** m answering machine
**anrufen** call, phone, telephone
**ansässig** resident
**Anschluß** m telephone extension; computer port
**Anschlußflug** m connecting flight
**Anschrift** f address
**ansprechen** appeal to, attract
**Anspruch** m claim; right, legal title, entitlement
**anspruchsvoll** up-market, discriminating
**anstehend** pending
**ansteigen** rise, increase
**Anstellung** f employment
**Anstieg** m rise, increase
**Anteil** m proportion
**anteilig/anteilsmäßig** pro rata
**Antrag** m application, request
**Antragsformular** n application form
**antreiben** chase (an order)
**Antwort** f reply, answer, response
**antworten** reply, answer
**anwachsen** accrue
**Anwaltskosten** pl legal costs
**Anweisung** f order, instruction; payment, transfer
**anwesend sein** be present (at), attend (meeting)
**Anzahl** f number, quantity
**Anzahlung** f deposit, down payment
**Anzahlung, als** on account
**Anzeige** f advertisement

**Anzeigenkosten** pl advertising rates
**Anzeigenkunde** m advertiser
**Anzeigenraum** m advertising space
**Apparat** m telephone (extension)
**Arbeit** f work, job, employment
**arbeiten** work
**Arbeiter[in]** worker
**Arbeitgeber[in]** employer
**Arbeitgeber-Arbeitnehmer-
    Beziehungen** fpl industrial
    relations
**Arbeitnehmer[in]** employee
**Arbeitsbedingungen** pl
    working conditions
**Arbeitserlaubnis** f work permit
**Arbeitsgericht** n industrial tribunal
**Arbeitskämpfe** mpl
    labour/labor disputes
**Arbeitskosten** pl labour/labor costs
**Arbeitskräftemangel** m
    manpower shortage
**Arbeitslohn** m wage
**arbeitslos** out of work, unemployed
**Arbeitslosigkeit** f unemployment
**Arbeitsplatz** m place of work
**Arbeitsplatzsicherheit** f
    security of employment
**Arbeitsstunde** f man-hour
**Arbeitsunfall** m industrial accident
**Arbeitsvertrag** m
    contract of employment
**Arbeitsvertragsbedingungen** fpl
    conditions of employment
**Artikel** m article, item
**Attest** n doctor's certificate
**Attrappe** f mock-up, dummy
**Aufbewahrung** f
    storage, warehousing
**aufbringen** raise/obtain money
**Aufenthalt** m residence
**Aufenthaltsgenehmigung** f
    residence permit
**auffordern** invite, ask
**Aufforderung** f demand (for
    payment), invitation
**Aufgabe** f job, piece of work
**aufgeben** place (an order); post (a
    letter); check in (baggage)
**aufgeben, seine Arbeitsstelle** leave
    one's job
**aufgliedern** break down, itemize
**Aufgliederung** f
    breakdown (of items)

**aufgreifen** follow up
**aufhalten** hold up, delay
**aufheben** abolish, reverse, cancel
**Auflage** f condition (terms); batch;
    circulation, edition
**Auflagennummer** f batch number
**auflaufen** accrue
**auflösen, ein Konto** close an account
**auflösen, ein Unternehmen** liquidate
    a company
**Aufmerksamkeit** f attention
**aufnehmen** enter into (discussion)
**Aufpreis** m
    additional charge, surcharge
**aufrechterhalten** maintain,
    keep going
**Aufrechterhaltung** f der Versorgung
    maintenance of supplies
**aufrunden** round up
**Aufschlag** m surcharge
**aufschlüsseln** break down, itemize
**Aufschlüsselung** f breakdown
    (of items)
**Aufschub** m postponement, shelving
**Aufschwung** m rally,
    recovery, upturn
**Aufseher[in]** supervisor
**aufsetzen, einen Vertrag** draw up
    a contract
**Aufsicht** f supervisor; supervision
**Aufsichtsrat** m directorate,
    supervisory board
**aufteilen** share (out), divide (up)
**Auftrag** m order (for goods)
**Auftrag von, im** on behalf of
**Auftraggeber[in]** client, customer
**Auftragnehmer[in]** contractor
**Auftragsabwicklung** f
    order processing
**Auftragsausführung** f
    order fulfilment
**Aufwendungen** fpl
    expenditure, outgoings
**Aufwertung** f
    appreciation (in value), revaluation
**aufzeichnen** record
**Aufzeichnung** f record (of events)
**ausbilden** train (teach)
**Ausbildung machen** train (learn)
**Ausdruck** m printout
**ausdrucken** print out
**Ausfall** m breakdown (of machine)

## ausfallen

**ausfallen** break down *(machine)*
**Ausfuhr** f export
**ausführen** export
**ausführen, einen Auftrag** deal with an order, fulfil an order
**Ausfuhrgenehmigung** f export licence/license, export permit
**Ausführungsanzeige** f contract note
**Ausgabe** f issue, expense, copy
**Ausgaben** fpl expenditure, outgoings
**Ausgänge** mpl outgoing goods; out tray
**Ausgangspunkt** m starting point, initial position
**ausgeben** pay out, spend
**ausgebildet** qualified *(skilled)*
**ausgefallen** cancelled
**ausgenommen** excluding
**ausgezeichnet** excellent
**ausgleichen** balance *(a budget)*; make up for *(a loss)*
**aushandeln** bargain
**Aushilfskraft** f casual worker, temp
**Auskunft** f information *(bureau)*
**ausladen** unload *(goods)*
**Auslage** f (window) display
**Auslagen** fpl outlay, expenditure
**Ausland, ins/im** abroad
**ausländische Absatzmärkte** mpl overseas markets
**Auslands-** (cpd) international
**auslaufen lassen** phase out
**ausleihen** lend
**ausrüsten** equip
**ausschlaggebende Stimme** casting vote
**Ausschluß** m der Gewährleistung caveat emptor
**Ausschlußklausel** f exclusion clause
**ausschreiben, ein Stellenangebot** advertise a vacancy
**Ausschuß** m board, committee
**Ausschußware** f reject *(goods)*
**Außendienstleiter[in]** field sales manager
**Außenhandel** m foreign/external trade
**Außenstände** pl outstanding debts; accounts receivable, receivables
**außerbetrieblich** external
**Aussichten** fpl prospects
**ausstatten** equip

**Ausstattung** f equipment
**ausstehend** outstanding, unpaid
**ausstellen** exhibit, display; make out, issue *(invoice)*, write out *(cheque/check)*
**Aussteller[in]** exhibitor; drawer *(of cheque/check)*
**Ausstellung** f exhibition
**Ausverkauf** m sale(s), bargain sale
**Auswahl** f choice, selection, range
**auswählen** choose
**Auswahlliste** f shortlist
**ausweiten** expand, diversify
**Auswertung** f analysis, evaluation
**Auswirkung** f effect, influence
**auszahlen** pay out
**auszeichnen** label, mark
**Auszubildende(r)** trainee
**Avis** m/n advice note, dispatch note

## B

**Bahnhof** m railway station
**Balkendiagramm** n bar chart
**Bank-** (cpd) bank
**bankrott** bankrupt (adj)
**Bankrott** m bankruptcy
**bankrott gehen** fail *(go bust)*
**bar bezahlen** pay cash
**Bargeld** n (ready) cash
**Bar-** (cpd) cash
**Barzahlung** f payment in cash
**Barzahlungs-** (cpd) cash
**Beachtung** f observance, compliance, consideration, attention
**Beamte(r)/Beamtin** official
**beanstanden** complain (about), query
**beantragen** apply for, propose
**beantworten** answer
**bearbeiten** process, deal with
**Bearbeitungsgebühr** f handling charge
**beaufsichtigen** supervise
**Bedarf** m demand; requirements
**bedeutend** important, significant
**Bedeutung** f importance
**bedienen, einen Kunden** serve a customer
**bedienerfreundlich** user-friendly
**Bedienung** f service *(charge)*; waiter, waitress

**Bedienungsanleitung** f
operating instructions
**Bedingung** f condition, proviso
**Bedingungen** fpl requirements, terms
**beeinflussen** influence
**beenden** complete, end, finish
**Befähigung** f capability, ability
**befassen mit, sich** attend to, handle, deal with
**befolgen** comply with
**befördern** promote (give better job); carry, transport
**Beförderung** f
promotion (to better job); transport
**Befrachter** m shipper
**befreien** exempt
**befreit, von der Steuer** exempt from tax
**Befreiungsklausel** f escape clause
**befristeter Kredit** term loan
**Befugnis** f authority
**beglaubigen** certify
**beglaubigte Kopie** certified copy
**begleichen, eine Rechnung** settle an account/an invoice
**Begleichung** f settlement, payment
**Begleitbrief** m covering letter
**beglichen** paid (invoice)
**Begünstigte(r)** beneficiary
**begutachten** examine, inspect
**Begutachtung** f survey, examination
**Beherrschung** f control
**beifügen** enclose
**Beilage** f enclosure
**beilegen** enclose
**Beitrag** m contribution
**bejahend** affirmative, positive
**Beklagte(r)** defendant
**bekommen, zu** obtainable
**beladen (Lastwagen/Schiff)** load (a truck/a ship)
**belasten, ein Konto** debit an account
**Belastung** f debit entry
**Belastungsanzeige** f debit note
**belaufen auf, sich** total
**Beleg** m receipt, slip
**Belegschaft** f staff, workforce
**Benachrichtigung** f notification
**benutzerfreundlich** user-friendly
**Benutzer-** (cpd) operating
**Benutzerhinweise** mpl directions for use
**Benutzung** f use

**Benutzungsgebühr** f toll, (hire/ rental) charge
**Berater[in]** consultant
**Beratungsfirma** f consultancy firm
**berechnen** charge; calculate
**Berechnung** f calculation, evaluation
**berechtigen** entitle
**Berechtigung** f entitlement
**Bereich** m area, sector
**bereit** ready
**bergen** salvage
**Bergung** f salvage
**Bergungsgut** n salvaged goods
**Bericht** m report
**berichten** report
**Beruf** m occupation, profession, job
**berufen** appoint
**berufliche Qualifikationen** fpl professional qualifications
**Berufsbezeichnung** f job title
**berufstätig** working
**Berufung** f
vocation, appointment; appeal
**Berufung einlegen** appeal
**beschädigen** damage
**Beschädigung** f damage
**beschaffen** get, obtain
**beschäftigen** employ
**beschäftigt** busy, employed
**Beschäftigung** f employment
**Bescheid** m answer, notification
**bescheinigen** certify
**beschleunigen** hurry up
**beschlußfähige Anzahl** quorum
**beschränken** limit, restrict
**beschränkte Haftung**
limited liability
**beschriften** mark, label
**Beschwerde** f complaint
**Beschwerdebrief** m letter of complaint
**beschweren, sich** complain (about)
**besetzen** man
**besetzt** engaged (tel.); manned
**Besetztzeichen** n engaged tone
**besitzen** possess, own
**Besitzer[in]** proprietor (-tress)
**besprechen** discuss
**Besprechung** f discussion, meeting
**Besprechungszimmer** n
conference room
**Bestandsaufnahme** f stocktaking
**Bestandsliste** f stock list

# bestätigen

**bestätigen** confirm, acknowledge; check, verify; witness *(document)*
**bestätigter Scheck** certified cheque/check
**Bestätigung** f confirmation, acknowledgement; verification
**bestechen** bribe
**Bestechungsgeld** n bribe
**bestellen** order, book
**bestellt** on order
**Bestellung** f order *(for goods)*
**besteuern** tax
**Bestimmungsort** m destination
**bestrafen** penalize
**Besuch** m call, visit
**Beteiligung** f shareholding
**Betrag** m amount, sum
**Betrag, zu zahlender** amount owing
**betreffen** apply to, affect, concern
**betreffend** regarding
**betreiben** run/manage *(a business)*
**Betrieb** m business, concern; factory
**Betrieb, in** in operation, in use
**Betriebs-** (cpd) operating/trading
**betriebsintern** in-house, internal
**Betriebsunfall** m industrial accident
**Betrug** m fraud, deceit, deception
**Beurteilung** f judgment, assessment
**Bevollmächtigte(r)** authorized representative
**Bevollmächtigung** f authorization
**bewerben, sich um eine Stelle** apply for a job
**Bewerbungsformular** n application form
**bezahlen** pay
**bezahlt** paid *(invoice)*
**Bezahlung** f settlement, payment
**bezeugen** witness *(a document)*
**beziehen** obtain, get, receive
**beziehen auf, sich** refer *(to item)*
**Beziehungen** pl connections, relations
**Bezirk** m area/territory *(of salesman)*
**Bezirksleiter[in]** area manager
**Bezogene(r)** drawee
**bezüglich** regarding, relating to
**Bezugsrechtsemission** f rights issue
**bieten** bid, offer *(to buy)*
**Bilanz** f balance *(sheet)*
**bilden** form, set up, establish
**Bildschirm** m monitor, screen
**billig** cheap(ly)

**Billigwaren** fpl cut-price goods
**binden, Kapital** lock up capital
**Binnenmarkt** m domestic market
**BIP (Bruttoinlandsprodukt)** n GDP (gross domestic product)
**bitten** ask (for)
**Blankokredit** m open credit
**Blankoscheck** m blank cheque/check
**Bodenfläche** f floor space
**Bon** m voucher
**Bonität** f creditworthiness, financial standing
**Bord gehen, an** board (v)
**Bordkarte** f boarding card/pass
**Börse** f stock exchange/market
**Börsenmakler[in]** stockbroker
**Boß** m boss *(informal)*
**Branche** f industry, trade, line of business
**Branchenverzeichnis** n classified/trade directory
**brechen** break *(an agreement)*
**Briefwechsel stehen, in** correspond with someone
**Briefwerbeaktion** f mailing shot
**bringen** bear/earn *(interest)*
**brutto verdienen/einnehmen** gross (v)
**Brutto-** (cpd) gross
**Bruttoinlandsprodukt** n (**BIP**) gross domestic product (GDP)
**Bruttosozialprodukt** n (**BSP**) gross national product (GNP)
**buchen** book
**Buchführung** f bookkeeping
**Buchgewinn** m paper profit
**Buchhalter[in]** bookkeeper
**Buchhaltung** f accounting; accounts department
**Buchprüfung** f audit
**Buchwert** m book value
**Budgetkontrolle** f budgetary control
**bürgen für** underwrite, guarantee
**Büro** n office
**Bürokratismus** m red tape
**Büropersonal** n office staff

# C

**Charterflug** m charter flight
**Chef[in]** boss *(informal)*
**Chiffre** f code; box number

**Computer-** (cpd) computer
**Couponanzeige** f coupon ad
**Couponsteuer** f withholding tax

## D

**D-Mark** f Deutschmark
**Dachgesellschaft** f holding company
**Dankesworte** pl vote of thanks
**Darlehen** n advance, loan
**Datei** f file (computer)
**Daten** pl data
**Daten eingeben** input information
**Datenkasse** f electronic point of sale
**datiert, nicht** undated
**Datum** n date
**Datumsstempel** m date stamp
**Dauerauftrag** m banker's/
    standing order
**Dauerkarte** f season ticket
**Debatte** f discussion, debate
**Debitoren** mpl accounts receivable
**decken den Bedarf/die Nachfrage**
    meet a demand
**decken, die Kosten** cover costs
**Deckung** f cover, collateral
**Deckungszusage** f cover note
**deponieren** deposit
**Devisen** pl foreign/foreign currency
**Diebstahl** m theft
**Dienstleistungsgewerbe** n
    service/tertiary industry
**dienstlich** official(ly), on business
**Dienststunden** fpl office/
    working hours
**Direktor[in]** director
**Direktverkauf** m door-to-door selling
**Direktversand** m direct mail
**Diskettenlaufwerk** n disk drive
**Diverses** sundries
**Dividendenertrag** m dividend yield
**Dokument** n document, instrument
**dolmetschen** interpret
**Dolmetscher[in]** interpreter
**Doppel-** (cpd) double
**dreifacher Ausfertigung, in**
    in triplicate
**dringend** urgent
**Dritte(r)** third party
**drucken** print
**Drucker** m printer
**Durchführbarkeitsbericht** m
    feasibility report

**durchführen** carry out,
    implement, effect
**Durchführung** f implementation
**Durchsatz** m throughput
**Durchschlag** m carbon copy
**Durchschnitt** m average, mean
**durchschnittlich** average (adj)
**durchschnittlicher Jahreszuwachs**
    mean annual increase
**Dutzend** n dozen

## E

**Ebene** f level
**Eckwert** m benchmark
**Eckzins** m bank base rate
**Ecu/ECU** m/f ecu/ECU (European
    currency unit)
**EDV-Service** m computer services
**Effekten** pl securities
**Effektivertrag** m; **Effektivrendite** f
    effective yield
**Eigenmarkenwaren** fpl own
    label goods
**Eigentum** n ownership, property
**Eigentümer[in]** owner, proprietor
**Eignung** f
    suitability, aptitude, qualification
**Eilauftrag** m/**Eilbestellung** f express
    order, rush order/job
**Eilbote** m courier, messenger
**Eilbrief** m express letter
**eilig** urgent
**Eilzustellung** f express delivery
**einberufen** convene
**einbringen** earn/yield (interest)
**Einbuße** f loss
**einchecken** check in (at airport)
**Eincheckzeit** f check-in time
**eindringen, in einen Markt** penetrate
    a market
**einfache Zinsen** pl simple interest
**Einfluß** m influence
**einfrieren** freeze (prices)
**Einfuhren** fpl imports
**einführen** introduce; import
**Einfuhrkontingent** n import quota
**Einführungsangebot** n
    introductory offer
**Einführungslehrgang** m
    induction training
**Einfuhrzoll** m import duty
**Eingang** m entry (going in)

### Eingangssteuersatz

**Eingangssteuersatz** *m* basic rate of tax

**eingeben, (in den Computer)** input, keyboard (v)

**eingehen** fold up *(of a business)*; arrive *(goods)*

**eingehen (einen Vertrag)** enter into (an agreement)

**eingehender Bericht** detailed account

**eingestellt sein auf** cater for

**eingetragen** registered

**einhalten, einen Termin/eine Frist** meet a deadline

**Einheitstarif** *m* flat rate

**Einkauf** *m* buying, purchasing

**einkaufen gehen** go shopping

**Einkaufsabteilung** *f* buying department

**Einkaufsbuch** *n* bought/ purchase ledger

**Einkommen** *n* income, earnings, revenue

**Einkommensteuer** *f* **und Lohnsteuer** *f* income tax

**Einkommensteuererklärung** *f* declaration of income, income tax return

**Einkünfte** *pl* earnings, income

**einladen** invite

**Einlage** *f* bank deposit, investment

**einlagern** store, keep in a warehouse

**Einleger[in]** depositor

**einleiten, die Diskussion** open the discussion

**einlösen** cash *(a cheque/check)*; honour/honor *(a bill)*

**einmalig** one-off

**einmalige Summe** *f* lump sum

**Einnahmen** *fpl* receipts, takings, revenue

**Einnahmequelle** *f* source of income

**einpacken** pack, wrap up

**einpendeln, sich** level off/out

**Einreisevisum** *n* entry visa

**einrichten** arrange/set up *(meeting)*

**Einrichtung** *f* equipment

**Einrichtungen** *fpl* facilities

**Einschiffungshafen** *m* port of embarkation

**einschließen** include

**einschließlich** inclusive

**einschränken** restrict, limit

**Einschreiben** *n* registered post, recorded delivery;

**einseitig** one-sided; unilateral

**einziehbare Außenstände** *pl*, **nicht** bad debts

**einsparen** save, economize

**Einstandspreis** *m* cost price

**einsteigen** get on, board

**einsteigen, in das Geschäftsleben** go into business

**einstellen** employ; discontinue (production, payments)

**einstellen, allmählich** phase out

**Einstellungsbedingungen** *fpl* conditions/terms of employment

**einstufen** classify, grade

**Eintrag** *m* entry *(writing)*

**eintragen** enter *(write in)*, register

**einträglich** profitable

**Eintragung** *f* registration

**Eintragungsgebühr** *f* registration fee

**eintreten** enter *(go in)*

**Eintritt** *m* entry *(going in)*

**Eintrittsgebühr** *f* admission charge

**einverstanden sein, mit etwas** agree with something

**Einweg(ver)packung** *f* non-returnable packing, disposable wrapping

**einwickeln** wrap up *(goods)*

**einzahlen** pay in, deposit

**Einzahler[in]** depositor

**Einzahlung** *f* bank deposit

**Einzahlungsbeleg** *m* deposit/paying-in slip

**Einzelhandelspreis** *m* retail price

**Einzelhändler[in]** retailer

**Einzelheit** *f* detail

**Einzelheiten** *fpl* particulars

**einziehen** collect, levy, seize, withdraw *(from circulation)*

**Einziehung** *f* collection, seizure

**einzigartiges Verkaufsargument** unique selling point/proposition

**elektronische Post** *f* electronic mail

**elektronisches Kassenterminal** *n* electronic point of sale

**Empfang** *m* receipt; reception desk

**empfangen** receive

**Empfangsbestätigung** *f* receipt *(piece of paper)*

**empfehlen** recommend

**Endbenutzer** *m* end user

**Endbetrag** m final amount, grand total
**Endsaldo** m closing balance
**Endverbraucher** m end user
**energiesparend** energy-saving (adj)
**Engpaß** m bottleneck
**Enteignung** f compulsory purchase
**enthalten** contain, hold; include
**entladen** unload (goods)
**entlassen** dismiss, discharge, release (employee)
**Entlassung** f dismissal; redundancy
**Entleiher[in]** borrower
**entschädigen** compensate, indemnify
**Entschädigung** f compensation, damages, indemnification
**entscheiden** decide, adjudicate, rule
**Entscheidung** f decision, adjudication, ruling
**entsprechen** meet/comply with/correspond to (requirements)
**entwerfen** design/draw up/draft (a contract)
**entwickeln** develop
**Entwurf** m design, draft, rough plan
**Erdöl** n oil (petroleum)
**erfahren** experienced
**Erfolg** m success
**erfolglos** unsuccessful
**erfolgreich** successful
**Erfolgs- und Leistungsnachweis** m track record
**erfüllen** fulfil, meet, satisfy; implement (an agreement)
**Erfüllung** f fulfilment, implementation
**ergänzen** supplement, amend
**Ergänzung** f supplement, amendment
**ergeben** total (v)
**ergeben aus, sich** result from
**Erhalt** m receipt, receiving
**erhalten** obtain, receive; win (a contract)
**erhältlich, (nicht)** (un)available, (un)obtainable
**erheben** charge, levy; file (charges)
**erhöhen** mark up, raise, increase
**Erhöhung** f increase n, rise
**erholen, sich** recover (get better)
**Erinnerungsschreiben** n follow-up letter, chaser

**erkundigen, sich** inquire
**erlauben** allow, permit
**Erlaubnis** f permission, permit
**erlaubter Handel** lawful trade
**erlöschen** expire
**Erlöschen** n expiration, expiry
**Ermächtigung** f authority, authorization
**ermäßigter Tarif** reduced rate
**ernennen** appoint
**ernsthafte(r) Käufer[in]** genuine purchaser
**erobern** capture
**eröffnen** open, initiate
**Eröffnungs-** (cpd) opening
**erreichen, ein Ziel** meet a target
**Ersatz** m replacement (item); compensation
**Ersatzteil** n spare part
**erstatten** refund, repay
**Erstattung** f rebate, refund
**Erstattung in voller Höhe** full refund
**erstes Quartal** first quarter
**erteilen, eine Konzession/Lizenz** license (v)
**erteilen, einen Auftrag** place an order
**Ertrag** m profit, return, yield
**Ertragszentrum** n profit centre/center
**erwartet** due (awaited), expected, projected
**Erwerb** m acquisition, purchase; earnings
**erwerben** purchase; earn
**Erwerber[in]** purchaser
**Erzeugnis** n product
**Etage** f floor (level)
**Etikett** n label
**etikettieren** label
**Europäische Union** f (EU) European Union (EU)
**Euroscheck** m/**Eurocheque** m Eurocheque/Eurocheck
**Exklusiv-** (cpd) exclusive
**Export-** (cpd) export
**Exporteur** m/**Exportfirma** f exporter
**exportieren** export

## F

**F&E (Forschung und Entwicklung)** R&D (research and development)

## Fabrik

**Fabrik** f factory
**Fabrikant[in]** manufacturer
**Fabrikationsnummer** f serial number
**Facharbeiter[in]** skilled worker
**Fachhändler** m specialist supplier/stockist
**Fachmann/Fachfrau** professional, expert, specialist
**Fachzeitschrift** f specialist/ trade journal
**Factor** m factor *(person, company)*
**Fähigkeit** f ability, capability, efficiency
**Fahrplan** m timetable
**Fahrpreis** m fare
**Fahrstuhl** m lift
**Faktor** m factor *(influence, maths)*
**Fall** m decrease, drop, fall
**fallen** decrease, depreciate, drop, fall
**fällig** due, owing
**fällig sein/werden** fall due
**fälliger Rechnungsbetrag** balance due
**Fälligkeitstermin** m maturity date
**falsch** false, wrong, incorrect
**falsch berechnen/kalkulieren** miscalculate
**fälschen** forge, falsify
**Fälschung** f fake n, forgery; faking
**Fassungsvermögen** n capacity *(space)*
**Fazilität** f credit facility
**fehlende Geldmittel** pl lack of funds
**Fehler** m error, mistake
**fehlerhaft** imperfect; incorrect
**Fehlkalkulation** f miscalculation
**fehlschlagen** fall through, go wrong
**Feierabend machen** stop work, knock off
**Fernflug** m long-haul flight
**Fernsprechauftragsdienst** m answering service
**fertig** ready
**fertigen, (maschinell)** manufacture, produce
**Fertigkeit** f skill
**fertigstellen** complete (v)
**Fertigungsgemeinkosten** pl manufacturing overheads
**Fertigwaren** fpl finished goods
**fest** (adj) fixed
**festangestellt** permanent, salaried
**festgelegt/festgesetzt** set (adj)

**festigen, (sich)** stabilize
**festlegen** stipulate/fix *(rate)*
**festlegen, Kapital** lock up capital
**Festplatte** f hard disk
**Festpreis** m firm price
**Festpreisvereinbarung** f fixed-price agreement
**festsetzen, einen Preis** price (v)
**Feuerschaden** m fire damage
**Filiale** f multiple/chain store, branch
**Filialleiter[in]** branch manager
**Finanz-** (cpd) financial
**finanzieren** finance, fund
**Finanzierung** f financing
**finanzpolitische Maßnahmen** fpl fiscal measures
**Firmenimage** n corporate image
**Firmenwert** m goodwill
**Firmenzeichen** n logo
**flau** slack
**florierend** flourishing
**Flug-** (cpd) flight
**Flughafengebühr** f airport tax
**Flugzeug** n plane, aircraft
**Fluktuation** f fluctuation/turnover *(of personnel)*
**flüssiges Vermögen** liquid assets
**Flußdiagramm** n flow chart
**Folge haben, zur** result in
**Fonds** m fund
**fordern** ask, claim, demand
**fördern** promote, stimulate, support, sponsor
**Forderung** f claim/demand *(for payment)*; amount owing
**Forderungen** fpl receivables
**Förderung** f promotion, support, sponsorship
**formell/förmlich** formal
**Formular** n form
**Formulierung** f form of words, wording
**Forscher[in]** researcher
**Forschung und Entwicklung** f (F&E) research and development (R&D)
**fortsetzen** continue
**Fracht** f freight *(carriage)*, cargo
**Fracht gegen Nachnahme** freight forward
**Fracht- und Löschungskosten** pl landed costs
**Frachtbrief** m bill of lading, waybill
**frachtfrei** carriage free, carriage paid

**Frachtkosten** pl freight costs
**Frachtkosten per Nachnahme** carriage forward
**Frage** f query, question; matter
**Franchise-Geber[in]** franchiser
**Franchise-Nehmer[in]** franchisee
**Franchise-Basis vergeben, auf** franchise (v)
**Franken** m Swiss franc
**frankieren** frank, stamp
**frei an Bord (f.o.b.)** free on board
**freiberuflich** self-employed, freelance
**freie Stelle** vacancy
**freier Markt** open market
**freier Wechselkurs** floating exchange rate
**Freihandelszone** f free trade area
**freistellen** exempt, release (v)
**Freizeichen** n dialling tone
**Freizeichnungsklausel** f exclusion clause
**Fremdkapital** n outside capital, loan capital
**Fremdwährung** f foreign currency
**Frist** f notice; term
**führen** conduct, direct, run; carry, have in stock
**führen zu** result in
**Führung** f management, direction
**Führungsgruppe** f management team
**Führungskraft** f executive
**Funktelefon** n cellular telephone
**Fusion** f merger
**fusionieren** merge

## G

**Gabelstapler** m fork-lift truck
**gängiger Satz** going rate
**ganztags** full-time
**Gebiet** n area/field/region/territory (of salesman)
**Gebietsleiter[in]** area manager
**Gebrauch** m use
**Gebrauchsanweisung** f directions for use
**Gebrauchsartikel** m article of daily use
**gebraucht** secondhand
**Gebühr** f charge, fee; rate
**Gebühr bezahlt** postpaid

**gebührenfrei** free of charge, postage paid
**Gebührenordnung** f scale of charges
**gebührenpflichtig** subject to a charge
**gebührenpflichtige Verwarnung** fine
**Gedeck** n place setting; set menu; cover charge
**gefälschte Papiere** npl faked documents
**Gegen-** (cpd) contra/counter
**Gegenbuchung** f contra entry
**Gegenteil, im** on the contrary
**gegenwärtig** present (adj)
**gegenzeichnen** countersign
**Gehalt** n pay, salary
**Gehalts-** (cpd) salary
**geheim** secret (adj)
**Gelände** n site
**Geld** n money
**Geldautomat** m cash dispenser
**Gelder flüssigmachen** mobilize capital
**Geldgeber[in]** financial backer, sponsor
**Geldmenge** f money supply
**Geldsendung** f remittance
**Geldstrafe** f fine
**Geldstrafe verurteilen, zu einer** fine (v)
**Geldstück** n coin
**Geldüberweisung** f transfer of funds
**Gelegenheitsarbeit** f casual work
**Gelegenheitskauf** m bargain
**gelten** apply to, affect, be in force, be valid
**gemäß** under, according to
**gemäß dem Muster** as per sample
**gemäßigt** moderate (adj)
**Gemeineigentum** n common property, collective ownership
**Gemeinkosten** pl fixed costs, overhead costs, overheads
**gemeinnützig** non profit-making, charitable
**gemeinsames Konto** joint account
**Gemeinschaftsunternehmen** n joint venture
**genau** exact
**genaue Angabe** specification
**genehmigen** approve, authorize, permit, license

## Genehmigung

**Genehmigung** f permission, authorization; permit, licence
**Generaldirektor[in]** chief executive
**geöffnet** open
**Gepäck** n luggage
**Gepäckträger** m porter
**gerecht** fair
**Gericht** n (law) court
**gerichtliche Verfügung** writ
**Gerichtskosten** pl (court) costs
**Gerichtsverfahren** n legal proceedings
**geringer Absatz** low sales
**geringfügige Ausgaben** fpl petty expenses
**gesamt** total (adj)
**Gesamt-** (cpd) total
**Geschäft** n business; deal, transaction; business concern; shop, store
**Geschäfte tätigen** transact business
**geschäftlich** (on) business
**Geschäfts-** (cpd) business
**Geschäftsbank** f clearing/commercial bank
**geschäftsführend** managing, executive
**Geschäftsführer[in]** managing director (MD); manager (of shop)
**Geschäftsjahr** n financial year
**Geschäftsschluß** m closing time
**Geschäftsstelle** f office, branch
**geschätzter Absatz** estimated sales
**Geschenk** n gift, present
**Geschenkgutschein** m gift voucher
**geschlossen** closed
**Gesellschaft** f mit beschränkter Haftung (GmbH) limited (liability) company
**Gesellschafter[in]** associate, partner
**Gesellschaftsgründung** f (an der Börse) incorporation, flotation
**gesetzlicher Feiertag** legal/statutory holiday
**gesetzlicher Kündigungsschutz** security of tenure
**gesichertes Darlehen** secured loan
**gesondert** separate(ly)
**gesperrtes Konto** frozen account
**Gespräch** n conversation, discussion; (telephone) call
**Gestehungskosten** pl prime cost
**Gesuch** m request, application

**getrennt** separate (adj)
**Gewerbe** n business, occupation, trade
**gewerbliche Räumlichkeiten** business premises
**Gewerkschaft** f trade union
**Gewerkschaft(l)er[in]** trade unionist
**Gewicht** n weight
**Gewinn** m profit, gain, return
**Gewinn nach Steuern** after-tax profit, profit after tax
**Gewinn vor Steuern** pretax profit, profit before tax
**Gewinn- und Verlustrechnung** f profit and loss account
**Gewinnaufschlag** m mark-up, profit margin
**gewinnbringend** profitable
**Gewinnspanne** f profit margin
**gewogener Index** weighted index
**girieren, einen Scheck** endorse a cheque/check
**Girokonto** n current account
**Gläubiger** m creditor; lender
**Gläubiger ohne Sicherheiten** unsecured creditor
**gleich** immediately
**GmbH (Gesellschaft mit beschränkter Haftung)** f Ltd (limited company)
**Gratisprobe** f free sample
**Grenze** f border; limit
**Grenzkostenkalkulation** f marginal pricing
**grob** rough
**Großeinkauf** m bulk buying
**Größendegression** f/**Größenvorteile** mpl economies of scale
**Großhandel** wholesale trade
**Großhandelspreis** m trade price
**Großhandelsrabatt** m wholesale discount
**Großhändler[in]** wholesaler
**Großraumbüro** n open-plan office
**Grundbesitz** m property, real estate
**gründen** establish, found, set up
**Grundfläche** f floor space
**Grundfreibeträge** mpl personal allowances
**Grundgebühr** f basic/standing charge
**Grundlage** f base, initial position
**Grundrabatt** m basic discount

**Grundriß** m floor plan
**Grundstück** n property
**Gründungskapital** n initial/start-up capital
**Gruppenbuchung** f block booking
**gültig** valid
**günstig** convenient, favourable/favorable
**günstige Bedingungen** fpl easy terms
**günstige Preise** mpl keen prices
**Gutachter[in]** surveyor, assessor; expert, consultant
**Güter** pl goods
**gutgehend** flourishing
**Guthaben** n credit balance; asset
**Gutschein** m voucher, coupon
**gutschreiben** credit
**Gutschrift** f credit entry
**Gutschriftanzeige** f credit note

## H

**Habenbuchung** f credit entry
**Habensaldo** m credit balance
**Hafen** m harbour/harbor, port
**haftbar sein für/haften für** liable for
**Haftungsablehnungserklärung** f disclaimer
**Halbfabrikate** npl work in progress
**Haltbarkeitsdatum** n sell-by date
**halten, ein Versprechen** keep a promise
**Handel** m commerce, trade, trading; bargain, deal, transaction
**Handel treiben** trade, deal (v)
**handeln** bargain
**handeln (mit)** trade (in), deal (in), handle
**Handelskammer** f Chamber of Commerce
**Handelsmarke** f trademark, trade name
**Handelsmesse** f trade fair
**Handelspartner** m trading partner
**Handelsrecht** n commercial law
**Handelssperre** f (trade) embargo
**handelsüblich** standard, usual
**Handelsverkehr** m commerce, trade
**Handelsvertreter** m salesman, representative
**Handelsvolumen** n volume of trade

**Handelsware** f merchandise, commodity
**handgeschrieben** handwritten
**handhaben** handle, deal with, administer
**Händler[in]** merchant, dealer, trader
**Händlerrabatt** m trade discount/terms
**Handlungsvollmacht** f power of attorney
**häufig** frequent
**Hauptaktionär[in]** major shareholder
**Hauptbelastungszeit** f peak period
**hauptberuflich** full-time
**Hauptbuch** n ledger
**Hauptgebäude** n main building
**Hauptgeschäftsstelle** f head/main office
**Hauptpost** f general post office
**Hauptsitz** m headquarters
**Hauptverkehrszeit** f rush hour; peak period
**Haushalts-** (cpd) budget
**Haustelefon** n internal telephone
**Haustürverkauf** m door-to-door selling
**Havarie** f collision/crash (ship, plane); average (insurance)
**Hefter** m stapler; binder, file
**herabsetzen** mark down/reduce (a price)
**heraufsetzen** raise, increase
**Herkunft** f origin
**Herkunftsbescheinigung** f certificate of origin
**herstellen** make, manufacture
**Hersteller** m manufacturer
**Herstellungskosten** pl manufacturing costs
**herunterhandeln** knock down, reduce
**hervorragend** excellent, outstanding
**hinausgehen über** exceed
**hochbezahlt** highly-paid
**Höchstgewinne** mpl record profits
**Höchstpreis** m maximum/ceiling price
**hochwertig** high-quality/-grade
**hohe Kosten/Ausgaben** fpl heavy costs/expenditure
**hohe Miete** high rent
**hohe Zinsen** pl high interest

## höhere Führungskraft

**höhere Führungskraft** senior manager/executive
**höhere Gewalt** act of God, force majeure
**Holdinggesellschaft** f holding company
**Honorar** n royalty; fee
**Hülle** f cover, top
**Hypothek** f mortgage
**hypothekarisch belasten/eine Hypothek aufnehmen** mortgage (v)

## I

**immaterielle Vermögenswerte** mpl intangible assets
**Immobilien** pl property, real estate
**importieren** import
**Indexbindung** f indexation
**indexgebunden** index-linked
**indirekte Besteuerung** indirect taxation
**Indossament** n endorsement
**Indossant** m endorser
**Indossat(ar)** m endorsee
**Indossierung** f endorsement
**Industrielle(r)** industrialist
**Inhaber[in]** bearer, holder; proprietor, proprietress
**Inhaberschuldverschreibung** f bearer bond
**Inhalt** m contents
**Inkassobeauftragte(r)** (debt) collector
**Inkassobüro** n debt collection agency
**Inlands-** (cpd) domestic
**Innenrevision** f internal audit
**innerbetrieblich** in-house, internal
**Inserent** m advertiser
**inserieren, ein Stellenangebot** advertise a vacancy
**Insiderhandel** m insider dealing/trading
**Instandhaltung** f maintenance
**institutionelle Anleger** mpl institutional investors
**Inventarverzeichnis** n/**Inventarliste** f inventory, list of contents
**Inventur** f stocktaking
**Inventur machen** take stock
**Inventurausverkauf** m stocktaking sale

**Investition** f investment
**Investitions-** (cpd) capital
**Inzahlungnahme** f part exchange
**Irrtümer und Auslassungen vorbehalten** errors and omissions excepted (e. & o.e.)
**Ist-Kosten** pl plus prozentualer Gewinnaufschlag cost plus
**Ist-Zahlen** fpl actuals

## J

**Jahr, im/pro** per annum
**Jahres-** (cpd) annual
**Jahreszeit** f season (time of year)
**jährlich** annual, annually, yearly
**jetzig** present (adj)
**juristisch** legal (referring to law)
**juristisch beraten lassen, sich** take legal advice

## K

**Kapital schlagen aus** capitalize on
**Kapitalanlage** f investment
**Kapitalertrag** m return on capital
**Kapitalertragssteuer** f capital gains tax
**Kapitalgesellschaft** f corporation, joint-stock company
**Kapitalsammelstellen** fpl institutional investors
**Kapitalsumme** f principal
**kaputtgehen** break down (machine)
**Kartei** f card index
**Karteikarte** f filing card
**Kartenverkäufer[in]** booking clerk
**Kassageschäft** n cash sale
**Kasse** f cash; cash desk/checkout; cash register/till; ticket/box office
**Kassenbestand** m cash balance
**Kassierer[in]** cashier, teller
**Katalogpreis** m catalogue/list price
**Kauf** m purchase
**kaufen** buy, purchase
**Käufer[in]** buyer, purchaser; shopper
**Kaufhaus** n department store
**Kaufkraft** f purchasing power
**Kaufoption** f option to purchase, call option
**Kaufvertrag** m bill of sale, sale contract
**Kettenladen** m chain/multiple store

**Kiste** f case *(box)*
**Klage** f complaint, action, lawsuit
**klagen** complain; sue
**Kläger[in]** claimant, plaintiff
**Klausel** f clause, article; provision, stipulation
**Kleinanzeigen** fpl classified advertisements
**Kleinbetriebe** mpl small businesses
**kleine Kasse** f petty cash; float
**knapp an** short of
**kommen, zu einer Entscheidung/ Vereinbarung** reach a decision/ an agreement
**Kompensationsgeschäfte machen** barter (v)
**Konferenzschaltung** f conference phone, link-up
**Konjunktur-** (cpd) economic
**konjunkturbedingt** cyclical
**konjunkturelle Entwicklung** economic trend
**Konjunkturindustrie** f boom industry
**Konkurrent[in]** competitor
**Konkurrenz** f competition
**konkurrenzfähig** competitive
**Konkurrenzfähigkeit** f competitiveness
**Konkurrenz-** (cpd) competing, rival
**konkurrierend** competing
**Konkurs** m bankruptcy, liquidation
**Konkursschuldner[in]** bankrupt
**Konkursverwalter[in]** receiver, liquidator
**Konnossement** n bill of lading
**Konstruktionsabteilung** f design department
**konsultieren** consult
**Konsument[in]** consumer
**Konsumgüter** npl consumer goods
**Kontakt aufnehmen zu** contact (v)
**Kontaktperson** f contact *(person)*
**Kontingent** n quota
**Konto** n account
**Konto mit Habensaldo** account in credit
**Kontoauszug** m bank statement
**Kontokorrentkonto** n open/ drawing account
**Kontokorrentkredit** m advance on account
**Kontostand** m bank balance
**Kontrollabschnitt** m counterfoil

**Kontrolle** f control; supervision; check, inspection
**Kontrolleur** m supervisor, inspector
**kontrollieren** control, check, inspect
**Kontrolltaste** f control key
**Konzept** n draft, rough copy; plan, concept
**Konzession** f concession, licence/license
**körperliche Arbeit** manual work
**Körperschaftsteuer** f corporation tax
**Kosten, Versicherung, Fracht (cif)** cost, insurance and freight
**Kosten** pl expense(s), cost(s), charge(s)
**kostendeckend arbeiten** break even (v)
**Kostendeckungspunkt** m break-even point
**kostenlos** free of charge
**Kostenrentabilität** f cost-effectiveness
**Kostenstelle** f cost centre/center
**Kostenvoranschlag** m estimate, quotation
**Kostenwirksamkeit** f cost-effectiveness
**kostspielig** costly, dear
**Kraftfahrzeugversicherung** f motor insurance
**Kredit** m credit; loan
**Kredit aufnehmen** borrow
**Kredit mit kurzer/langer Laufzeit** short/long credit
**Kreditauskunft** f credit/ status inquiry
**kreditieren** credit, grant credit
**Kreditinstitut** n financial institution
**Kreditnehmer[in]** borrower
**Kreditoren** mpl accounts payable; liabilities
**Kreditumschuldung** f restructuring of a loan
**Kreisdiagramm** n pie chart
**Kreislauf** m cycle, circulation
**Krisenplan** m contingency plan
**Kühlhaus** n cold store
**Kunde/Kundin** customer, client
**Kundendienst** m after-sales service, customer service department
**Kundenkarte** f charge card
**Kundenkreis** m clientele

# kündigen

**kündigen** resign; terminate *(agreement)*
**Kündigungsklausel** f termination clause
**Kundschaft** f clientele
**Kurier** m courier, messenger
**Kurs** m price, rate; course, policy; class
**Kurs-Gewinn-Verhältnis** n price/earnings ratio (P/E ratio)
**Kurszettel** m stock list, list of quotations
**kurze Sicht, auf** on a short-term basis
**kürzen** cut, shorten
**kurzfristig** short-term, at short notice
**kurzfristige Verbindlichkeiten** fpl current liabilities
**Kürzung** f cut(back), reduction, retrenchment

## L

**Ladeliste** f manifest
**laden** load
**Ladendieb[in]** shoplifter
**Ladendiebstahl** m shoplifting
**Ladenpreis** m retail price
**Ladenschluß** m closing time
**Ladentisch** m counter
**Laderaum** m hold *(on ship)*
**Ladung** f cargo; shipment
**Lage** f situation
**Lagebericht** m progress report
**Lager** n warehouse, store, storeroom
**Lager-** (cpd) storage
**Lager halten, auf** carry/stock *(goods)*
**Lagerbestand** m stock *(of goods)*
**Lagerbestände flüssigmachen** liquidate stock
**Lagerfähigkeit** f eines Produktes shelf life of a product
**Lagerhaltungskontrolle** f inventory control
**lagern** store, warehouse, keep in a warehouse
**Lagerraum** m storeroom
**Lagersteuerung** f stock control
**Lagerung** f storage, warehousing
**Land** n land, country; state
**landesweit** nationwide
**langfristig** long-term

**langfristiger Wechsel** long-dated bill
**Lastschriftanzeige** f debit note
**laufen** run, be in force
**laufend** (adj) running
**laufendes Konto** current account
**Laufzeit** f term *(of validity)*
**laut Avis/laut Versandanzeige** as per advice
**laut Rechnung** as per invoice
**Leasinggeber[in]** lessor
**Leasingnehmer[in]** lessee
**Lebenshaltungskosten** pl cost of living
**Lebenslauf** m curriculum vitae/resumé
**Lebensversicherungspolice** f assurance policy
**leer** empty
**Leerpackung** f dummy pack
**Lehrling** m trainee
**leihen** lend, advance; borrow, hire
**Leihgebühr** f hire/rental charge
**leistungsfähig** capable, efficient
**Leistungsfähigkeit** f effectiveness, efficiency
**Leistungszulage** f merit award, productivity bonus
**leiten** run, manage, direct
**leitende(r) Angestellte(r)** senior manager/executive
**leitendes Personal** managerial staff, key personnel
**Leiter[in] der Finanzabteilung** finance director
**Leiter[in] des Finanzamtes** tax inspector
**Leitung** f control, management, direction; *(telephone)* line
**Leitzins** m bank base rate
**letzte Mahnung/Zahlungsaufforderung** final demand
**letzter Termin** closing date
**Liefer-** (cpd) delivery
**Lieferant** m supplier
**liefern** deliver, supply
**Lieferung** f delivery *(of goods)*; consignment, delivery
**Lieferung frei Bestimmungsort** free delivery
**Linienflug** m scheduled flight
**Liste** f list, catalogue/catalog
**Listenpreis** m list price
**Lockartikel** m loss-leader

**Lohn** m wage, pay
**Lohn-** (cpd) wage, pay
**Lohnkosten** pl labour/labor costs
**Lohnsteuer** f (earned) income tax
**Los** n batch (of products),
   lot (auction)
**Löschungskosten** pl **und**
   **Löschungszölle** mpl landing charges
**lose** loose
**lösen** solve (problem);
   terminate (agreement)
**Lösung** f solution; termination
**Luftfracht** f air freight
**Luftfracht befördern, als**
   airfreight (v)
**Luftpost** f airmail
**Luftpost schicken, per** airmail (v)

## M

**Magazin** n store; magazine
**Maklergebühr** f
   (broker's) commission
**Mangel** m shortage; fault, defect
**Manifest** n manifest; manifesto
**Marge** f (profit) margin
**Marke** f brand, make
**Markenname** m brand name
**Markentreue** f brand loyalty
**Marketing-** (cpd) marketing
**Markt-** (cpd) market
**Marktdurchdringung** f
   market penetration
**Marktentwicklung** f market trend
**Marktforschung** f market research
**Marktkräfte** fpl market forces
**Marktlücke** f gap in the market
**Maschinen** fpl plant, machinery
**Maschinist[in]** operator, machinist
**mäßig** moderate (adj)
**Maßstab** m benchmark,
   standard, yardstick
**materielle Vermögenswerte** mpl
   tangible assets
**Maut** f toll
**mehrfach** multiple (adj)
**Mehrheit** f majority
**Mehrheitsaktionär[in]**
   majority shareholder
**Mehrwertsteuer** f **(MwSt.)** value
   added tax
**Meinungsumfrage** f opinion poll

**Meinungsverschiedenheit** f
   misunderstanding
**melden** report (for); answer (phone)
**Menge** f quantity
**Mengeneinkauf** m bulk buying
**Mengenrabatt** m quantity/
   volume discount
**Miete** f rent, rental
**mieten** hire, lease, rent
**Mieter[in]** lessee, tenant
**Mietkauf** m hire purchase
**Mietverhältnis** n tenancy
**Mietvertrag** m lease n,
   rental agreement
**Mietvertragsverlängerung** f renewal
   of a lease
**Milliarde** f thousand million,
   (US) billion
**Minderheit** f minority
**Minderheitsaktionär[in]**
   minority shareholder
**minderwertige Qualität** poor quality
**Mindestbetrag** m
   minimum amount
**Mindestlohn, (garantierter)**
   guaranteed minimum wage
**Mindestnachbestellung** f
   reorder level
**Mindestpreis, (garantierter)**
   intervention price (in EU)
**Mineralöl** n oil (petroleum)
**Minusbetrag** m deficit
**mißlingen** fall through, fail
**Mißverständnis** n misunderstanding
**Mitarbeit** f co-operation
**Mitarbeiter[in]** assistant,
   colleague, employee
**Mitbewerber[in]** competitor
**mitteilen** notify, inform
**Mitteilung** f note, message,
   memo; notification
**Mittel** pl means, resources, funds;
   means, way; average, mean
**mittelfristig** medium-term
**mittelgroß; mittelständisch**
   medium-sized
**Mittelständler** m
   middle-sized business
**Mittelwert** m mean, average
**Mitunterzeichner[in]** joint signatory
**monatlich** monthly
**monopolistischer Absatzmarkt**
   captive market

## mündliche Vereinbarung

**mündliche Vereinbarung**
   verbal agreement
**Münze** f coin
**Münzfernsprecher** m pay phone
**Muster** n swatch, sample, pattern
**Mustervertrag** m model agreement,
   standard contract
**Muttergesellschaft** f
   parent company
**Mutterschaftsurlaub** m maternity leave
**MwSt. (Mehrwertsteuer)** f VAT
   (value added tax)

## N

**nachbestellen** reorder, repeat
   an order
**Nachbestellung** f reorder,
   repeat order
**Nachfrage** f demand
**Nachfrage stillen/befriedigen** satisfy
   a demand
**nachgehen** follow up
**nachlassen** knock down/
   reduce (price)
**nachmachen** copy, imitate; forge
**Nachnahme, per** cash on delivery
**nachrangiger (Konkurs-)Gläubiger**
   deferred creditor
**Nachricht** f message, (piece of) news
**Nachtrag** m rider, endorsement;
   supplement, addendum; codicil
**natürlicher Arbeitskräfteabgang**
   natural wastage
**Naturschätze** pl natural resources
**Nebenausgaben** fpl incidental
   expenses, incidentals
**Nebenbeschäftigung** f sideline,
   spare-time job
**Nebenkasse** f petty cash
**Nebenkosten** pl extra
   charges, extras
**Nebenprodukt** n by-product, spinoff
**nebensächlich** subsidiary,
   secondary, minor
**Nebensaison** f off-/low season
**Nennwert** m face/nominal value, par
   value; denomination
**Netto-** (cpd) net
**Nettoverdienst** m net earnings,
   take-home pay
**Neuordnung** f reorganization

**Nichtbezahlen (einer Verbindlichkeit)**
   non-payment
**Nichterfüllung** f default
**nichtig** null, void, not valid
**niedriger Tarif** cheap rate
**Niedrigpreis** m low/cut price
**Niedrigstpreise** mpl rock-
   bottom prices
**Nische** f niche
**Niveau** n level
**nominelle Gebühr** token charge
**Nominierte(r)** nominee
**Norm** f standard
**normale Abnutzungserschei-
   nungen** fpl wear and tear
**normen** standardize
**Notar[in]** notary public
**Notenbank** f central bank
**Notiz** f memo, note
**Notverkauf** m distress/forced sale
**numerieren** number
**Nutznießer[in]** beneficiary
**Nutzung** f use, utilization

## O

**oberste Preisgrenze** price ceiling
**Obligation** f bond, debenture
**öffentlich** (adj) public
**Öffentlichkeitsarbeit** f
   public relations
**offiziell** official, formal
**Öffnungszeit** f opening time
**ohne Steuer** exclusive of tax
**operativer Gewinn**
   operating profit
**ordentliche Jahreshauptversamm-
   lung** annual general meeting
**Orderpapier** n (bank) order
**Ordnung bringen, in** put in order,
   sort out, clear up
**Organigramm** n/**Organisationsplan** m organization chart
**ortsansässige Arbeitskräfte** fpl local
   labour/labor
**Ortsgespräch** n local call
**Ortsnetzkennzahl** f area/
   dialling code

## P

**Pacht** f lease; rent, rental
**pachten** rent, lease

**Pächter[in]** tenant, lessee
**Pachtverhältnis** n tenancy
**Pachtvertrag** m lease
**packen, fertig**
  prepack, prepackage (v)
**Packer[in]** packer
**Packliste** f packing list
**Papierkram** m paperwork
**Papierkrieg** m red tape
**Pappkarton** m cardboard box
**Paragraph** n paragraph,
  article, section
**paraphieren** initial
**Patent angemeldet, zum** patent
  pending/applied for
**Patentverletzung** f infringement
  of patent
**Pauschalangebot** n package deal
**Pauschalbetrag** m lump sum
**Pauschale** f inclusive charge, flat rate
**Pauschalpreis** m all-in price
**pendeln** commute (travel)
**Pendler[in]** commuter
**Pension** f pension;
  retirement; guesthouse
**Pension gehen, in** retire
**Pensionsalter** n retirement age
**Peripheriegeräte** npl peripherals
**Personal** n personnel
**Personal einstellen** hire staff
**Personalbestand** m manpower,
  number of staff, personnel
**Personalchef[in]/Personalleiter[in]**
  personnel manager
**Personalstärke** f manning levels
**persönliches Interesse**
  vested interest
**Pfandrecht** n lien
**Pfund** n pound
**Platte** f disk
**Platz** m room, space; seat;
  place, site
**platzen** bounce (cheque/check)
**Pleite** f bankruptcy, collapse,
  business failure
**Pleite sein, eine** flop (v), be a flop
**Politik** f policy; politics
**Port** m (computer) port
**Porto** n postage
**Porto bezahlt** postage paid
**portofrei** post free
**Portokasse** f petty cash (box)
**Position** f position, job; entry, item

**Postanweisung** f money/
  postal order
**Postausgang** m outgoing mail
**Posten** m post, job; item, entry;
  quantity, lot
**Postfach** n P.O. box
**Postgebühren** fpl postal charges
**postlagernd** poste restante
**Postleitzahl** f postcode, zip code
**Postversand** m mail-order
**Postwurfsendung** f direct mail,
  mail shot
**praktisch** practical,
  convenient, handy
**Prämie** f bonus, premium
**Prämienzuschlag** m
  additional premium
**Präsentationsstand** m display stand
**Präsident[in]** president, chairman
**Preis** m price, rate
**Preis ab Lager** price ex warehouse
**Preis ab Werk** factory price, price
  ex works
**Preis bei Inzahlungnahme** trade-
  in price
**Preis nach Abzug des Rabatts**
  discount price
**Preisabsprache** f price fixing,
  common pricing
**Preisangebot** n quotation/quote
**Preisangebot machen, ein** quote (v)
**Preisbindung** f price control
**preisgünstig** good value
  (for money)
**Preis-** (cpd) price
**Preisnachlaß** m
  price reduction, discount
**preiswert** cheap, good value
**Pressemitteilung/Presseverlaut-
  barung** f press release
**privat** private
**Privatisierung** f privatization
**pro Stunde/Tag/Woche/Jahr** per
  hour/day/week/year
**Pro-forma-Rechnung** f pro
  forma (invoice)
**Probe, auf** on approval
**Probebilanz** f trial balance
**Probeentnahme** f sampling (testing)
**Probestück** n trial sample
**Problembereich** m problem area
**Produktgestaltung** f product design
**Produktionsleistung** f output

## Produktionsleiter

**Produktionsleiter[in]**
 production manager
**Produktionsmittel** *pl* capital
 equipment, means of production
**Produktionsziel** *n* production target
**Produktmix** *m*/**Produktpalette** *f*
 product mix/range
**Produktwerbung** *f*
 product advertising
**Prognose** *f* forecast
**prognostizieren** forecast
**Programm** *n* programme, agenda,
 timetable; computer program
**Projektleiter[in]** project manager
**prolongieren** extend *(make longer)*,
 renew *(bill of exchange)*
**prompte Bedienung** *f*/**prompter
 Service** *m* prompt service
**Prospekt** *m* prospectus;
 pamphlet, brochure
**Protokoll** *n*
 record/minutes *(of meeting)*
**Protokoll nehmen/protokollieren, zu**
 minute, record (v)
**Provenienz** *f* origin
**Provenienzzertifikat** *n* certificate
 of origin
**Provision** *f* commission
**Provisionsvertreter[in]**
 commission rep
**Prozentsatz** *m* percentage rate
**prozentualer Rabatt**
 percentage discount
**Prozeß** *m*
 legal proceedings, lawsuit
**prüfen** examine, inspect, test; audit
**Prüfung** *f* examination,
 test; inspection
**Punkt** *m* point; item *(on agenda)*
**pünktlich** on time
**pünktliche Zahlung** prompt payment

## Q

**qualifiziert** qualified, skilled
**Quartal** *n* quarter *(three months)*
**quartalsweise** quarterly (adj)
**Quellensteuer** *f* tax deducted
 at source
**Quittung** *f* receipt *(piece of paper)*
**Quittungsduplikat** *n* duplicate
 (of a) receipt
**Quote** *f* quota

## R

**Rabatt** *m* discount
**Rabatt gewähren** discount (v)
**Rate** *f* instalment; rate
**raten** advise, recommend; guess
**rationell** efficient; economical
**räumen** clear, vacate
**Räumlichkeiten** *fpl* premises
**Räumungsverkauf** *m*
 (clearance) sale
**Raumverteilungsplan** *m* floor plan
**Realeinkommen** *n* real income
**realisierbare Vermögenswerte** *mpl*
 realizable assets
**Reallohn** *m* real wages
**Rechenschaft** *f* **ablegen** account for
**Rechner** *m* computer; calculator
**Rechnung** *f* account, bill, invoice
**Rechnung ausstellen** invoice (v)
**Rechnung stellen, einen Kauf in**
 charge a purchase
**Rechnungsjahr** *n* financial year
**Recht** *n* right *(legal title)*
**rechtlich** legal *(referring to law)*
**rechtliche Stellung** legal status
**rechtmäßige(r) Besitzer[in]**
 rightful owner
**Rechtsanwalt[-in]** lawyer
**Rechtsberatung** *f* legal advice
**rechtsgültig** valid
**rechtshängig** sub judice
**Rechtsmittel** *n* appeal *(against
 a decision)*
**Rechtsmittel einlegen** appeal/lodge
 an appeal *(against a decision)*
**Rechtsposition** *f* legal status
**reduzieren** cut, reduce
**Referenz** *f*
 (letter of) reference; referee
**Regel** *f* rule
**regelmäßig** regular
**regeln** regulate *(by law)*; sort
 out, settle
**Register** *n* register; index
**Registratur** *f* registration; registry;
 filing cabinet
**Reinertrag** *m* net yield
**Reinfall** *m* flop
**Reingewinn** *m* clear/net profit
**Reinvermögen** *n* net assets/worth
**Reiseleiter[in]** courier *(guide)*,
 tour leader

**reizen** appeal to, attract
**Reklamation** f complaint
**Reklamations-** (cpd) complaints
**Reklame** f advertisement; publicity
**Reklame machen** promote, advertise, publicize
**Rekordverluste** mpl record losses
**Rendite** f yield (on investment)
**rentabel** profitable, viable
**Rentabilitätsmessung** f measurement of profitability
**Rente** f pension
**Rente gehen, in** retire (from job)
**Rentenalter** n retirement age
**Rest** m rest/remainder (things left)
**Restbetrag** m balance
**Restdividende** f final dividend
**Retourwaren** fpl returns (unsold goods)
**Revision** f audit
**Revisor[in]** n auditor
**R-Gespräch** n reverse charge call, collect call
**richtig** right, correct
**Richtlinien** fpl guidelines
**Risiko** n risk
**Risiko (des) Käufers, auf** caveat emptor
**Risikokapital** n risk/venture capital
**Rohgewicht** n gross weight
**Rohstoffe** mpl raw materials
**rückdatieren** backdate
**Rückerstattung** f rebate, refund
**Rückgabe** f return, restitution
**Rückgang** m drop, decline, fall
**rückgängig machen** call off, revoke, cancel
**Rückkaufwert** m surrender value
**Rückkehr** f return (going back)
**Rücklage** f reserve(s)
**Rückschlag** m setback, reverse
**Rückstand** m backlog; arrears
**Rückstand geraten, in** fall behind, be late
**Rücktrittsklausel** f cancellation/escape clause
**Rückvergütung** f refund, rebate
**rückzahlbar** repayable
**Rufnummer** f telephone number
**Ruhegehalt** n pension
**Ruhestand treten, in den** retire (from one's job)
**ruhig** calm, quiet, slack

**ruinieren** ruin, bankrupt
**Rumpfbelegschaft** f skeleton staff
**Rundschreiben** n circular, mail shot, mailing shot

# S

**Sachbearbeiter[in]** specialist, person in charge
**Sache** f affair, business, matter
**sachkundig** experienced, (well-) informed
**sachlich** objective (adj)
**Sachverständige(r)** expert; surveyor
**saisonbedingt** (adj) seasonal
**Saldo** m balance
**sättigen, den Markt** saturate the market
**Satz** m rate
**säumige(r) Schuldner[in]** defaulter
**säumiger Zahler** slow payer
**Schaden** m damage
**Schadenersatz** m damages, compensation for damage
**Schadenersatzklage** f action for damages
**Schadenfeststellung** f assessment of damages
**Schadenfreiheitsrabatt** m no-claims bonus
**schadhaft** defective, faulty
**schaffen** achieve, manage; create, establish
**Schalterbeamte(r) [-beamtin]** booking clerk
**Schalterstunden** pl hours of business, opening hours
**scharfer Wettbewerb** m keen/stiff competition
**Schattenwirtschaft** f black economy
**schätzen** assess, value; estimate, calculate; appreciate, value
**Schätzung** f estimate, calculation; valuation, assessment, rating
**Schaufenster** n shop window
**Schaupackung** f dummy pack
**Scheck** m cheque/check
**Scheckheft** n cheque/check book
**Schein** m banknote; ticket; certificate
**scheitern** fail, break down
**Scheitern** n failure, breakdown
**schenken** give (as gift)

## Schicht

**Schicht** f shift *(team of workers)*; layer, echelon
**Schichtarbeit** f shift work
**schicken** dispatch, send
**Schild** n sign; tag, ticket
**Schleuderpreise** mpl rock-bottom prices
**Schlichtungskommission** f arbitration board/tribunal
**schließen** close, close down, conclude; compromise; fill *(a gap)*
**Schloß** n lock
**Schluß-** (cpd) closing
**Schlußdividende** f final dividend; terminal bonus
**schlüsselfertiges Projekt** turnkey operation
**Schlüssel-** (cpd) key
**Schlußnotierung** closing price/quotation
**schmieren** bribe
**Schmiergeld** n bribe
**Schnäppchen** n bargain
**Schnittstelle** f interface
**Schnitzer** m slip, blunder
**Schreibarbeit** f paperwork, clerical work
**Schreibfehler** m clerical error
**schriftlich abfassen** put in writing
**schriftliche Vereinbarung** written agreement
**Schriftverkehr** m correspondence
**schrittweise einführen** phase in
**Schuld** f debt; fault
**schulden** owe
**Schulden** fpl debts, liabilities
**Schulden einziehen/eintreiben** collect a debt
**Schulden machen/in Schulden geraten** get/run into debt
**Schuldeneintreibung** f debt collection
**Schuldner[in]** debtor
**Schuldschein** m promissory note, IOU
**Schuldverschreibung** f debenture
**Schutz** m protection
**schützen** protect, safeguard
**schwanken** fluctuate
**Schwankung** f fluctuation
**schwarze Liste setzen, auf die** blacklist (v)
**Schwarzmarkt** m black market

**schwebend** pending
**Schwellenpreis** m threshold price
**Schwemme** f glut
**Schwertransporter** m heavy goods vehicle
**Schwund** m wastage, shrinkage
**See-** (cpd) maritime; marine
**selbständig** self-employed, independent
**Selbstkostenpreis** m cost price
**Selbstläufer** m fast-selling item
**Sendung** f shipment, consignment; broadcast, programme
**senken** cut/mark down/reduce *(prices)*
**Senkung** f cut, reduction
**Serie** f batch *(of products)*, series
**serienmäßige Herstellung** mass production
**seriös** serious, reliable, reputable
**sichere Kapitalanlage** safe investment
**Sicherheit** f reliability; safety
**Sicherheit des Arbeitsplatzes** job security, security of employment
**Sicherheitsvorkehrungen** fpl safety precautions
**Sicherheitsvorschriften** fpl safety regulations
**sichern** safeguard, back up, save *(computer file)*
**sichern, sich finanzielle Mittel** secure funds
**Sicherungskopie** f backup copy
**sichtbarer Handel** visible trade
**Sitz** m headquarters, base
**Sitzung** f meeting
**Skonto** m/n cash discount
**sofortige Bezahlung** spot cash
**Sofortkredit** m instant credit
**Soll** n debit
**Sollbuchung** f debit entry
**Sollzinsen** mpl interest charges
**Sommerschlußverkauf** m summer sale(s)
**Sonderangebot** n special offer
**Sonderausgaben** fpl extras
**Sonderzubehör** npl optional extras
**Sorge** f concern, worry
**Sortiment** n product range
**Sozialhilfe** f social security
**Sozius** m partner
**sparen** save *(money)*

**Sparkonto** n deposit/savings account
**sparsam** economical, thrifty
**sparsam wirtschaften** economize
**Sparsamkeit** f economy (saving)
**spät** late (adv)
**Spediteur** m shipper, carrier, haulier
**Spedition** f carrier, freight forwarder; removal company
**Speicher** m store, memory (on computer)
**sperren** stop (a cheque/check)
**Spesenkonto** n/**Spesenrechnung** f expense account
**spezifizierte Rechnung** detailed account
**Spitzenqualität** f top quality
**Spitzenumsätze** mpl record sales
**Sponsern** n sponsorship
**Spontankäufer[in]** impulse buyer
**Staatsanleihen** fpl government bonds
**Staatsanwalt[-in]** prosecution counsel
**Staatsfinanzen** pl public finance(s)
**Stabdiagramm** n bar chart
**stabile Währung** stable currency
**Stammaktien** fpl equities, ordinary shares
**Stammkunde [-kundin]** regular/long-standing customer
**Stand** m level, position; stand (at exhibition)
**Stand, auf dem neusten** up to date
**Stand bringen, auf den neuesten** update (v)
**Standardgröße** f regular/stock size
**ständig** continual(ly); regular (income)
**Standort** m base, site
**Stange** f carton, box
**stapeln** batch, stack, pile up
**stattfinden** take place
**Stecker** m electric plug
**steigen** increase, rise, climb, gain
**Stelle** f job, employment; place, spot
**Stellenangebote** npl job vacancies, situations vacant
**Stellenbeschreibung** f job description
**Stellung** f position, job; status
**stellvertretende(r) Leiter[in]** acting/assistant manager

**Stellvertreter[in]** proxy, representative; deputy, assistant
**Stempelgebühr** f stamp duty
**stetig** steady, continuous
**Steuer** f tax, duty, levy
**Steuer-** (cpd) tax
**Steuer belegen, mit einer** tax (v)
**Steuerbegünstigung** f tax concession/shelter
**Steuerbescheid** m (notice of) tax assessment
**Steuererklärung** f tax return/declaration
**steuerfrei** free of tax, tax-free
**Steuerhinterziehung** f tax evasion
**steuerlich absetzbar/abzugsfähig** tax-deductible
**Steueroase** f tax haven
**steuerpflichtiges Einkommen** taxable income
**Steuerschuld** f back tax
**Stichprobe** f random check/sample
**Stichtag** m deadline
**stille Reserven** fpl hidden reserves
**stille(r) Teilhaber[in]** sleeping partner
**stillegen** close/shut down
**stillschweigende Genehmigung** tacit approval
**Stillstand** m standstill, deadlock
**Stock** m floor (level)
**Stockung** f stoppage, hold-up, delay
**stoppen** stop, block, freeze
**stornieren** cancel/contra (an entry)
**Störung** f disturbance, disruption; defect
**Stoßzeit** f peak period, rush hour
**Strafe belegen, mit einer** penalize
**Strafklausel** f penalty clause
**Strafverteidiger[in]** defence counsel
**streben nach** strive for, aspire to
**streichen** cut, cancel; cross off, delete
**Streik** m strike
**streiken** strike
**Streikende(r)** striker
**Strichkode** m bar code
**Stückkosten** pl unit cost(s)
**Stücklohnsatz** m piece rate
**Stückpreis** m unit price
**stufen** grade, graduate, stagger
**Stundenlohn** m hourly rate/wage
**stützen, Preise** peg prices

## Stützungspreis

**Stützungspreis** m support price
**Substanzwert** m asset value
**Subunternehmer** m subcontractor
**Subunternehmervertrag** m
   subcontract
**Subvention** f subsidy, subvention
**subventionieren** subsidize

## T

**Tageskurs** m current rate of
   exchange; current price (of shares)
**Tagesordnung** f agenda
**Tarif** m tariff, rate, charge
**Tarifverhandlungen** fpl
   wage negotiations
**Taste** f key (on keyboard)
**tätig werden** take action
**Tausch** m/**Tauschgeschäft** n
   exchange, swap, barter
**tauschen/Tauschhandel treiben**
   exchange, swap, barter (v)
**Teil** m part, piece; proportion, share
**teilabschreiben** write down (assets)
**teilen, (sich)** divide, share
**Teilhaber[in]** associate, partner
**Teilzahlung** f partial payment
**Teilzahlungskauf** m hire purchase
**Teilzeitarbeit** f/**Teilzeitbeschäfti-
   gung** f part-time work/employment
**Telefonleitung** f telephone line
**Telefonzentrale** f telephone
   switchboard; telephone exchange
**Termin** m appointment
**Termin, (letzter)** deadline
**Termin kaufen/verkaufen, auf**
   buy/sell forward
**Termineinlage** f time/term deposit
**Terminjäger** m progress chaser
**Terminkurs** m forward rate,
   futures price
**Terminlieferung** f future delivery
**Terminmarkt** m forward/
   futures market
**teuer** dear, expensive, highly-priced
**Textverarbeitung** f word-processing
**Thema** n subject, matter, topic
**tilgen** pay off, amortize, redeem
**Tilgung** f repayment, amortization,
   redemption (of loan)
**Tilgungstermin** m redemption date
**Tochtergesellschaft** f subsidiary
**Totalverlust** m dead/total loss

**tragbar** portable
**tragen** bear/defray (costs)
**Transport** m transport, carriage
**Transportflugzeug** n freight/
   cargo plane
**Transportkosten** pl carriage,
   haulage/freight costs
**Transportunternehmen** n
   carrier/haulage firm,
   shipping company
**Trassant** m drawer (cheque/check)
**Trassat** m drawee
**Tratte** f draft, bill of exchange
**treffen (mit), sich** hit, affect;
   meet (so.)
**Tresen** m counter
**Tresor** m safe n; strongroom,
   bank vault
**Trinkgeld geben** tip, give a tip
**tüchtig** efficient, capable, competent

## U

**Überbestand** m
   excess stock, overstocks
**Überbringer[in]** bearer
**Übereinkunft** f
   understanding, arrangement
**übereinstimmen (mit)**
   agree/correspond (with)
**überfällig** overdue
**überflüssig** redundant, superfluous
**übergeben** hand over
**übergehen, in andere Hände**
   change hands
**Übergewicht** n overweight;
   excess baggage
**Übergröße** f outsize
**Überhang** m surplus, glut
**übermäßig** excessive
**Übernahme** f acquisition, takeover;
   assumption (of responsibility)
**Übernahmeangebot** n takeover bid
**Übernahmeobjekt** n takeover target
**übernehmen** take over (from so.);
   bear/defray (costs)
**übernehmen, für etwas Haftung**
   accept liability for something
**überprüfen** check, inspect, verify
**Überprüfung** f check,
   inspection, verification
**Überschlag** m estimate,
   rough calculation

**überschreiten**
exceed, overrun, overspend

**überschüssige Warenbestände veräußern** dispose of excess stock

**Überschuß** m excess, surplus

**Überseehandel** m overseas trade

**übersetzen** translate

**Übersetzer[in]** translator

**Übersetzung** f translation

**Überstunden** fpl overtime

**übertragbar** transferable

**übertragbares Wertpapier** negotiable instrument

**übertragen** carry forward/ over; transfer

**übertragener Saldo** balance carried over/forward

**überwachen** monitor, supervise

**Überwachung** f control, supervision

**Überweisung** f remittance, transfer

**überzählig** surplus, spare

**Überziehungskredit** m advance on account; overdraft facility

**überzogenes Konto** overdrawn account

**übliche Satz** going rate

**übrigbleiben** remain, be left

**Ultimoabrechnung** f month-end accounts

**umgehend** immediate(ly), prompt(ly)

**Umlauf** m circulation; circular (letter)

**Umlaufvermögen** n current assets

**Umrechnungskurs** m conversion price/rate

**Umsatz** m turnover, sales

**Umsatz, erwarteter** projected turnover

**umsatzloses Konto** dead account

**Umsatzrückgang** m drop in turnover

**umschulden** refinance, reschedule, roll over (a debt)

**umschulen** retrain

**umsehen, sich** shop around

**umsetzen** turn over (make sales)

**umsonst** gratis, free (of charge)

**Umstrukturierung** f restructuring, reorganization

**umtauschen** change, convert; exchange

**unabhängig** independent; self-sufficient

**unabhängige Revision** external audit

**unabhängiges Unternehmen** independent company

**unbesetzt** vacant, unoccupied; free

**unbewohnt** unoccupied, vacant

**unbezahlt** unpaid, outstanding

**uneinbringliche Forderung** bad/irrecoverable debt

**unerledigte Aufträge** mpl back/outstanding orders

**unfähig** incapable, unable; incompetent, inefficient

**unfrei** unfranked

**ungeachtet** despite, regardless of

**ungefähr** approximate(ly)

**ungelernte Arbeitskraft** unskilled worker, manual labourer/ laborer

**ungenau** inaccurate, inexact

**ungeprüfte Geschäftsbücher** npl unaudited accounts

**ungesetzlich** illegal

**ungültig** invalid, null, void

**ungültig erklären, für** void (v), invalidate

**unkündbare Anleihe** irredeemable bond

**unlauterer Wettbewerb** unfair competition

**unmittelbar** direct(ly), immediate(ly)

**Unregelmäßigkeiten** fpl irregularities

**unsichtbar** invisible

**unter Preis verkaufen** undersell

**unterbewerteter Vermögenswert** undervalued/hidden asset

**unterbieten, einen Konkurrenten** undersell/undercut a rival

**Unterhändler[in]** negotiator, mediator

**Unterlagen** pl records, documentation, papers

**unterliegen** liable to, subject to

**Untermiete haben, in** sublease (v)

**Unternehmen** n company, firm, business

**unternehmen, etwas** take action

**Unternehmensbereich** m division (part of a company)

**Unternehmensgewinne** mpl corporate profits

**Unternehmensleitung** f management, managers

## Unternehmensplan

**Unternehmensplan** *m*
corporate plan
**Unternehmensspitze** *f*
top management
**Unternehmenszusammenschluß** *m*
merger
**Unternehmer[in]** entrepreneur;
employer, industrialist
**unternehmerisch** entrepreneurial
**Unternehmertum** *n*
enterprise; employers
**unterschreiben** sign
**Unterschrift** *f* signature
**unterstehen, jdm**
be subordinate to/report to so.
**unterstellt sein, jdm** be
answerable/responsible to so.
**unterstützen** support, help, assist
**untersuchen** examine, inspect
**Untersuchung** *f*
examination, inspection
**untervermieten** sublet, sublease
**Untervermietung** *f* sublease
**Untervertrag** *m* subcontract
**unterworfen** liable to, subject to
**unterzeichnen** sign
**Unterzeichner** *m* signatory
**Unterzeichnete(r)** (the) undersigned
**unwiderrufliches Akkreditiv**
irrevocable letter of credit
**unzeitgemäß** outmoded, out of date
**Urkunde** *f*
deed, document, certificate
**Ursprungsland** *n* country of origin
**Urteilsschuldner[in]**
judgment debtor

## V

**Verabredung** *f*
appointment, engagement
**veraltet** obsolete, out of date
**Veranlagung** *f* assessment *(of tax)*
**veranschlagen** estimate, budget
**verantworten, sich** account for
**verantwortlich für** responsible (for)
**Verantwortlichkeit** *f/*
**Verantwortung** *f* responsibility
**Veräußerung** *f* disposal
**Veräußerungsgewinn** *m*
capital gains
**verbieten** ban, prohibit
**verbindlich** compulsory, binding

**verbindliche Gebührenordnung**
fixed scale of charges
**Verbindlichkeiten** *fpl* accounts
payable; liabilities
**Verbindung** *f* connection, contact;
telephone line
**Verbindung setzen mit, sich in**
contact (v)
**Verbindungen** *fpl* communications
**Verbot** *n* ban
**Verbraucher[in]** consumer
**Verbraucher-** (cpd) consumer
**Verbrauchssteuer** *f* excise duty;
purchase tax
**verbringen** spend *(time)*
**verbunden** associated, affiliated
**verbürgen, sich** guarantee, vouch for
**verderbliche Waren** *fpl/***verderbliche
Fracht** *f* perishable goods/cargo
**verdienen** earn
**verdoppeln** double
**vereinbaren** agree, arrange
**vereinbarter Preis** agreed price
**Vereinbarung** *f*
agreement, arrangement
**Verfahrensregeln** *fpl* code
of practice
**Verfall** *m* expiry, forfeiture; maturity
date *(of bill)*
**verfallen** lapse, expire
**Verfallsdatum** *n* expiry/use-by date
**Verfolgung, strafrechtliche**
prosecution *(legal action)*
**verfügbar, (nicht)** (un)available
**Verfügbarkeit** *f* availability
**Verfügung** *f* disposal; order, decree
**vergeben, einen Auftrag an jdn**
award a contract to someone
**Vergleich** *m* comparison;
arrangement, settlement
**vergleichbar** comparable
**vergleichen mit** compare with
**vergrößern** enlarge, expand
**vergüten** pay, remunerate;
reimburse, compensate
**Vergütung** *f* payment, remuneration;
compensation, indemnity
**Verhältnis** *n*
proportion, ratio; relationship
**verhandeln** negotiate
**Verhandlung** *f* negotiation
**Verhandlungen abbrechen**
break off negotiations

**Verhandlungen wiederaufnehmen**
resume negotiations
**Verhandlungsführer[in]** negotiator
**Verhandlungsposition** f
bargaining position
**verhängen, ein Embargo** embargo
**Verjährungsfrist** f
statute of limitations
**Verkauf** m sale, selling
**verkaufen** sell
**verkaufen, zu** for sale
**Verkäufer[in]** shop assistant;
seller, vendor
**verkäuflich** saleable, sellable
**Verkaufs-** (cpd) sales
**Verkaufsförderung** f merchandizing,
sales promotion
**Verkaufsstelle** f point of sale
**Verkehrsverbindungen** fpl
communications
**verklagen** sue, take legal action
**Verladekosten** pl shipping
charges/costs
**verlangen** ask, demand
**verlängern** extend, prolong; renew
(a lease)
**Verlängerung** f extension, renewal
**verleihen** lend; hire, rent (out)
**Verleiher** m lender, hire firm
**verletzen** infringe (a patent)
**verlieren** lose
**verlieren, an Wert** depreciate,
lose value
**verlockendes Gehalt**
attractive salary
**Verlust** m loss
**Verlustfaktor** m downside factor
**vermarkten** market/merchandize
(a product)
**Vermarktung** f
marketing, merchandizing
**vermieten** lease/let (v) (of landlord)
**Vermieter[in]**
lessor; landlord, landlady
**vermindern, sich** decrease
**Verminderung** f decrease, reduction
**vermitteln, in einem Streitfall**
arbitrate in a dispute
**Vermittler[in]**
intermediary, mediator
**Vermögenswerte realisieren/**
**veräußern** realize assets
**vernetzen** network (computers)

**veröffentlichen** release, publish
**Verordnungen** fpl regulations
**verpachten** lease, rent out
**Verpächter[in]** lessor
**verpacken** pack, package
**Verpackung** f packing, packaging
**verpassen** miss
**verpflichten, sich vertraglich**
contract
**Verpflichtung** f
obligation, commitment
**Verpflichtungen** fpl responsibilities
**verringern**
decrease, reduce, scale down
**Versagen** n failure
**Versand** m dispatch,
consignment, shipment
**Versandanweisungen** fpl
forwarding/shipping instructions
**Versandanzeige** f advice note
**Versandhauskatalog** m mail-order
catalogue/catlog
**Versandkosten** pl transport charges,
shipping costs
**Versandschein** m dispatch note
**Versäumnis** n default n; omission
**verschicken** send, dispatch
**verschieben** postpone, hold over,
put back
**verschieden** different,
miscellaneous, sundry
**Verschiedenes** n sundries; any
other business
**verschiffen** ship
**Verschiffung** f shipping, shipment
**Verschleiß** m wear (and tear)
**verschlossene Angebote** npl
sealed tenders
**verschulden, sich** get into debt
**verschuldet** indebted
**verschwenden** waste, squander
**Versehen** n slip, mistake
**versenden** send, dispatch, ship
**Versetzung** f transfer
**Versicherer** m insurer, underwriter
**Versicherung** f insurance
**Versicherung abschließen/**
**versichern** insure
**Versicherungs-** (cpd) insurance
**Versicherungsbeitrag** m
insurance premium
**Versicherungsmakler[in]**
insurance broker

## Versicherungspolice

**Versicherungspolice** f
insurance policy
**Versicherungsträger** m
insurer, underwriter
**versorgen** supply, provide, furnish
**Versorgung** f supply
**verspätet** late, delayed
**verstaatlichte Industrie**
nationalized industry
**verständigen, sich** communicate;
come to an understanding
**verständlich** clear, understandable
**versteigern** auction
**Versteigerung** f auction
**versteuert** tax paid
**Versuchsprojekt** n pilot scheme
**versuchsweise** on trial, on approval
**vertagen** postpone, adjourn
**Vertagung** f
postponement, adjournment
**Verteiler** m distributor
**Verteilung** f distribution
**Vertrag** m contract, agreement
**Vertrag, durch** contractually,
by contract
**Vertrag abschließen, einen**
contract (v), enter into a contract
**vertraglich** contractual(ly)
**vertraglich vereinbaren**
covenant (v), stipulate
**vertraglich verpflichtet**
under contract
**Vertragsbruch** m breach of contract
**Vertragshaftung** f
contractual liability
**Vertragshändler[in]** authorized/
appointed dealer, distributor
**vertraulich** confidential(ly)
**vertreiben** distribute, market, sell
**vertreten** represent; deputize
**Vertreter[in]**
(sales) representative; deputy
**Vertreter fungieren, als jds** deputize
for someone
**Vertretung** f
agency; representation; proxy
**Vertrieb** m distribution; sale(s)
**Vertriebs-** (cpd) distribution/sales
**Vertriebsabteilung** f
sales department
**Vertriebswege** mpl
channels of distribution
**Verwahrung geben, in** deposit (v)

**Verwaltung** f administration
**Verwaltungskosten** pl
administrative costs/expenses
**verweigern** refuse
**Verweigerung** f refusal
**Verwendung** f use, utilization
**verwirken** forfeit (a deposit)
**Verwirkung** f forfeiture
**verzeichnen** record
**Verzeichnis** n register, record;
index; directory
**verzichten auf** renounce, waive
**Verzichterklärung** f
disclaimer, waiver
**Verzichtklausel** f waiver clause
**verzögern** hold up, delay (v)
**Verzögerung** f hold-up, delay
**Verzug** m delay; default, arrears
**Verzug geraten, in** fall behind/
into arrears
**Veto gegen eine Entscheidung
einlegen, ein** veto a decision
**Viertel** n quarter (25%); area, district
**Vierteljahr** n quarter (3 months)
**vierteljährlich** quarterly
**Visitenkarte** f business card
**Visum** n visa
**Völkerrecht** n international law
**Vollabschreibung** f write-off (loss)
**voller Rechnungsbetrag** total
invoice value
**Vollmacht** f power of
attorney; proxy
**vorantreiben** hurry up/chase
(an order)
**voraus bezahlen/zahlbar, im**
pay/payable in advance
**vorausbezahlt** prepaid
**vorausgesetzt, daß** provided
that, providing
**voraussagen** forecast, predict
**Vorauszahlung** f advance payment,
money up front
**Vorbehalt** m reservation,
qualification, proviso
**Vorbehalt, unter** conditional
**vorbehaltlos** unconditional
**Vorbestellung** f advance
order/booking
**Vorbestellungen** fpl dues (orders)
**Vorbeugung** f prevention
**Vordruck** m form (to fill in)
**vorführen** demonstrate, display

**Vorführung** f demonstration, display

**vorgelagert, der Küste** offshore

**vorgetragener Saldo** balance
brought down/forward

**Vorhand** f first option

**Vorhersage** f forecast

**Vorlage** f presentation, production

**vorläufiger Etat** provisional budget

**vorläufiger Versicherungsschein** m
cover note

**vorlegen** present, produce, submit;
render (an account)

**Vorrat** m reserve(s), stock(s)

**Vorrat anlegen, einen**
stock up, stockpile

**vorrätig, nicht** out of stock

**vorschießen** advance (lend)

**Vorschriften** fpl rules, regulations;
instructions, directions

**Vorschriftswidrigkeit** f irregularities

**Vorschuß** m advance (loan)

**Vorschußzahlung** f
advance payment

**Vorsitzende(r) und Geschäfts-
führer[in]** chairman and
managing director

**Vorstand** m executive (committee),
board (of directors); chairman,
managing director

**vorstellen** introduce, present

**Vorstellung** f
introduction, presentation

**Vorstellungsgespräch** n
interview (for a job)

**Vorstellungsgespräch führen, ein**
interview (v) (for a job)

**vorübergehende Anstellung**
temporary employment

**Vorverkauf** m advance booking

**Vorwahl** f area/dialling code

**Vorzugsaktien** fpl preference shares

**Vorzugsgläubiger** m
preferred/secured creditor

## W

**Wachstum** n growth

**Wachstumsrate** f growth rate

**Wagniskapital** n venture capital

**Währung** f currency

**Wandelanleihe** f convertible
loan stock

**Waren** fpl goods, merchandise

**Waren im Einzelhandel verkaufen**
retail (v) goods

**Warenbestand** m stock, inventory

**Warenbestand aufnehmen, den**
take stock

**Warenbörse** f commodity (market)

**Warenhandel** m visible trade

**Warenprobe** f sample

**Warenzeichen** n trademark

**warten** service (a machine)

**warten, auf Anweisungen**
await instructions

**Warteraum** m departure lounge

**Wartung** f service/maintenance
(of machine)

**Wartungshandbuch** n
service manual

**Wechsel** m change (difference); bill
of exchange, draft

**Wechselforderungen** fpl
bills receivable

**Wechselgeld** n change, cash float

**Wechselkurs** m exchange rate, rate
of exchange

**wechseln** change (money)

**wechseln, den Besitzer**
change hands

**Wechselprolongation** f renewal of
a bill

**Wechselstube** f bureau de change

**Wechselverbindlichkeiten** fpl
bills payable

**Wegerecht** n right of way

**Wegwerf-** disposable

**weiche Währung** soft currency

**Weihnachtsgeld** n Christmas bonus

**weiterleiten** refer, pass on, forward

**weitervergeben** farm out (work)

**weitervergeben, einen Auftrag**
subcontract (v)

**Weiterverkauf** m resale

**Welthandel** m international trade

**Werbe-** (cpd) publicity/advertising

**Werbebeilage** f magazine insert

**Werbeetat** m advertising/
publicity budget

**Werbefläche** f advertising space

**Werbegeschenk** n free gift,
premium offer

**Werbeleiter[in]** advertising/
publicity manager

**Werbematerial** n **an der
Verkaufsstelle** POS material

## werben

**werben** promote, advertise, publicize
**Werbespot** *m* commercial *(TV, radio)*
**Werbung** *f* advertisement, *(TV)* commercial; advertising, promotion, publicity
**Werbung durch Postwurfsendung** direct-mail advertising
**Werbung für ein neus Produkt machen** advertise a new product
**Werk** *n* works, factory, plant
**Werkzeug** *n* implement, tool
**Wert** *m* worth, value
**wert sein** be worth
**Wertminderung** *f* decrease in value, depreciation
**Wertpapiere** *npl* securities, stocks and shares
**Wertpapiermakler[in]** stockbroker
**Wertzuwachs** *m* appreciation, gain
**Wettbewerb** *m* competition
**wettbewerbsfähig** competitive
**wettbewerbsfähig im Preis** competitively priced
**Wettbewerbsfähigkeit** *f* competitiveness
**wettmachen** make good *(a defect/loss)*
**Wichtigkeit** *f* importance
**Widerklage** *f* counter-claim
**Widerklage erheben, eine** counter-claim (v)
**widerrufen** cancel, countermand, revoke, withdraw
**widrigenfalls** failing that, failing which
**wieder auffüllen** restock
**Wiederbelebung** *f* recovery, revival
**Wiederbeschaffungswert** *m* replacement value
**Wiedereinfuhr** *f* reimport
**wiedereinführen** reimport
**wiedereinstellen** reappoint, reinstate
**Wiedererlangung** *f* recovery, retrieval
**wiederernennen** reappoint
**wiedergewinnen** regain
**wiedergutmachen** make up for
**Wiederverkauf** *m* resale
**Winterschlußverkauf** *m* winter/end of season sale

**wirksam werden** take effect, become operative
**Wirksamkeit** *f* effectiveness
**wirtschaftliche Entwicklung** economic development
**Wirtschaftlichkeit** *f* economy, economic efficiency
**Wirtschaftsentwicklung** *f* economic trend(s)
**Wirtschaftsprüfer[in]** auditor; chartered accountant
**Wirtschaftsspionage** *f* industrial espionage
**Wirtschaftswachstum** *n* economic growth
**Wirtschaftszweig** *m* branch of industry
**wöchentlich** weekly
**wohnhaft** resident (adj)
**Wohnung** *f* flat
**Wunsch, auf** on request

## Z

**Zahl** *f* number, figure
**zahlbar bei Lieferung** payable on delivery
**zahlbar bei Sicht** payable on demand
**Zahler** *m* payer
**Zahlung f anweisen** authorize payment
**Zahlungsanweisung** *f* money order
**Zahlungsaufschub** *m* deferment of payment, moratorium
**Zahlungsbedingungen** *fpl* terms of payment
**Zahlungsbilanz** *f* balance of payments
**Zahlungseinstellung** *f* suspension of payments
**Zahlungsempfänger[in]** payee
**Zahlungserleichterungen** *fpl* easy terms
**zahlungsfähig** solvent (adj)
**Zahlungsfähigkeit** *f* solvency
**zahlungsunfähig** bankrupt, insolvent
**Zahlungsweise** *f* method/mode of payment
**Zeichen** *n* sign, mark; reference *(on letter)*
**Zeichnungsberechtigte(r)** authorized signatory

**Zeitarbeit** f
temporary work/ employment
**Zeitarbeiter[in]** temp
**Zeitarbeitskräfte** fpl temporary staff
**Zeitkarte** f season ticket
**zeitlicher Rahmen** time scale
**Zeitplan aufstellen, einen**
timetable (v)
**Zeitraum** m period
**Zeitschrift** f magazine
**Zentrale** f main office, headquarters
**Zentraleinkauf** m/**zentraler Einkauf**
central purchasing
**Zettel** m slip, note, piece of paper
**Zeuge [-in]** witness
**Zeugnis** n
(letter of) reference, testimonial
**Ziel** n aim, objective, target
**Zielmarkt** m target market
**Ziffer** f figure, digit
**Zimmer** n room
**Zins und Zinseszins** m
cumulative interest
**Zinsbelastung** f interest charges
**Zinsen** mpl
interest (paid on investment)
**Zinseszins** m compound interest
**Zinssatz** m interest rate
**Zoll** m customs; customs duty
**Zollabfertigung** f customs clearance
**Zollanmeldesstelle** f customs
entry point
**Zollbeamte(r)/-beamtin** customs
official/officer
**Zollbehörde** f customs (authorities)
**Zollerklärung** f customs declaration
**zollfrei** duty-free
**Zollkontrolle** f customs examination
**Zollschranken** fpl tariff barriers
**zufällige Stichprobe** random sample
**Zufallsfehler** m random error
**zufriedenstellen** satisfy (customer)
**Zug** m train
**Zulage** f bonus, allowance; rise
(in salary)
**Zulassungsbescheinigung** f test
certificate, certificate of approval
**Zulieferer** m supplier
**Zunahme** f rise, increase, gain
**zunehmen** rise, increase, grow
**Zurückbehaltungsrecht** n lien
**zurückerstattbare Kaution**
refundable deposit

**zurückgehen** decline, drop, fall away
**Zurückstellung** f shelving, deferment
**zurücktreten** withdraw (from
contract); resign, step down
**zurückzahlen** pay back,
refund, repay
**zurückziehen** withdraw (an offer);
abandon (an action)
**Zusammenarbeit** f
collaboration, co-operation
**zusammenarbeiten**
collaborate, co-operate
**zusammenbrechen** collapse,
break down
**zusammenfassen** bracket, group
together; summarize
**Zusammenhang** m
connection; context
**zusammenhängend mit** relating to
**zusammenlegen** combine,
consolidate, amalgamate
**zusammenrufen** convene
**zusammenschließen** merge,
amalgamate, combine
**Zusammenschluß** m tie-up,
merger, amalgamation
**zusammensetzen aus, sich**
consist of
**Zusatz** m supplement,
addition; appendix
**zusätzlich** supplementary
**Zusicherung** f
assurance, undertaking
**Zustand** m condition, state, situation
**zuständig (für)** responsible (for)
**Zuständigkeit** f
responsibility, jurisdiction
**zustellen** deliver
**zustimmen** agree, approve
**zuverlässig** reliable
**Zuverlässigkeit** f reliability
**Zuwachs** m growth, gain, increase
**Zuwendung** f subsidy, donation
**Zwangsverkauf** m forced sale
**Zweigstelle** f branch (office)
**zweiseitiger Handel**
bilateral/reciprocal trade
**Zweitschrift** f duplicate
**Zwischenhändler** m middleman
**Zwischensumme** f subtotal
**zyklische Faktoren** mpl
cyclical factors
**Zyklus** m cycle